Grant Rodwell

While a Tasmanian school principal, Grant Rodwell completed his BA(Hons), MEd and PhD at UTAS. His interests are deeply imbedded in schools and in academia. Following the completion of his first PhD he moved to the Australian university sector, where he taught and researched in a number of universities. He is committed to lifelong learning, and consequently he has gone on to complete a total of four PhDs.

Grant's research interests include curriculum studies, especially History curriculum, the subject of his fourth PhD. This was undertaken at the University of Adelaide, and will be submitted through publication during mid-2013. Specifically it involves a non-fiction publication with the University of Adelaide Press concerning the place of historical novels in the History curriculum, and the way in which they may be used to enhance student interest. The second component of this PhD is a time-slip novel set in wartime Sydney. Grant's other novels include *Fortunes of Fire: a Historical Saga* (Crawford House), *Goulburn's Deliverance, Gommera Woman* and *Blood Her Maiden Sword* (all Sid Harta Publishing).

Grant draws much of his inspiration for research and teaching from his passion for working with student teachers and schools in the Practicum, an area of his work as member of the School of Education Executive at the University of Adelaide.

This book is available as a free fully-searchable PDF from
www.adelaide.edu.au/press

Whose History?

Engaging History Students through Historical Fiction

Grant Rodwell
School of Education, The University of Adelaide

THE UNIVERSITY
of ADELAIDE

UNIVERSITY OF
ADELAIDE PRESS

This book is dedicated to my mother, Hilary, who left me with many cherished values, not least of which was a passion for history.
This book is also dedicated to my wife, Julie, and my son, Carl, and daughter, Jahna, who augment my life in untold ways.
And that now is sustained with my grandchildren.

Published in Adelaide by

University of Adelaide Press
The University of Adelaide
Level 1, 230 North Terrace
South Australia 5005
press@adelaide.edu.au
www.adelaide.edu.au/press

The University of Adelaide Press publishes externally refereed scholarly books by staff of the University of Adelaide. It aims to maximise the accessibility to the University's best research by publishing works through the internet as free downloads and as high quality printed volumes on demand.

© 2013 Grant Rodwell

This book is copyright. Apart from any fair dealing for the purposes of private study, research, criticism or review as permitted under the *Copyright Act 1968* (Cth), no part may be reproduced, stored in a retrieval system, or transmitted, in any form or by any means, electronic, mechanical, photocopying, recording or otherwise without prior written permission. Address all inquiries to the Director at the above address.

For the full Cataloguing-in-Publication data please contact the National Library of Australia: cip@nla.gov.au

ISBN (paperback) 978-1-922064-51-6
ISBN (ebook) 978-1-922064-50-9

Cover design: Emma Spoehr
Cover image: Courtesy of the University of Adelaide Archives
Cover photograph: Sarah Ahern
Book design: Zoë Stokes

Contents

List of Abbreviations and Acronyms		ix
Acknowledgements		xi
Introduction		1

Part I — The Challenges of Compulsory History in the Australian School Curriculum

1	Compulsory History: the Issues Confronting Teachers	7
2	Student Engagement through Historical Narratives	17
3	Pedagogical Dimensions of Historical Novels and Historical Literacy	29

Part II — Understanding the Genre of Historical Novels

4	Defining the Historical Novel	47
5	The Increase of History as a Subject for Novels: Memory and the Context of Interpretation	55
6	'The plot against the plot': Page-turners for Students	71
7	Counterfactual Histories and the Nature of History	81
8	Alternate Histories in the Classroom	99
9	'Caught in time's cruel machinery': Time-slip Novels in the History Lesson	117

Part III — Deconstructing the Historical Novel

10	Whose History? Historical Fiction and the Discipline of History in the Classroom: Varying Views of the Past	129

11	Understanding the Past through Historical Fiction	**151**
12	Unpacking Historical Novels for their Historicity: Historical Facts and Historical Agency	**171**
13	Key Themes in Australian History and their Reflection in Historical Novels	**183**

Conclusion   **231**

References   **235**

List of Abbreviations and Acronyms

ABC	Australian Broadcasting Commission
ABS	Australian Bureau of Statistics
ACARA	Australian Curriculum and Reporting Authority
ACT	Australian Capital Territory
AHA	Australian History Association
CIB	Criminal Investigation Bureau
CSIRO	Commonwealth Scientific and Industrial Research Organisation
ERA	Excellence in Research for Australia
FECCA	Federation of Ethnic Communities' Councils of Australia
HTAA	History Teachers' Association of Australia
K-10	Kindergarten to Year 10
HSIE	Human Society and its Environment
NAPLAN	National Assessment Plan — Literacy and Numeracy
NISH	National Inquiry into School History
NSW	New South Wales
NT	Northern Territory
POW	Prisoner of War
SA	South Australia
SACE	South Australian Certificate of Education

SOSE	Study of Society and Environment
UK	United Kingdom
USA	United States of America
WA	Western Australia

Acknowledgements

This study comprised a part of a PhD by publication submission at the University of Adelaide. My special thanks are due to my supervisor, Dr Margaret Secombe, and my co-supervisor, Emeritus Professor John Ramsland from the University of Newcastle, both of whom provided wise and gentle guidance, reflecting an understanding of my work on a fourth PhD. Both academics continue to offer a highly consistent, knowledgeable and professional level of advice for the researching and writing of a PhD thesis. Professor Tom O'Donoghue, Winthrop Professor, Graduate School of Education at the University of Western Australia, has also provided much encouragement.

My thanks are due also to a team of librarians in a vast number of libraries around Australia, but particularly to the staff at the Barr Smith Library of the University of Adelaide.

I would like to thank the many people who, in an informal manner at such gatherings as the History Teachers' Association, both at State and national conferences provided me with insights into many of the issues confronting History teachers in Australian schools.

I would also especially like to thank Professor Tania Aspland from the School of Education, the University of Adelaide, who with great erudition has provided marvellous academic leadership and professional support in the School of Education, where I have worked since 2011.

Dr Patrick Allington, Commissioning Editor for the University of Adelaide Press, particularly has been very helpful in preparing the work for publication.

Finally, my deep appreciation and thanks go to my wife, Julie, who has shared the trials and tribulations of six postgraduate theses, including a fourth PhD, with me and who, as usual, has been most supportive during the writing of this thesis.

Introduction

I once was taking a unit of work on Napoleon in Moscow with my university History Curriculum and Methodology students. What sources could we use? A group of students wanted Tolstoy's *War and Peace* (1869/2010), an iconic historical novel. What about Adam Zamoyski's *1812: Napoleon's Fatal March on Moscow* (2005), one of the best nonfiction sources on the topic? The class group then debated the relative merits of historical novels versus nonfiction as teaching/learning sources in schools and colleges — a huge and multi-layered topic.

Motivation, however, to write this book came from other sources. First, there was the continued demonstrated concern for the decline in students undertaking History courses in Australian schools. Curiously juxtaposed to this has been the clear evidence of the popularity of history as the subject matter for books, either in their fictional or nonfictional forms, and in feature films, television films and television mini-series as dramas. Then there has been the Commonwealth legislation mandating the teaching of History from the first year of schooling to Year 12, and the demonstrated fact that mandating the teaching of the subject does nothing to increase students' interest in the subject and consequently to pursue its study in university. Last, my motivation to write this book stemmed from my deeply held passion for the historical novel in its various genres, and a well-founded belief that the genre can stimulate students' interests in studying the subject at school.

This book aims to illustrate how historical novels and their related genres may be used as an engaging teacher/learning strategy for student teachers in pre-service teacher education courses, the vast majority of which simply provide for a single unit in order to prepare student teachers for the classroom. It does not argue all teaching of History curriculum in pre-service units should be based on the use of historical novels as a stimulus, nor does it argue for a particular percentage of the use of historical novels in such courses. It simply seeks to argue the case for this particular approach, leaving the extent of the use of historical novels used in History curriculum units to the professional expertise of the lecturers responsible for the units.

At the time of the writing of this book, historical fiction is enjoying boom times in the Australian book industry. The genre's massive retail sales, however, is not reflected in the use of historical fiction in Australian schools. This is possibly because so little History was taught in Australian schools prior to the advent of the Australian Curriculum and Reporting Authority's (ACARA) History, with only Victoria and New South Wales having a mandatory secondary school History curriculum. It has the potential to engage students in discussion of historical events and broader themes.

ACARA is definite about how it sees the possibility of the use of historical fiction in the Australian History Curriculum: 'Historical narrative is used so that students experience the "story" in History, and this can be extended to investigations of cause and consequence, historical significance and contestability' (National Curriculum Board, 2009, p. 6).

Somebody once quipped that any work of Australian historical fiction is a 'burning fuse', travelling over decades through Australian culture and society. In some manner, every newly published Australian historical novel is connected to what it has preceded. Each work belongs to a proud history. The writing of Australian historical fiction dates back well into the nineteenth century, and most authors are aware of this. Generally, authors of Australian fiction also pride themselves on their research of the historical terrain they are including in their art. These points inform the structure and organisation of this book. Through examples, readers are encouraged to see how a work of historical fiction has evolved. Thus, under various themes, this book examines the traditions in Australian historical fiction, and how Australian historical novels can engage student teachers in Australian universities and teachers generally in Australian schools, to use historical fiction in their History lessons.

This book is organised into four parts. Part One deals with the challenges of compulsory History in the Australian school curriculum. How can Australian teachers of History from the early years of schooling through to senior grades in schools and colleges? An analysis of overseas experience shows mandated History in the Australian curriculum is both a huge challenge and a wonderful opportunity for teachers. While mandating History in schools does not bring with it increased student engagement in the subject, the use of historical fiction as a teaching/learning strategy is a proven means to engage students. I conclude this part of the book with an examination of the pedagogical dimensions of historical novels in the development of historical literacy.

There is no definite, single genre which we might call the historical novel. Part Two examines issues with understanding the genre of the historical novel. First I define the historical novel. Then I attempt to understand the increase in history as a subject for novels. But in line with broader socio-cultural changes, the nature of the historical novel has undergone many changes over the decades. Recent years have witnessed an increase in the importance of plot in the genre. Other important developments have come with the rising popularity of the sub-genres of counterfactual novels, alternate novels and time-shift novels, all of which provide wonderful opportunity for the teachers of History in Australian schools.

How close can readers, and teachers of History, expect historical novels to be to historical 'truth'? Part Three of this book assesses the historical novel, particularly in respect to the many questions teachers of History may pose concerning their use in the History curriculum. This part of the book attempts to answer questions concerning how close teachers of History may rightfully expect a historical novel to explain to students what happened in the past, in a manner that is beyond the scope of History textbooks.

Australian authors have long written in the genre of historical novels. Part Four looks at the way in which they are represented in some key themes in Australian history, all of which have a prominent place in the ACARA national curriculum: national character and our convict heritage; European inland exploration and pastoralism; Indigenous Australian/European relations; patriotism, nationalism and society; and militarism and war.

PART I

THE CHALLENGES OF COMPULSORY HISTORY IN THE AUSTRALIAN SCHOOL CURRICULUM

PART 2

1 Compulsory History: the Issues Confronting Teachers

The Australian Curriculum Assessment and Reporting Authority (ACARA), through a rolling program, has been mandating the teaching of History in Australian schools. However, this comes at a time when students' interest in studying History in schools is at a low ebb. While I will pursue these topics later in this chapter, here I address the issues associated with having Australian History students engage with historical novels.

The internationally acclaimed Australian children's novelist, Jackie French, titled her presentation to the 2010 History Teachers' Association of Australia (HTAA) Conference in Sydney 'Turning History into Stories and Stories into History — Subtitle: What We can learn from Queen Victoria's Underpants'. She advertised her paper as:

> From the World War I trenches of *A Rose for the Anzac Boys* to the social revolution begun by Queen Victoria's public approval of underpants, or how our view of 1770s exploration can be changed by the tale of Captain Cook's goat, this session looks at the true stories behind the novels, and the difference between writing history books and creating historical fiction, and the role both can play in education. (French, 2010)

The inclusion of French's paper in the national conference of the HTAA signifies that Australian teachers of History are recognising the value of the historical novel as a pedagogical strategy in the History classroom. For me, this is all about engaging students in History and cultivating their imagination generally, and in particular their historical imagination.

Engaging with historical novels

It is common now for historical novelists, particularly those writing for children, adolescents and young adults, to link with teachers. One example is Valerie Tripp, a US author best known for her American Girl historical characters Felicity, Kit, Josefina, Molly and Samantha. Writing on the *Teaching History.org* blog, she asks: 'how do we capture the children's interest? How do we pique their curiosity? How do we engage their imaginations?' For Tripp, historical fiction attempts all these things, and that is the principal reason why she writes it, why she thinks 'it is good to use in the classroom'. For her, 'good historical fiction':

- 'exercises a child's imagination through a vicarious experience'
- 'leads children to use themselves and their own lives as comparisons to the characters that lived long ago'
- leads students 'to reflect on their own experience'
- leads students 'to ask their families questions'
- 'awakens awareness'
- 'perks up perception'
- 'sparks conversations'
- leads students 'to ask " what's my voice?"'
- leads students to ask 'What's my view?'
- leads students to ask 'Which side should I be on?'; and
- leads students to ask 'Is there a right side?'

For Tripp, 'what we're trying to do through historical fiction is to help our students realize they are what history is. What they do matters. ... What we're trying to do is to sort of tickle a moral intelligence, a mindfulness, a sense of responsibility, into being' (Tripp, 2011).

Academic historians, too, are increasingly paying attention to the relationship of historical fiction to their discipline. At the 2011 Australian Historical Association conference held in Launceston, a plenary conversation session was devoted to the topic of 'Is Fiction History?' Chaired by Professor

Graeme Davison from Monash University, and in conversation with Professor Ann Curthoys from the University of Sydney, it featured Rohan Wilson, winner of *The Australian*/Vogel's Literary Award for his novel *The Roving Party* (2011) (Australian History Association, n.d.). Through their professional associations, historians have long debated the relationship between their work and that of the historical novelist. One particularly insightful discussion was published by the American Historical Research Association in their 1998 *AHR Forum: Histories and Historical Fictions* (Atwood, 1998; Hunt, 1998; Spence, 1998; Demos, 1998).

But how do these discussions and arguments in historical fiction relate back to the teaching of History in schools? Most enthusiasts of the use of historical fiction as a pedagogical strategy in the History curriculum will say it is all about generating imagination in students. Maxine Greene (1995, p. 36) writes of the importance of imagination in 'the lives of teachers as it is in the lives of students', partly because an imaginative teacher with a passion for her/his subject matter will excite and motivate students in the same way. For me, teachers have a special role in connecting their students with creative literature, but they must themselves be first connected to creative literature. Herein is the unique place historical novels and their related genres have in awakening in children a passion for history.

Changes in the History curriculum in Australia: issues of teacher quality

The teaching of History from grades K-10 in Australian schools underwent a massive change when in 2008 the federal government instructed ACARA to develop and implement a national curriculum in History. On 24 February 2010, Julia Gillard, then Deputy Prime Minister and Minister for Education, addressed the National Press Club in Canberra on this topic.

Justine Ferrari in *The Australian* reported that all states and territories would be forced to follow a set curriculum in English, History, Science and Maths: 'Announcing its release ... she [Gillard] said the curriculum set out the essential content for each year of learning as well as the achievement standards students should be expected to perform. "It will be a comprehensive new curriculum, providing a platform for the highest quality teaching"' (Ferrari, 2010). Full national implementation was scheduled for the start of 2011. However, due to circumstances in the various States and territories, full implementation did not occur until the beginning of 2012. Soon after Gillard's speech to the National Press Club, Dan Harrison in Melbourne's *The Age* alerted readers: 'History teachers are warning that the national History curriculum could be a failure if the subject is placed in the hands of bored or ill-trained teachers' (Harrison, 2010).

Apparently, children are very poorly engaged with the study of History in Australian schools. Clark's 2008 national survey of senior History students' attitudes to the way in which the subject was being taught to them, showed most senior school History students in the 35 schools from a variety of socio-economic settings across Australia showed most students despised Australian history. Australian newspapers continue to highlight the demise of interest in Australian history in our schools and universities, with the result that courses implode at an alarming rate. For example, Christopher Bantick wrote in *The Age* that 'after being bored witless, students have no interest in the past by the time they arrive at university' (2012). The same week as this article was published, Andrew Trounson wrote in *The Australian* that:

> historians like to joke that to attract students you have to put 'sex' or 'death' into the course title. But languishing enrolments in Australian history may require more than the tales of courtesans adrift on convict ship. (2012)

Clearly, in the light of History becoming compulsory for Australian children from 2012, a drastically fresh approach to the development of engaging teaching/learning strategies will be needed.

Of course, falling subject enrolments have many complex causes, but students' perceived views on the quality of teaching, as Clark (2008) has demonstrated, must remain one of these causes. How has this manifested itself in enrolments in History in Australian schools and colleges? Sheradyn Holderhead (2012), writing in *The Advertiser* (Adelaide), recorded the alarming decline in some Humanities subjects and an accompanying increase in Mathematics and Sciences. This was confirmed by the SACE Board of SA (2012), which reported declines in South Australian schools offering Australian History from 18 in 2008 down to eight in 2011, while schools offering Modern History in South Australia fell from 108 in 2008 to 87 in 2011. These were alarming statistics, indeed, for SACE History teachers.

Gillard's announcement and Harrison's warning came as no surprise to the HTAA. In its February 2010 Newsletter the HTAA 'expressed concern about the capacity of current pre-service training programs to prepare History teachers capable of successfully implementing [the] new national courses'. The HTAA reminded its members that this concern was 'shared by Professor Stuart Macintyre, an imminent historian', and that Professor Barry McGaw, Chair of ACARA, had expressed the same concern (HTAA, 2010, February). In its March Newsletter, the HTAA reiterated its concerns, adding:

> The proposal for new national history courses relies on the assumption that teachers will have a sophisticated grasp of significant knowledge, historical understandings and historical skills. It could also be argued that history is a 'passion thing' and that this passion is built on confident expertise. Indeed, particularly with history, if a teacher is not a passionate expert there is the danger that any teaching of a mandatory subject will be counter-productive. If we are developing ambitious national history courses, there must be a focus on teacher qualifications. Since the start of the process in 2008, HTAA has been voicing concern about the urgent need to address the issue of teacher pre-service training. (HTAA, 2010, March)

The challenge for teachers

How can these concerns about the quality of teaching be best addressed? There is little empirical research to show the level of preparedness in Australia's teacher education institutions for the teaching of the new History curriculum, particularly in primary schools. As early as 2000, in his report on the National Enquiry into School History (NISH), Taylor expressed concerns about the preparedness of many graduate teachers to teach History. He noted 'there was widespread concern about the quality of many recently trained graduate teachers who were applauded for their enthusiasm but who were a source of anxiety because of an apparently deficient knowledge-base in historical studies'. For Taylor, 'this anxiety applied both to primary and secondary trainees' (Taylor, 2000, p. vii).

The record of teachers' knowledge base in the teaching of History shows a similarly mixed picture. In their study of four beginning social studies teachers, Wilson and Wineburg (1988) found the varied disciplinary backgrounds of each of the teachers influenced their perspective on the teaching of American history. Each of the teachers differed concerning factual knowledge, the place of interpretation, chronology and continuity, reflecting each teacher's particular disciplinary background. Their teaching reflected what they knew (or did not know) about History. Wilson and Wineburg concluded that as social studies teachers teach a variety of disciplines they need knowledge of the structures of the social science disciplines in addition to their own. In Australia, the NISH report, *The Future of the Past*, indicates similar issues with subject knowledge.

Some teacher-educators are making efforts to address the problem of teacher preparation in History. For example, Sim (2001) reports on a two-year action-research study she undertook with her pre-service History teachers 'to integrate pedagogical factors with the learning of particular discipline knowledge' (Sim, 2001, p. 1). Drawing on transformative learning theory, Sim had positive results with student teachers who were encouraged to think as professional historians and had to 'clarify and justify' their purpose and approach to teaching History (Sim, 2001, p. 8). Commenting on pre-service teacher education of History/SOSE (Study of Society and Environment) teachers, Triolo argues against 'the indiscriminate placement of all "newly-trained graduates teachers" in a category of concern' (Sim, 2001, p. 6). She argues that pre-service teachers who take a History Curriculum Methods course at university or have strong History academic prerequisites will have a good knowledge base. This learning, she asserts, extends to the broader SOSE curriculum: 'History Method students are more likely than not to have specialised in the teaching and learning of History and the use of historical resources [and] … developing understandings of the wider curriculum perspective/focuses, values and issues of the SOSE learning area' (Sim, 2001, p. 90).

She qualifies these comments, however, by referring to the NISH finding that secondary teachers across Australia are grouped into SOSE Method courses with little or no discipline-based methods in the teaching of History, while 'Pre-service training of primary teachers would appear to cater even less for "History in SOSE"' (Sim, 2001, p. 9). Middle school SOSE teachers are drawn from both primary and secondary school, so it is possible that in terms of the teaching of History in SOSE that the grasp of the disciplinary base of History is likely to vary considerably.

In his long-standing and widely used SOSE/HSIE (Human Society and its Environment) undergraduate textbook, Marsh (2008) contends that History is poorly received by students in schools. He suggests that 'perhaps, one of the reasons is that teachers prefer to use only a limited number of teaching techniques — ones that they have experienced or with which they are most comfortable — and these may not be very challenging or exciting for students' (Marsh, 2008, p. 70). Marsh then cites research done by Yeager (2000, cited in Marsh, 2008, p. 70) to suggest that 'teachers may believe that they are varying their teaching, but their students see it as stultifying routine'.

Student response to compulsory History

How are teacher educators to engage pre-service teachers in History curricular? Lack of training is not the only threat to the successful teaching of History. The introduction of the National Curriculum for History has made History a compulsory subject for all students until the end of Year 10. The very idea that History is a compulsory subject is a threat, as this carries a certain stigma for students. If a student 'has to' study a subject, they can sometimes lose motivation and become disengaged with the topic. This leads to students who are not passionate about history, and passion for history is certainly something a History teacher should strive to awaken in students. This is a challenge in itself for teachers, and one that the compulsory nature of the National Curriculum only heightens. As Taraporewalla (2011, p. 2) points out, 'with all Australian students soon to be obliged to study History, and the subject set to become one of the fundamental academic domains, the History classroom now will be filled with a much more diverse group of learners, representing greater variation in learning styles and motivation'. As most teachers will attest, this in itself provides many new challenges.

Legislating for the mandatory status of History does not necessarily ensure its acceptance by students. A key factor directly related to the motivation of students is 'student perceptions and beliefs concerning the value of academic tasks and domains' (Taraporewalla, 2011, p. 1). To optimise student engagement and in order to be motivated and to achieve in the History classroom, students need to identify that there is some intrinsic value beyond the mandated teaching of the subject. In the United Kingdom (UK), where History became a compulsory subject in 1991 for students under the age of fourteen years, Ferguson (2011), for example, found that the value and purpose of History had not been transmitted to the students (see further discussion below, this chapter). Student perception regarding the value of History will directly relate to achievement in the subject, and by transmitting the value of History to the students, the teacher will uncover learners who are engaged and motivated.

According to Ofsted, the official body for inspecting schools in the UK, 'History is successful in schools' (Ferguson, 2011). But Niall Ferguson, who also appears in this book as the champion for counterfactual histories, took issue with the report. For him, 'the inspectors are missing the ruination of the subject' (Ferguson, 2011). Ferguson is Professor of History at Harvard University and William Ziegler Professor at Harvard Business School. He is also a Senior Research Fellow of Jesus College, Oxford. Readers, of course, should recognise Ferguson's position, in the above instance, as an author of an opinion piece, and his is a contested point of view.

The Ofsted report, as Ferguson puts it, stated that

> based on evidence from inspections conducted between 2007 and 2010 in 83 primary schools and the same number of secondary schools, the report begins on a reassuringly positive note. 'There was much that was good and outstanding' in the History lessons the inspectors observed. 'Most pupils enjoyed well-planned lessons that extended their knowledge, challenged their thinking and enhanced their understanding.' (Ferguson, 2011, including quote of Ofsted report)

Ferguson interrogated the data, went into schools and concluded the teaching of History in UK schools was never in such a pitiful state. Moreover, he 'laments the fact that history has never been more popular outside schools as it is today, yet never more unpopular inside schools' (Ferguson, 2011). As Chapter 2 shows, if the sale of historical fiction is any index, history enjoys the same popular support in Australian society-at-large. In schools, apparently, students widely avoid it.

* * *

Australian teachers of History, and the academics training student teachers in faculties and schools of education, are faced with enormous challenges as they attempt to ameliorate the drastic decline in students undertaking History in post-secondary years.

Simply mandating History in schools and colleges does little to achieve student interest in the subject. How can we best engage students in the subject, encouraging them to think like professional historians?

Through their readings of historical fiction, students can develop an appreciation of the powerful and engaging medium of historical narrative, and one that is in tune with its rising popularity in our society and culture. This book will argue that while historical fiction has a wonderful readership amongst the general public, History teachers in schools and colleges need to develop the confidence and understanding to engage their students with this genre and that students will then respond with fresh and lively understandings in history.

2   Student Engagement through Historical Narratives

As the teaching of History in Australia undergoes substantial changes through the implementation of the national History curriculum, undergraduate student teachers and teachers in classrooms are being required to re-think their teaching/learning strategies for the teaching of History. With the developments in SOSE/HSIE since the 1970s, curricula researchers have found that during the last few decades the teaching of History has drifted almost into oblivion in many Australian schools. More recently, with the implementation of the National History curriculum undergraduate teachers and teachers in classrooms have been asked to re-engage with the subject (Rodwell, 2010). In this chapter, I argue historical narrative offers many effective possibilities for this re-engagement process.

Developments in the use of the historical novel in History classrooms

In this book's Introduction I looked at several authors of historical fiction who were passionate about the use of their genre in the classroom. Some teachers are also passionate about the use of the genre in their teaching. For example, Moran (2005) writes about why she decided to use historical fiction in her classroom. It relates to the curiosity and discourse that the reading of historical fiction generates amongst students:

> For many of my tenth graders, it was historical novels that had them coming to me even after the school day had ended. They wanted to ask if Henry VIII had really sent Anne Boleyn to the chopping block after failing to give him a son; if three hundred Greeks had really slayed

eighteen thousand Persian warriors before being killed themselves, as depicted in Steven Pressfield's *Gates in Fire*. I wondered: if their reading at home sparked such enthusiasm, why not extend it to the curriculum as well? (2005, n.p.)

Internationally, some educators and researchers have long argued for the use of historical fiction in the teaching of History (Freeman, 1988; Macdonald, 2008). Norton has argued:

> Through historical fiction, children can begin to visualize the sweep of history. As characters in historical fiction from many different time periods face and overcome their problems, children may discover universal truths, identify feelings and behaviors that encourage them to consider alternative ways to handle their own problems, empathize with viewpoints that are different from their own, and realize that history consists of many people who have learned to work together. (1999, p. 523)

In the United Kingdom, Dave Martin, at one time an Adviser for History for Dorset County Council, has long championed the use of historical novels in the History Curriculum. For example, his website (http://davemartin46.wordpress.com/) offers teachers at all levels a variety of advice on the how they might use historical fiction in the classroom. Hicks and Martin have argued for an interdisciplinary use of historical fiction in classrooms: History teachers working with English teachers on studies using historical novels, and vice versa (Hicks & Martin, 1997).

The pedagogical reasons for doing this, I argue, are clear. For example, Herz contends:

> When students examine the past as outlined in a historical novel, they become immersed in characters moving through time and place and they begin to perceive the continuity of time. The events in a novel become more significant because the student is required to understand them in order to appreciate the novel. By reading about a historical character in a novel, students begin to place that character's life in the

past and begin to connect this section of the past to the society they live in and soon realise how studying the past helps them to understand the present. (2010, n.p.)

Students are able to recall the historical information more easily because it has been associated within the context of the plot, character, setting and theme of the novel. According to Herz, 'They begin to absorb the historical details in the novel without even realizing they are being instructed' (2010, n.p.).

Hedeen (2010) states that historical fiction will form lasting impressions and foster more authentic learning than a textbook. Moreover, Nawrot (1996, p. 343) argues that History textbooks tend to treat history as a 'science', requiring an analytical and objective response by students. Hedeen (2010) argues that the study of History can become more relevant to students when presented as a story. If students engage with an accurate and well-written historical novel, their interest can be maintained, and students may be motivated to research further.

Adams (2001) argues the youth of today live very much in the present, yet, ironically, that they have little to no understanding of how they got to where they are now. This is where historical fiction can make an important connection with the events of the past, giving them meaning and relevance to the present. Furthermore, Adams (2004) suggests that using a variety of books about the same period but told from different perspectives is just one thought-provoking way of using historical fiction. Such a strategy allows students to explore a historical period from different avenues, allowing them to get a feel for what it would have been like to be in another place and time.

There are a growing number of web-based articles, located in the UK, Canada and the USA, that provide support to teachers in their practical use of historical fiction in the classroom. Examples of these include K. Steele (n.d.), 'Historical Fiction', *Kim's Korner for Teacher Talk*; J. Britt (n.d.), 'Historical fiction in the next generation's method of how we learn about history', *Ezine@rticles*; M. Brewer (2007), 'Using Novel Studies in the Classroom', *Teacher Timesavers*; 'What Are the Benefits of Using Historical Fiction to

Teach History?' (n.d.), *eHow.com*; and Moran (2005) 'Why Historical Fiction Belongs in Your Classroom', *Random House, For High School Teachers*.

Historical novels assist in integration with other curriculum areas

Not only does using historical fiction promote understanding and knowledge of past historical events, it can also be integrated to fit into the English curriculum. Students can analyse the novel, its structure and content (Herz, 2010). Groce and Groce (2005) argue students engage in interdisciplinary activities when reading historical fiction, practising research skills and critical thinking in their quest to validate the information presented by the author.

But Groce and Groce (2005) have another important reason for arguing in favour of teachers choosing the reading of historical fiction as a teaching/learning strategy for an integrated classroom. This reason — newly developing pressures of time as a result of system-wide testing — has particular relevance in Australian schools as the imperatives of the National Assessment Program Literacy and Numeracy (NAPLAN) begin to bite into teachers' time for the teaching of SOSE/HSIE. Evidence from several Australian educational jurisdictions show how much SOSE/HSIE-allocated time teachers were devoting to developing literacy and numeracy skills demanded from the NAPLAN testing (Kersey Group, 2010).

The role that historical novels can play in alleviating these pressures on time available to teachers for the teaching of History is obvious. Integrating History with literacy — children reading historical novels during literacy time — might reduce the pressure on teachers and children in their required allocation of time for History.

Ruth Reynolds, an Australian History curriculum academic, has long argued for the use of historical fiction as a teaching/learning strategy in primary grades as a strategy that greatly enhances values education: 'the study of historical fiction allows for a study of different cultures, separated by time

— not necessarily place — and as such allows for student involvement' (R. Reynolds, 2006, p. 28).

For Reynolds (2008, p. 6), stories provide a link between the teaching of History and the teaching of Civics:

- Stories behind contemporary issues and the context through which students make meaning of current events and develop perspectives on the future.
- Narratives behind Australia's civic past so that students gain a sense of change, time, continuity, causation, motivation and heritage.
- Insight into human experience in other times and societies which provide a basis for evaluating students' own life experiences.
- Individual stories and models of citizenship which enable students to understand decision-making processes and choices made by individuals when confronted with challenges.
- Development of skills and abilities and a means of understanding and valuing principles of democracy, social justice and ecological sustainability.

Reynolds (2008) argues the gateway opened by historical fiction provides students with the opportunity to vicariously experience the emotions of characters, thus creating a deeper connection between past and present historical perspectives. For students, there is an element of 'safety' or 'non-threatening nature' in the narratives of the past: 'historical fiction's ability to display solutions and accommodations to conflicting situations in the past — allowing for safe distancing for children to explore similar situations in their own lives — that is its great contribution to citizenship understanding' (R. Reynolds, 2008, p. 7).

Reynolds (2008) also shows how this 'distancing' that comes with the use of historical fiction in History teaching is also important for teachers who may need to 'distance issues when dealing with sensitive matters that may generate strong feelings or polarise students' (R. Reynolds, 2008, p. 7). She suggests 'teachers can consider analogies and parallels to current controversial situations either by removing themselves in time or in place' (p. 7). By having students look to how Indigenous issues emerge in other cultures — for example, the Native Americans — through their reading of historical novels, students can better understand the corresponding issues here in Australia. Reynolds finds that these issues are often very confronting for students. The use of historical novels may alleviate this problem and can lead to new understandings and perspectives on current issues:

> The distancing allows for principles to be explored without including the emotional aspects that current issues often incite. It is historical fiction's ability to provide distancing that probably explains its power to inform in terms of current citizenship issues. (R. Reynolds, 2008, p. 7)

Reynolds (2008, p. 7) goes on to contend that 'historical fiction deals with some difficult citizenship issues'. She shows historical fiction is accessible as well as motivational and that, increasingly, it examines 'social themes and views on citizenship issues' (R. Reynolds, 2008, p. 7).

The legacy of the past: History in past SOSE/HSIE curricula in Australia

It is relevant to consider how the discipline of History has fared in Australian schools since its demise as a mandatory subject in many jurisdictions as far back as the early 1970s. The very complexity of the past SOSE/HSIE pedagogy and content, and the various systemic demands on schools and teachers nationally, prompted Tony Taylor, author of the Commonwealth Government-commissioned publication, *An Overview of Teaching and Learning of Australian History in Schools* (2006) to comment: 'as for detecting any coherence in delivering Australian history in both syllabus construction and implementation, there are several issues which have been highlighted in this survey and which were originally outlined in the National Inquiry' (Taylor, 2006, p. 33). First, for many teachers it comes as no surprise to learn Taylor's (2006) survey found 'in generic SOSE or Essential Learnings curriculum' History had lost its identity as 'a unique and complex discipline'

(p. 33). For Taylor, a prime reason for this was that individual schools and teachers exercised considerable autonomy on what was taught and what was not taught. Taylor (2006) argues that 'the permissive nature of the generality of primary school teaching means that individual teachers call the shots about what exactly is taught and when' (p. 33). Consequently, Taylor (2006) found it difficult to discover what exactly was being taught in Australian history in Australian primary schools prior to the introduction of the national History curriculum in Australian primary schools in 2012. Moreover, with the development of middle schools throughout Australia, this state of affairs was rapidly extending into post-primary education.

Taylor mentions the systemic demands on teachers leading them to lose focus on History teaching. A later example of this would be the stress schools have come under from NAPLAN results as shown on *MySchool*, the Australian Curriculum and Reporting Authority (ACARA) website: Key Learning Areas (KLAs) such as SOSE/HSIE increasingly paled in importance in comparison to greater demands in literacy and numeracy. Then Taylor reminds us of the perennial problems associated with teachers' professional preparation, noting that both primary and secondary teachers often have had little pre-service or professional development in History pedagogy. My own anecdotal evidence suggests there are many teachers in schools, and certainly many undergraduates studying SOSE/HSIE curriculum, who sought out proven teaching/learning strategies in History (Kersey Group, 2010).

Leadbetter (2006) paints a bleak picture of the past teaching of History in our schools: 'very few people, including teachers, know what SOSE really is. I have to explain it in some detail to my trainee teachers, and they're quite taken aback by the complexity of it' (Salusinszky, 2006, cited in Leadbetter, 2006). While SOSE/HSIE pedagogies and curricula vary from one Australian educational jurisdiction to another, Leadbetter (2006) highlights a central difficulty with History teaching in the past SOSE/HSIE curricula: 'History is not readily extractable from SOSE, as historical concepts are embedded within the learning area, and in turn the learning area seeks to develop concepts and processes which empower students to be their own historians, or sociologists, or geographers' (Leadbetter, 2006).

In extracting History from SOSE/HSIE, and at the same time developing an understanding of history for students, Leadbetter (2006) maintains a central issue is a consideration of the ways in which children develop an understanding of the past and of history. For me, the use of narratives has had a long and successful history in developing in students an understanding of the past. For example, Seixas (2001) describes three different approaches to teaching History, which all involve storytelling. The first involves the teacher telling the students the 'best' or most appealing story, the second requires the students to investigate how a story came about, and the third considers stories from different perspectives, and debates their merits. These considerations support the idea that history is a moral story, drawing a further similarity to children's fiction, which often has a moral imperative.

The significance of narrative and personal experience

How can an understanding of the notion of narrative enhance our appreciation of the role of the historical novel in the teaching of History? Narrative essentially is a precious relationship between the author and the reader. It is a socially symbolic act, a 'form of reasoning' about experience and society, whose task is to produce fictional resolutions to real social contradictions (Jameson, 1977, cited in Dixon, 1986). Narrative is a personal engagement between the author and the reader, often embracing real and enduring social and personal contradictions, such as injustice and betrayal, love and revenge, dream and disillusion. Often these spring from an author's own worldview and value system.

For example, Kate Grenville was motivated by the dispossession and other injustices inflicted on Australian Aborigines. Miriam Cosic (2011) writes:

Grenville's shift into the colonial era, and to the relations between black and white in the founding years of the country, began when she made the Sydney Harbour Bridge walk for reconciliation in 2000, for which hundreds of thousands of people turned out. While on it, she made eye contact with an Aboriginal woman. They didn't speak, but it set off a train of thought. She began researching her own family history: the arrival of Solomon Wiseman, after whom Wiseman's Ferry is named, a convict from the East End of London, and his development of a land grant received from Governor Macquarie in 1817. The two trains of thought coalesced in *The Secret River*.

These contradictions provide for powerful and engaging reading. Grenville is second only to Patrick White as a prescribed novelist in Australian schools (Cosic, 2011).

Engaging the audience in historical images and memory through the narrative

A work of fiction is complex in its public meaning. First, it is 'a *public* utterance, telling a story about characters' emotions … [that] mediates *private* experiences to make it *public*' (Cohen & Shires, 1998, p. 1, added emphasis). Thus, fictional narrative provides the audience with a private statement, able to communicate its meaning by *engaging* its audience and bringing the audience into what amounts to a private discussion. In this way the 'paradigm of a language maintains its operation as a system by keeping its conventions stable and continually recognisable to users of the language — so stable and recognisable, in fact, one is rarely conscious of the elaborate grid of similarity and difference which the paradigmatic marking constructs for language use' (Cohen & Shires, 1998, p. 17). Indeed, it is the 'smoothness' — the seamlessness — of the grid that makes for memorable narrative. And of course it is the degree of the attainment of this goal that assists in determining the success of a particular novel.

According to Cohen and Shires, a 'language system does not prescribe right and wrong uses for discourses, so much as it establishes possible conditions of significance, metaphorical coherence, and thematic unity … [and] define[s] an agenda for reading which has political and social implications in what it excludes as well as includes' (Cohen & Shires, 1998, p. 24). Thus, fiction generally, and historical fiction in particular, provides a double layer of meaning: first, there is the present and everyday meaning, providing an entrée to the past; then there is the past used to interpret and add greater and more poignant understandings to the present.

Cohen and Shires also argue that 'the narrative system often appears totally to determine a given text's meaning by containing the play of narrativity within a closed structure, thereby centering it through a story, or point of view' (Cohen & Shires, 1998, p. 52). The values underpinning the narrative are always imbedded in the set of contemporary socio-cultural values in which the narrative is written.

Cohen and Shires contend that in fiction a 'narrative recounts a story, a series of events in a temporal sequence' (Cohen & Shires, 1998, p. 1). However, in nonfiction 'language represents reality in a transcription, whereas fictional language represents it in facsimile' (Cohen & Shires, 1998, p. 2). I suggest that historical fiction does both, and it does neither, remaining both history, or nonfiction, and non-history, or fiction.

* * *

This chapter has argued that the use of historical fiction provides a powerful and engaging opportunity for student engagement in the History curriculum. As Australian schools move into the full-implementation phase of the ACARA national History curriculum, History teachers in Australian schools and colleges as well as lecturers teaching about History curriculums in university education schools and faculties, will look to use historical novels as a teaching/learning strategy.

There are manifest challenges facing teachers of the ACARA national History curriculum. Teachers and teacher educators will face the legacy of the past: History in past SOSE/HSIE curricula has been absent or almost non-existent in many Australian schools. Given the significance of the unique connection of the narrative and personal experience — the matchless and precious relationship between the author and the reader of historical fiction — students are able to engage with contentious issues and points of view in a historical context. Values change over the generations, and historical accounts also change. So, too, do the ways in which historical novelists deal with their subject matter.

3 Pedagogical Dimensions of Historical Novels and Historical Literacy

As many teachers and educators seriously question the role of textbooks in the History lesson, teachers and educators are looking increasingly to alternative and more engaging teaching/learning strategies (Villano, 2005). Recognising the significant pedagogical advantages of using historical fiction in their classrooms, some teachers have long used historical fiction as a central teaching/learning strategy in the History classroom. Now, however, student teachers and teachers are advantaged — and consequently, should be reassured — by an emerging amount of research showing how the teaching of historical literacy through historical novels can be achieved. There is, I argue, ample evidence of the many pedagogical advantages of using historical novels in their teaching.

Consider this classroom scenario: there is a Year 9 class researching different aspects of medieval history. One group is researching the design of a typical castle. The teacher reads a short section of Ken Follett's *The Pillars of the Earth* (1989) to the group. The selection describes the layout and design of a castle as seen through the eyes of William, a potential attacker. The goal is for students to design their own castle based on the description from the novel. This is a challenging lesson, requiring students to envision text. The teacher reads the excerpt, a few sentences at a time. At appropriate points, she pauses and gives the students time to sketch. Follett (1989) describes the moat as a figure 8. The teacher instructs the students to draw the moat, leaving space inside the circles for the rest of their castle. The rest of the scene describes the castle bridges, gatehouse, towers and keep. She reads through and pauses as students illustrate the description and label each section. She gives students time to complete their design. This activity is student-based, with the teacher being the facilitator using a constructivist approach. The teacher chooses to make the actual assessment of the entire drawing, as students interpret the content of the text.

The power of the pedagogies: constructivist pedagogy and essential learnings

Considerable changes to teaching and classroom practice in History have come about during the past fifteen or so years because of new understandings of the notion of pedagogy. As Williams (1994, p. 57) shows, the term 'pedagogy' was revitalised in the 1980s so as to be conceptually quite distinct from the notion of 'teaching' as a set of behavioural techniques. Not only was the term 'pedagogy' revitalised, it was enlarged, so that now our understanding of the meaning of the term 'teaching' is imbedded in our conceptual understanding of the term 'pedagogy'.

Now, educators conceive of the notion of pedagogy as addressing the process of production and exchange that takes place in the interaction of teacher, learner, and the knowledge jointly produced (Lusted, 1986, p. 3, cited in McWilliams, 1994, p. 57). Referring to Lusted's (1986) research, McWilliams states that 'critical writers insisted that such a concept refused the instrumentalization of these relations, highlighting instead "exchange between and over categories ... render[ing] the parties within them as active, changing and changeable agencies"' (McWilliams, 1994, p. 57, including quotation of Lusted, 1986, p. 3). McWilliams (1994) goes on to observe that in focussing on knowledge production in this way, pedagogical concerns were 'to draw attention to the conditions necessary to maximize opportunities for affecting appropriate change. In particular, such conceptualization of the role of education called attention to the power relations within which knowledge is produced' (McWilliams, 1994, p. 57).

How does this translate into a History classroom? First, there are the students with their varying cultural backgrounds, including the historical knowledge they bring to the classroom; then there is the curriculum; and then there is the teacher with his/her cultural values. The pedagogy comprises the way in which these three elements come together, through the various teaching/learning strategies the teacher employs, in a dynamic fashion in the production of knowledge. Now, the teacher understands knowledge is a personal and individual thing, dependent upon a multitude of dynamic and interacting factors in any classroom. This understanding of pedagogy leads into our understanding of constructivist pedagogy.

Developing during the late 1980s, by the beginning of the twenty-first century constructivist pedagogy had impacted in various ways on most Australian classrooms. By 2012, it had a strong place in many schools, and State and Territory educational authorities endorse its use in schools. For example, in New South Wales, in 2001, Gore perceived constructivist pedagogy as being a something that would re-engage secondary school students with History. As Gore put it:

> These moves to a student-centred pedagogy come mainly from a constructivist approach to learning. This approach requires students to build their own knowledge and not to be simply passive recipients of information. Being active, students construct their own meaning by modifying existing knowledge, exploring meaning with others and addressing content in a variety of contexts. (Gore, 2001)

Constructivist learning has brought massive changes in classrooms around Australia since the 1980s. As Gore reminds us, now 'teachers need to help students construct understanding of concepts for themselves' (Gore, 2001). Gone are the days of 'memorising material, filling in worksheets, and repetitiously doing the same sort of task' (Gore, 2001). Instead, 'students solve new problems, research and integrate information, and create knowledge for themselves. A constructivist view of teaching and learning requires changes in other components of schooling, namely, curriculum and assessment' (Gore, 2001).

If teacher educators and academic historians were pessimistic about the future of the teaching of History in Australian schools in 1997 — see, for example, Critical Dialogue (1997), the constructivist developments in Australian classrooms during the next decade has had at least the potential to significantly ameliorate their views. I argue that the most powerful effect on classrooms during the last twenty years came from constructivist pedagogy. Those years saw the proliferation of essential learnings, which imbeds constructivist pedagogy, in the curricula of most Australian States and Territories. It was, as Gore (2001) argues, a significant move away from a passive, repetitious approach to learning, towards a pedagogy based on personalised knowledge, actively developed by students.

The constructivist model of knowledge views knowledge as personal, subjective, perpetually evolving and non-absolute. Papert (1993) insisted engagement by the learner and manipulation of materials was the cornerstone to real learning. He championed the idea of manipulative materials to the idea that learning is most effective when part of an activity the learner experiences as constructing a meaningful product. With catch-cries such 'Children don't get ideas, they make ideas' and 'Better learning will not come from finding better ways for the teacher to instruct, but from giving the learner better opportunities to construct', essential learnings flourished in most of Australia's education systems during the first decade of the twenty-first century (Rodwell, 2008, Chapter 6).

In 2005, John Graham, research officer with the Victorian Branch of the Australian Education Union (AEU), briefly reviewed the growth of essential learnings in Australian education jurisdictions. The AEU saw the essential learnings as a '"movement", for that is what it appears to be, [that] has spread around the country over the past few years. Tasmania, South Australia,

Northern Territory and Queensland have all implemented variations of essential learnings' (Graham, 2005).

With these major developments in pedagogy, and in the context of a national History curriculum, many teacher educators and academic historians have argued for a constructivist pedagogy to underpin its use in classrooms. The Australian discourse of a national History curriculum has far from ignored discussion on pedagogy during the last decade or so (see, for example, Schultz, 2007; Harris-Hart, 2008). The following section will show how the federal government's National Centre for History Education (n.d.) has nurtured many of these ideals.

Teaching historical literacy through historical novels

In the National Centre for History Education, Taylor (n.d.) addressed the issue of developing 'historical literacy' in our school students. Rightly, he first examined what comprised 'historical literacy', describing the following elements:

- **Events of the past** — knowing and understanding historical events, using prior knowledge, and realising the significance of different events.
- **Narratives of the past** — understanding the shape of change and continuity over time, understanding multiple narratives and dealing with open-endedness.
- **Research skills** — gathering, analysing and using the evidence (artefacts, documents and graphics) and issues of provenance.
- **The language of History** — understanding and dealing with the language of the past.
- **Historical concepts** — understanding historical concepts such as causation and motivation.
- **ICT understandings** — using, understanding and evaluating ICT-based historical resources (the virtual archive).

- **Making connections** — connecting the past with the self and the world today.
- **Contention and contestability** — understanding the 'rules' and the place of public and professional historical debate.
- **Representational expression** — understanding and using creativity in representing the past through film, drama, visual arts, music, fiction, poetry and ICT.
- **Moral judgement in History** — understanding the moral and ethical issues involved in historical explanation.
- **Applied science in History** — understanding the use and value of scientific and technological expertise and methods in investigating past, such as DNA analysis or gas chromatography tests.
- **Historical explanation** — using historical reasoning, synthesis and interpretation (the index of historical literacy) to explain the past. Historical understanding is incomplete without explanation. (Taylor, 2003, bold headings in original)

How can the use of historical fiction as a teaching/learning strategy develop and enhance historical literacy in students? Clearly, the use of historical fiction in the classroom can connect directly to many of these elements of historical literacy (p. 5).

Crawford and Zygouris-Coe (2008) endorse these points by arguing that

> the use of historical fiction within the curricular context promotes a stronger engagement between the reader and the text than does use of the traditional social studies textbook. In turn, student engagement with the text promotes comprehension. Thus, instead of wading through lists of dates and isolated historical events, readers of historical fiction find themselves 'walking in the shoes' of a particular character and seeing the historical world through this unique perspective. This type of viewpoint can make a tremendous difference not only in readers' understanding of historical events, but also in their understanding of the social consequences of these events. (p. 197)

While I have no research base to substantiate my claims, I assert that the use of historical fiction can be is a powerful teaching/learning strategy at the undergraduate level in History curriculum studies, achieving the same outcomes as shown by Crawford and Zygouris-Coe (2008, p. 197). However, I suggest that the establishment of historical literacy must start with practising History teachers and with student teachers at universities. This is one of the reasons why I choose to use historical novels written for an adult audience with my undergraduate student teachers in my History Curriculum and Methodology course. Many of these students would choose to read these kinds of novels outside of their university study. Strong anecdotal evidence suggests that when I have used historical as teaching/learning strategies in these units, undergraduate student teachers truly begin to develop an appreciation of what comprises historical literacy.

Developing abstract thinking

However, many of the elements of historical literacy presuppose the development of abstract thinking in younger students, particularly those in primary schools. Thinking mathematically, linguistically and logically are important aspects needed to grasp historical timeframes, according to Taylor and Young (2003), who show historical timeframes go beyond a student's present life experiences. This results in higher cognitive demands, which when combined with unfamiliar social and cultural situations, introduces learners to abstract concepts.

Because of historical timeframe, as one such abstract concept, teachers have long developed their pedagogy according to Piaget's (cited in Hoge, 1988) ideas about how younger students may struggle to grasp abstract ideas. Piagetian theory insists that most primary school-aged children are still in the stage of concrete thought. However, since the late 1980s many educational researchers have turned their attention to children's development of historical understanding. Resulting from this research, Egan (cited in Hoge, 1988) insists students' ability to grasp the concept of an historical timeframe is reflective of how they are taught. Egan encourages the use of historical fiction to develop a stronger emotional connection. Thus, the abstract understanding of historical timeframes develops through the concrete example of fictional forms.

On the basis of these types of inquiries, Taylor and Young (2003, p. 40), while modifying research by Sansom (1987, as cited in Taylor & Young, 2003, p. 20), show historical reasoning develops gradually, rather than in age-related stages. They contend gradual advances occur in four key aspects of young people's historical thinking:

Causation

- Initially, the learner's thinking is linear; any event is seen as the inevitable cause of what went before.
- As thinking develops, causation is seen as multiple acts working in combination
- With increased awareness, the learner understands causation as a unique combination of factors.
- Finally, causes are seen as an intricate network of actions and factors; the learner understands the whole story can never be known.

Change and continuity

- Initially, the learner sees changes as unrelated, rather than as progressions.
- As thinking develops, change is seen as traceable to one cause.
- Finally, the learner understands change as the gradual transformation of a situation.

Motivation and intentions of historical actors

- Initially, the learner finds it difficult to understand the motives of people in the past.
- As thinking develops, the learner explains people's actions from his or her own perspective.
- Finally, the learner begins to reconstruct the perceptions and beliefs of people in the past by reasoning from available sources.

Evidence and historical method

- Initially, the learner equates factual information with evidence and often fails to notice contradictory evidence or is unable, or does not know how to make sense of it.
- Finally, the learner understands that evidence must be interpreted and that different sources of evidence may conflict. (Taylor & Young, 2003, p. 40)

Being exposed to the narratives of historical fiction, and through guided discussion by the teacher, students gain enhanced opportunities to develop these four elements of historical thinking.

Linking the past to the present and future

It is important to consider how and why historians attempt to explain causation, change and continuity, motivation and intention of historical actors, and evidence of historical method. Bateman and Harris (2008, p. 272) argue a modern approach is to conceptualise 'history as the extended present'. Instead of considering history as a chronological series of events, the past, present and future(s) history is viewed through 'intersecting and often conflicting narratives'. This multi-dimensional view of history provides multiple visions of the past and present, I suggest, and considers their influence on possible, probable and preferable outcomes in the future. Rather than being about acquiring historical facts, this form of history is about developing historical and futures consciousness, and should be taught within the contexts of the students' own life-world experiences. Bateman and Harris (2008, p. 272) propose the use of temporally inclusive pedagogies to achieve this, which includes considering an issue over several different time-frames, and also the explicit teaching of empathy, to allow the students to imagine being 'in the shoes' of another person. I argue that these aims would often be achieved with the inclusion of suitable historical fiction in the learning experience.

Connecting and engaging with students

There is, I contend, pedagogical value in immersing children in a rich variety of narratives, both fiction and nonfiction. Such immersion enhances their development of historical understanding. This is supported by researchers such as Routman (2003), who reports that when students read a text they develop a number of metacognition reading strategies to infer understanding, including making connections between the text and their life, other texts and world experiences.

With this research and understanding in mind, during the last decade in the US historical fiction has begun to dominate major children's book awards. Rycik and Rosler (2009) have heralded this development while describing the values of using high-quality historical fiction in the classroom. They also present different ways to respond to the historical fiction genre, including using modern technology. They argue:

> Reading historical fiction provides students with a vicarious experience for places and people they could otherwise never know. Often, they are able to see history through a child's point of view and identify with their emotions. They can experience the sadness Leah feels when she must sell her pony to provide money for her family during The Great Depression in *Leah's Pony* (Friedrich, 1998). They can sense the fear that Monique has when her family hides a girl pretending to be her sister from the Nazis in *The Butterfly* (Polacco, 2001). Historical fiction can also help students to gain an understanding of their own heritage and others. In *Virgie Goes to School With Us Boys* (Howard, 2005), students today can relive the exuberance of African American boys and girls who, after the Civil War, attend school for the first time. While reading *Esperanza Rising* (Ryan, 2000), children can understand the challenges of Latino and Hispanic immigrants from the past and the present. Good historical fiction creates an emotional connection between children of today and their historical counterparts. (Rycik & Rosler, 2009, p. 164)

Adams (2001) has argued selecting historical fiction as a teaching/learning strategy provides a literacy-rich environment, which is meaningful, authentic and an engaging approach for students to learn about historical issues and events.

Tarry Lindquist, an American fifth-grade teacher, who was recognised by the National Council for the Social Studies as Elementary Teacher of the Year (2002), offers several reasons why she teaches with historical fiction:

- it piques kids' curiosity about historical events;
- provides them with everyday details that a textbook would miss;
- gives students multiple perspectives on events; and
- assists students contemplating the complexities of an issue. (Lindquist, 2002)

For example, Lindquist (2002) has her students create cost-versus-benefit lists of historical decisions, such as whether an American colonist should join the rebels or stay with the loyalists. Although Lindquist (2002, p. 48) uses many teaching methods in the social studies classroom, she refers to historical fiction as the 'spice' that triggers student inquiry into the facts driving the fiction.

Lindquist (2002) finds the advantages of historical fiction lie with its ability to unfold the events in history in layers where the reader understands the values, actions and behaviours of historical characters. As a result, students are motivated to find out the *why*? This distinguishes historical fiction from the traditional textbook in which historical events are usually summarised briefly. Therefore, Lindquist argues, historical misconceptions and stereotypical attitudes are more likely to develop. Consequently, teacher/student discussions are vitally important in this teaching/learning process, where the teacher needs to question extensively and be alert to historical misconceptions.

McManus (2008) shares Lindquist's enthusiasm for the use of historical fiction as a teaching/learning device in the class, adding:

> Using historical fiction in my social studies classroom has changed my method of teaching. I am excited each time I assign a new novel

and look forward to the process of discovery that my students will encounter because of reading. The best part is that I know that reading is good for my students and that they will grow from the process. These books help me to build a relationship with my students by giving us a common topic for conversations. It may be difficult to verify whether this method improves state-mandated test scores, but I have seen how reading is good for these students in terms of their subject knowledge and motivation to learn.

Crawford and Zygouris-Coe (2008) concur with Lindquist (1995) and McManus (2008), arguing the authenticity of the language used in historical fiction to communicate to the reader is closer to everyday language than a textbook, and therefore is more engaging. This results in students developing abilities to connect historical events and values to their lives, and critically reflect on histories past, present and future. In addition, students' connection with the text encourages empathy towards the characters, which motivates students to engage positively in learning about historical events, issues and people.

Historical fiction with young readers

Typically, textbooks obscure issues of agency by presenting the past as the result of abstract and impersonal forces that appear beyond human control (Levstik & Barton, 2001). Levstik and Barton (2001, p. 117) state that when textbooks, for example, describe how the shift from feudalism to capitalism occurred, it can be difficult for students to view historical events as being shaped by individuals and groups of people. Even very well-used and well-received textbooks can fall into this category: witness Easton et al.'s *SOSE Alive 2*, Chapter 2. In contrast, children's literature, especially narrative, biography, autobiography and historical fiction, often personalises history, making historical events come to life. Children's literature evokes emotional and personal connections to historical characters and events and encourages readers to experience history through the experiences — the choices, trials, travails, and triumphs — of the characters.

Historical fiction can help students understand what happened in the past (what people did at the time of the event, specific actions taken, and so on), why the event took place (what the actions, beliefs, motivations and intentions of certain actors were), and the consequences of the event (how people were affected, how they responded, and so on). Historical fiction also can help students understand broader contexts, such as the social forces created and shaped by people, or the ways certain economic conditions affected people's lives. Historical fiction, moreover, can make visible the contributions of individuals and groups of people often marginalised by traditional heroes and great (military) leaders' accounts of history. Much like revisionist historical accounts, such as Howard Zinn's *A People's History of the United States* (2003), historical fiction, because of its multiple characters and perspectives, also can better provide voice to those who might have been silenced or adversely affected by a particular event, thus inviting students to question why some groups had less power, influence, or privilege than others.

A key example of this is Toni Morrison's novel *Beloved* (1987). *Beloved* can be read as 'an overt and passionate quest to fill a gap neglected by historians, to record the everyday lives of the disremembered' (Davis, 1998, p. 245). In this regard, Morrison's novel gives a voice to the unspoken, allowing students the opportunity to delve into the historical lives of those whose stories would otherwise be left untold and unrecorded. Here, the protagonist, Sethe, is representative of an actual historical figure, Margaret Garner, who, like Sethe in the novel, killed her daughter in order to protect her from a life of slavery. As Morrison has expressed, stories such as Garner's have been left untold (Ying, 2006, Chapter 2). Therefore, I suggest, historical fiction such as *Beloved* brings to life the stories of these slaves, allowing the reader to empathise with the psychological effects of slavery. If students do not engage in the reading of historical novels such as *Beloved*, I argue, it is unlikely they will ever be able to develop an understanding of issues deeper than those expressed within their textbooks, nor will they be given the opportunity to do key in-depth character studies of history's 'forgotten victims' (Davis, 1998, p. 2; Ying, 2006, Chapter 2). Furthermore, as Morrison herself is African-American, both Davis and Ying suggest that *Beloved* can serve as a historical representation of how one African-American in contemporary society feels the need to 'be a voice' and share with others the injustices many African-Americans suffered as slaves during the time the novel is set (Davis, 1998, p. 2; Ying, 2006, Chapter 2).

There are several additional reasons for using historical fiction in primary school and middle school History classrooms. A work of historical fiction provides a continuous narrative that is easier to follow than a set of loosely connected primary documents. Levstik and Barton (2001) suggest an important reason for using historical fiction is to ensure students have experiences with a range of texts and genres in social studies literature. Reading across a range of texts, including primary sources, textbooks, biographies, and fictional works helps teachers and students build a web of meaning in classrooms. According to Levstik and Barton (2001), historical fiction helps students develop mature historical understanding because it encourages readers to recognise the human aspects of history and gives students a sense of history as an ongoing, participatory drama (p. 120). They argue historical fiction can particularise and personalise history to help students make connections between past and present moral dilemmas. All of these factors, and the special role of speculation inherent in historical fiction, support the use of that genre to help middle school students understand historical agency and learn about the past.

The historical novel in early childhood classes

Stories are central to everyday life. Children are told stories from a very young age, whether it be orally or by sharing a story book. Young children are comfortable listening to stories and this process offers them the opportunity to expand their existing knowledge of the world around them (Cooper, 2002,

p. 66). Historical fiction allows children to compare the present with the past in a familiar format. There are a variety of historical stories, such as *Minnie and Ginger* (Smith, 1990) or *Timothy's Teddy* (Harrison, 1992), that explore changes in family life, following the generations. This is an aspect children can relate to and embrace through discussion about their own families, making comparisons between their own lives and that of their parents and grandparents. Cooper describes the use of historical text with children: 'stories are a wonderful way of making children aware of changes over time, within living memory in their own lives and families' (2002, p. 78). For an insight into the teaching of History in the early years of schooling, I refer readers to Cooper's (2002) work.

* * *

With the advent of 'the new pedagogies' — constructivist pedagogy and essential learnings — many Australian teachers have a new confidence in progressive methods in the classroom. Consequently, as they work towards the new national History curriculum, anecdotal evidence suggests many teachers across all grades are looking to the teaching of historical literacy through historical novels (Kersey Group, 2010).

Taylor and Young (2003) at the National Centre for History Education have argued that thinking mathematically, linguistically and logically are important aspects needed to grasp historical time-frames. This chapter argues that the use of historical novels as a teaching/learning strategy can assist in these objectives, especially in encouraging students to think beyond their present life experiences to more abstract historical time-frames, that is, encouraging abstract thought in students.

Many early childhood teachers have long recognised this as they immerse young students in a rich literary experience. Typically, early childhood teachers recognise the power of stories and how they are central to children's everyday lives. Using historical novels in primary and middle school grades as a teaching/

learning strategy simply builds on experiences with which students have long been comfortable.

Historical novels can be used in the classroom in ways textbooks, I argue, have been long found to be wanting. For example, leading our students to appreciate the role of agency in history ought to be a major objective in our teaching of History. Typically, I suggest, textbooks obscure issues of agency by presenting the past as the result of abstract and impersonal forces appearing beyond human control.

Historical novels, moreover, can link the past to the present and future. Researchers have found that encouraging students to think of 'history as the extended present' (Bateman and Harris, 2008, p. 272) rather than as a chronological series of events — the past, present and future — enhances their understanding of the historical process. Historical novels often provide a narrative that allows for intersecting and often conflicting narratives. Historical novels dealing with complex social and personal issues are examples of how authors of historical fiction cater for this ideal. This ideal is all about using historical novels to connect and engage with students. Engaging students with quality historical novels enhances their historical understanding through a number of metacognition reading strategies.

PART II

UNDERSTANDING THE GENRE OF HISTORICAL NOVELS

4 Defining the Historical Novel

The genre of historical fiction is continually expanding, adapting to new demands from readers and the creativity of authors. First, let us examine this phenomenon from its international perspectives.

The range of historical fiction

What is historical fiction? The United States-based Historical Novel Society acknowledges the complexity and proposes the following definition:

> There will never be a satisfactory answer to these questions, but these are the arbitrary decisions we've made.
>
> To be deemed historical (in our sense), a novel must have been written at least fifty years after the events described, or have been written by someone who was not alive at the time of those events (who therefore approaches them only by research). (Historical Novel Society, n.d.).

Perhaps to maximise membership, however, the society offers a much broader definition:

> We also consider the following styles of novel to be historical fiction for our purposes: alternate histories (e.g. Robert Harris's *Fatherland*), pseudo-histories (e.g. Umberto Eco's *Island of the Day Before*), time-slip novels (e.g. Barbara Erskine's *Lady of Hay*), historical fantasies (e.g. Bernard Cornwell's *King Arthur Trilogy*) and multiple-time novels (e.g. Michael Cunningham's *The Hours*). (Historical Novel Society, n.d.)

Historical fiction comprises several sub-genres, and their nomenclatures are quite arbitrary. In Chapters 7, 8 and 9 respectively, I will examine counterfactual histories, alternate histories and time-slip histories for their application to the History curriculum in Australian schools.

The range of historical fiction

Given the popularity of historical fiction as a literary genre, there are many historical fiction authors writing in the growing number of sub-genres. Convening international annual conferences, the Historical Novel Society is a robust group. It publishes annually two issues of *Solander* and four issues of *The Historical Novel Review*. Sarah Johnson, one-time editor of the Historical Novel Society's journals, elaborated on the difficulties of arriving at a consensus regarding an acceptable definition of the historical novel: 'the obvious definition that comes to mind is that historical fiction is simply "fiction set in the past"' (Johnson, 2002). There is certainly no consensus on a definition for the genre. For Dalton, 'the reality is, however, that almost everyone — and this includes readers, authors, publishers, agents, and the press — seems to have his or her own idea of what historical fiction is, and also what historical fiction should be'. It is a genre of some 'controversy and contradiction' (Dalton, n.d.). As Johnson puts it, 'While the usual generic definition — "fiction set in the past" — is true for the most part, this seemingly simple definition brings up a number of questions' (Johnson, 2002).

However, Jill Paton Walsh, a UK historical fiction writer, argues that 'a novel is a historical novel when it is wholly or partly about the public events and social conditions which are the material of history, regardless of the time at which it is written' (Paton Walsh, 1977, p. 221). MacKinlay Kantor, the author of the Pulitzer Prize winner *Andersonville*, is adamant about the novelist's obligation to history. He maintains 'the term "historical novel" has a dignity of its own, and should be applied to those works wherein a deliberate attempt has been made to recreate the past' (Kantor, 1967, p. 2, cited in Herz, 2010). He is enthusiastic about the historical novel being an important genre of literature because an awareness of the past can help the general reader confront the fear and perplexities of the present and future. He feels the historical novel helps the reader to profit from the lessons of the past with 'its agonies, its triumphs, its dreams, its disillusionments' (Kantor, 1967, p. 2, as cited in Herz, 2010).

Nevertheless, the very term 'historical fiction' ostensibly appears to embody a contradiction. This was something Richard Lee, founder of the Historical Novel Society, addressed in a paper given to the Romantic Novelists' Association at their annual conference in 2000. He began by referring to a *Daily Telegraph* (London) article by Andrew Graham Dixon, art critic, journalist, television presenter, novelist, lecturer, educationalist and nonfiction author: '"The historical novel has always been a literary form at war with itself. The very term, implying a fiction somehow grounded in fact — a lie with obscure obligations to the truth — is suggestive of the contradictions of the genre"' (R. Lee, 2000, quoting Dixon).

Lee, however, countered by reminding his audience that Dixon's claim 'can just as easily be said of something contemporary'. He asked his audience to think of *Trainspotting* (1996) or *Bridget Jones' Diary* (1996). No one thinks these two books are true: 'Yet no-one would bother to read them if they didn't believe that they were in some way drawn from life.' Lee claims this may be a 'contradiction' but 'it's an absolute fundamental — perhaps the absolute fundamental quality of art. Not just fiction, but sculpture, painting, poetry — all art'. For Lee, in this sense 'all art is, to use Dixon's words "at war with itself"'. For Lee, 'It [historical fiction] seeks, at the same time, both *accuracy* and *illusion*. It is ludicrous to say this is *only* a defining characteristic of historical fiction — it's a defining characteristic of *all* fiction' (Lee, n.d., emphases in original).

Historical fiction compared to History as a discipline

Scott H. Dalton (2006) offers another definition of historical fiction:
- real historical figures in the context of the challenges they faced.
- real historical figures in imagined situations.

- fictional characters in documented historical situations.
- fictional characters in fictional situations, but in the context of a real historical period.

Dalton (2006) adds that 'the market recognizes a few other permutations':

- Time-shift stories, in which a modern character is transported back in time, or more rarely, a historical character is transported to the present, or to a time period not his own.
- Alternate history or 'What if?' stories, usually set in a world in which an historic event did not occur, or occurred much differently, such as a Nazi victory in World War II, a Texan victory at the Alamo, or the death of William, Duke of Normandy, in 1065.
- Historical fantasy, in which characters, even historic figures, are depicted in historical periods or situations, but along with magic or dragons or some other element of fantasy.

Dalton (2006) goes on to state that 'historical fiction is a fictional story in which elements of history, be they persons, events, or settings, play a central role'. While Dalton suggests that historical fiction must possess 'elements of history', 'what differentiates historical fiction from history? … After all, does not all history contain an element of fiction, or at least speculation?' (2006). As she suggests, 'Ask four soldiers about the same battle an hour afterward, and you're likely to get four different recounts of the fight'. That said, historians write within their discipline while historical novelists are not so bound. Nevertheless, for Dalton 'it is the job of both the historian and the [historical] fiction writer to cut through the fog of perception and come as close to the truth as possible'. Much has to do with the audience to which the historian and historical novelist address their respective narrative, but for Dalton 'the difference lies in the *level* at which they seek the truth, the *focus* of their seeking. The historian focuses on the events. The fiction writer focuses on the persons — the characters, if you will — involved in those events' (Dalton, 2006). Of course, this is a contested point of view, but nevertheless one worthy of consideration.

History is a discipline of enquiry, while historical novels are acts of creativity. Dalton reminds us writers of nonfiction history (historians) seek at 'the most basic level' to answer the questions 'what happened?' and 'why it happened that way'. By contrast, the writer of historical fiction seeks to explore the question 'What was it like?' (Dalton, 2006).

In answering that last question, authors of historical fiction make full use of historical 'facts' as they choose to understand them. Vernay states that 'it is generally accepted that a work of imagination is built on reality contributing to the psychology of the characters, the historical context, fictional setting, the authenticity of certainly situations modelled on the author's life and so on' (2010, p. 181). However, real happenings — the substrata of all literature, I suggest — have multiple uses. As Vernay (2010) has it, 'when they [facts] are not inspiration for the basic structure of the intrigue, they are the engine that enables the narrative to unfold. They also take the reader back to a pre-text and an after-text when they do not legitimise the story' (2010, p. 181). However, for the historical novelist, facts have another purpose in their narrative: 'facts give the text substance so that the reader can read it literally or symbolically. Actual trivia feeds the historical novel' (p. 181). Vernay suggests that because of the short span of its recorded history, writers of Australian historical novels face another challenge in their use of facts, that is, they may be tempted to over-trivialise their use of facts. Without citing any evidence, Vernay asserts 'actual trivia feed the historical novel which, from an Australian perspective, reads like a compensatory strategy' (p. 181).

Historical fiction, however, serves other important purposes for the reader, all of which contribute to its uniqueness as a genre. Comparing two works on World War One can show this. Les Carlyon's *The Great War* (2006) is a brilliant and scholarly piece of nonfiction that explores the manifold motives of the Allies and the tragedy of high command. As Hutchinson describes, 'it reads easily, the prose lopes along and, if the occasional metaphor is strained and some battle descriptions hard to follow, most remains in the great tradition of plain, dignified writing' (Hutchinson, 2006). With great finesse, Carlyon takes the reader into the mud, vermin and filth of the trenches. He 'tells their stories, rescues ordinary heroes, lays judicious blame at the feet of butcher-generals, is fair to the British, points the finger at ignorant politicians and their secret agents and recounts the forgotten battles' (Hutchinson, 2006). Moreover, Hutchinson adds, his history is not flagrant patriotism: 'He is careful in measuring our contribution to the huge mincing machine on the Western Front and effective in sketching the bigger background in Europe and Australia' (Hutchinson, 2006).

But compare Carlyon's *The Great War* with such works of fiction as Erich Maria Remarque's *Im Westen Nichts Neues*, which translates into English as *All Quiet on the Western Front* (1929). Written only ten years after the events described in the novel, it is not strictly a historical novel by earlier definitions. But it was written only ten years after the events it describes, and now over eighty years have passed since its publication. Soon after its publication, in 1930, vast numbers of people around the Western world were fascinated with the outstanding blockbuster Hollywood film version of the novel, brilliantly directed by William Wallman. Theatres filled everywhere — it was a must-see film. Sales of Remarque's book soared. A feature article in *The Reveille* edition of 29 June 1930 affords a fascinating contemporary insight into the Australian Digger's response to the film. Diggers heaped praise on it for its honesty in portraying conditions at the Front and for not glorifying war.

Remarque puts the reader into the battlefront from the ordinary German soldier's perspective; readers can feel the weight of the mud on Paul Bäumer's pitifully worn boots, and the pathos of his dreams and disillusionment. Readers feel Bäumer's heavy pack digging into their shoulders, and curse as his feet slip on the worn and wet duckboards of the trenches. Reader hear the snap of the merciless passing rounds, and feel his fear as he and his fellow soldiers scramble into the man-made warrens of the trenches under heavy Allied bombardment. Readers fear for his life in the moments before he raises his head above the trench. Readers care about the things he cares about: not national strategy but his friends and family, as this dreadful war eats away at his soul. Thus, in

Dalton's words 'the writer of historical fiction is first a writer not of history, but of fiction, and fiction is about characters, not events' (Dalton, 2006).

'So historical fiction' Dalton concludes, 'is a close relative of history, but not simply a retelling of the lectures we learned to dread in high school.' Moreover, 'we write historical fiction, and read it, not to learn about history so much as to live it. It is the closest we can get to experiencing the past without having been there' (Dalton, 2006). Indeed, Dalton suggests, reading historical fiction is a wonderfully personal experience: 'We finish a history and think "So that's what happened!" We finish a work of historical fiction, catch our breath, and think "So that's what it was like!"' (Dalton, 2006).

Historical fiction defined for teachers

Groce and Groce (2005) are concerned with how any definition of historical fiction may fit with the needs of teachers in their development of integrated teaching/learning strategies as a part of their social studies programs. They refer to Galda and Cullinan's research (2002), which describes historical fiction as 'a distinctive genre consisting of "imaginative stories grounded in the facts of our past"' (Groce & Groce, p. 205). Groce and Groce go on to contend that 'historical fiction differs from nonfiction in that it not only presents facts or re-creates a time and place, but also weaves the facts into a fictional story. Historical fiction is realistic — the events could have occurred and people portrayed could have lived — but differs from contemporary realistic fiction in that the stories are set in the past rather than the present' (p. 205).

Groce and Groce (2005) then add additional thoughts for teachers on a definition of historical fiction The authors contend that Reed (1994) offers more clarification by differentiating between 'historic fiction' that purports to 'reveal history and true character of historic figures' from 'historical fiction', whose purpose is to 'bring history to life' (p. 121). Perhaps so, but the commentary is a little semantic. I prefer Armstrong's (1999) suggestion: 'historical fiction takes all those things that *were* (the history) and turns something that *was not* (an imagined story) into something that *could have been*' (p. 16, cited in Groce & Groce, 2005, p. 100, emphases in Groce & Groce). But clearly, any definition of historical fiction is contestable.

* * *

The terms 'historical fiction' and 'history' are far from synonymous. Each has its own purpose: History is a disciplined method of enquiry of the past; historical fiction is a creative act, making extensive use of historical personages and events. A comparison of Carlyon's *The Great War* with such works of fiction as Erich Maria Remarque's *All Quiet on the Western Front* shows what works of history and historical fiction seek to achieve.

Any definition of historical fiction will take into account the purpose of the definition, and for whom it is intended. For the purposes of this present study, I have used the Historical Novel Society (n.d.) definition and that provided by Dalton (2006). These definitions included 'what if' history — counterfactual history, alternate history — and their definitions. This book has two chapters devoted to these genres, specifically to attempt to explain how teachers can use these related genres in History classrooms as pedagogical devices.

5 The Increase of History as a Subject for Novels: Memory and the Context of Interpretation

History teachers have available to them a rising tide of popularity in the reading of historical novels. There is no sign of this popularity waning. As this chapter will demonstrate, the historical novel continues to develop as a literary genre as increasing numbers of authors are attracted to it.

The rising tide of popularity for historical fiction

In 2008 Richard Nile wrote an impressionistic article in *The Australian*: 'today, historical novels massively outsell even the finest [nonfiction] history, and readers continue to learn from their imaginative journeys into Australia's past' (Nile, 2008). Thus, for Nile, historical fiction serves to educate readers about our past in a manner that exceeds nonfiction. This nationwide interest in Australian historical fiction perhaps stems from the nationalistic upsurge in a general interest in the Australian past as reflected by the massive increase in attendance at such events as the Gallipoli Anzac Day dawn service on freezing mornings, treks along the steamy Kokoda Trail, or expeditions to the misty Flanders Fields.

Further to the argument that history sells, it is relevant to note that a number of historical nonfiction writers have had or continue to have a strong public appeal, including authorities such as Manning Clark, Geoffrey Blainey and Robert Hughes. Also relevant are writers such as Peter FitzSimmon, who writes popular narratives in historical nonfiction, with fresh works appearing in bookshops at almost an annual rate. History sells. Another commentator has noted this penchant for the past in Australian fiction. In reviewing Chris McCourt's historical novel, *The Cleansing of Mohammed* (2012), Ed Wright (2012) noted, 'For a nation with a fairly short history it's remarkable how much of our literature is backward looking.'

But not all commentators consider the growth and sales of Australian historical fiction as being positive developments. For example, Delia Falconer (2006) has reflected on concerns that some commentators have raised about the decline in numbers of the Australian novel with a contemporary setting. As Falconer put it, 'since early 2002 this anxiety about the state of the art has centred on the content of Australian literature and its apparent failure to confront the present. In *The Bulletin* (13 November 2002) Hannie Rayson called for a "theatre of engagement", while in the *Sydney Morning Herald*, Malcolm Knox (21 January 2002) and Drusilla Modjeska (8 August 2002) took the Australian novel to task for its retreat from modern life' (Falconer, 2006). Falconer noted that Modjeska 'was surprised recently to discover that she no longer enjoyed Australian novels, which she finds, on the whole, "tricksy and insubstantial". While our non-fiction writers have risen to the complexities of our times, she argued, the sheer rate of change seems to have overwhelmed the novel, which now confines itself almost exclusively to exotic settings or the past'.

Similarly, Falconer noted that 'Knox, too, was troubled by his own lack of interest in contemporary Australian fiction; novels written by French and American authors (Houellebecq, Franzen, Moody) seemed to capture his own reality far more effectively than, say, Peter Carey's *True History of the Kelly Gang*. This was because too many Australian novels have retreated into the "far-off, the period, the unfamiliar, the allegoric"' (Falconer, 2006).

Falconer herself doubted the usefulness of arguing for more novels about the present and less about the past. She found pexplexing any 'tacit agreement that the use of historical fiction is, ipso facto, politically complacent: by writing about history, swottish authors are aiming for gold stars (neatness, tick; cultural cachet, tick) while shrinking from the messiness of the present' (Falconer, 2006). But her essay certainly highlighted a perception held by some in the literary community, one that Richard Nile's 2008 article in *The Australian* set out to question.

What are the motives of these critics who criticise Australian historical fiction? Perhaps it has to do with a sweeping dismissal of the genre as well as urging authors to tackle issues associated with contemporary Australia. Separate to any critiques of individual historical novels, there appears to exist a sentiment that implies that all historical novels are somehow locked into a particular social and cultural setting: that with the glut of historical novels comes mediocrity.

The historical novel and memory

Just how should a reader appreciate a historical novel written during a particular period? At this point, it is appropriate to clarify the distinction between memory and history. As Seixas, Fomowitz and Hill write, 'much ink has been spilled in recent years on the subject of history and memory':

> An easy dichotomy can he drawn: memory is the construction of the past, which is immediately available, deeply held, profoundly meaningful and therefore impervious to critique. History is the product of evidence-based investigation, rational dialogue and dispassionate scholarship. Memory is the product of direct experience; history is the product of [a disciplined] questioning, inquiry and critique. (2005, p. 116)

However, Seixas, Fomowitz and Hill (2005) go on to argue that 'this simple bifurcation fails on many counts' (p. 116). It does not take into account the fiercely held ramifications of 'the structures of social memory, as well as the deeply felt passions that stir people to engage in history' (p. 116). The authors, however, seek to maintain the distinction, and go on to propose a careful scrutiny of 'the intersections between history and memory; passion, reason and meaning; dialogue and identity. These are the places where we will find the generative leaven that gives rise to our most thoughtful uses of the past' (p. 116).[1]

Perhaps, associated with baby-boomers, and imbedded in the rising tide of electronic media, there has been a proliferation of 'memory' literature since the 1980s. But what of suppressed social or collective memory? An example of this might be the way in which authors from western societies during the decades following World War Two were loath to write about or discuss anything concerning the history of eugenics, possibly because of the way in which western propaganda had connected eugenic excesses with the Nazis. It was not until the 1980s that there appeared any research and discourse on this subject. This was so in Australia, despite the obvious connection of eugenics with the White Australia policy and the Stolen Generations (see, for example, W. Anderson, 2002; Lake & Reynolds, 2008).

Olick (2007, Chapter 1) emphasises that memory is a politically loaded notion. His study is with the politics of regret — a study of Germany's memories of its Nazi past. But memory and the politics of regret exists in most countries: witness the political imbroglios concerning a national official apology to Australia's Stolen Generations by then Labor Prime Minister Kevin Rudd in February 2008. Fentress and Wickham (1992) also note that memory is socially, culturally and gender bound. Moreover, 'the essential subjectivity of memory is the key issue to begin with' (p. 88). Memories almost inevitably will change over time, and historians are alert to this. But as Fentress and Wickham (1992) state, 'even when they do not, they will certainly be selected, out of the potentially infinite set of possible memories, for the relevance to the individuals who remember them, for their contribution to personal identity and relationships' (p. 88).

It goes without saying that an Indigenous woman from the 1950s will have a different story to relate in a work of historical fiction than will

---

[1] For a detailed discussion on memory and history see P. Ricoeur (2004), pp. 385-93.

a non-Indigenous woman from the same period. Historical novels used in the History classroom can assist in ensuring these suppressed, ignored or disregarded memories of characters are brought to the surface and discussed.

Here, Kate Grenville's novel *The Secret River* (2005) offers much. In discussing *The Secret River*, teachers may wish to have their students research how Grenville came by the title of the novel. In his 1968 Boyer lectures entitled *After the Dreaming* (1968) W. H. Stanner asserted 'there is a secret river of blood in Australian history' — violence and silencing, or suppressed, memory. In his Boyer lectures, Stanner referred to this as 'The Great Australian Silence'.[2] As Kossew (2007) shows, these notions of suppressed memory, or silence, are manifest in *The Secret River*. Grenville 'acknowledged the influence of Stanner's lectures, not only by quoting his words in her title but also in a number of interviews' (p. 8). Grenville 'uses the term "the great Australian silence" in a newspaper interview in which she suggests, too, that "until we go back and retell our stories and put the shadows in we won't grow up as a society"' (Kossew, 2007, p. 8).

In *The Secret River*, Grenville confronts a central issue in the Australian identity, what Hodge and Mishra term the 'dark side of the dream' (Hodge & Misha, 1991, p. 1, quoted in Kossew, 2007, p. 8). The dream is about the role of pastoralism in the development of the Australian (white) identity. The myth has it that pastoralism has a central role in this sense of who Australians are. As Kossew argues, quoting from Paul Carter's *The Road to Botany Bay*,

> There are two competing narratives in collision in uncovering this occluded place: the Aboriginal stories of violent encounters with settlers that are transmitted orally and are unwritten and those European historical accounts whose 'primary object is not to understand or to interpret' but to 'legitimate', thereby demonstrating 'the emergence of order from chaos'. (Kossew, 2007, p. 8, quoting Carter, 1987, p. xvi)

---

[2] For details of the Boyer lectures, including a short extract from Stanner's 1968 lectures, see the ABC Radio National website, http://www.abc.net.au/rn/boyers/index/BoyersChronoIdx.htm. The lectures also appeared in book form.

The history of the Australian pastoral industry is riddled with this same terrible reality. Kossew (2007) states 'what Grenville is trying to reconcile in her novel is her own convict ancestor's implication in acts of Indigenous dispossession and an acknowledgement of the strength and courage of such acts of settlement' (p. 8). For generations in schools, colleges and universities the history of the Australian pastoral industry was portrayed as one of immense opportunity. In Kossew's words, 'while the space of the settler colony can be viewed ... as a place of opportunity and egalitarianism where convicts were able to transform themselves into landowners, it was also necessarily a place of violent encounters that left scars on the land and on the psyche of the people, both Indigenous and non-Indigenous Australians' (2007, p. 8). This is also about collective suppressed memory in collision with the very real memories and contemporary experiences of Indigenous Australians.

Historians have long taken memory as the raw material for history, as a means to getting at the truth of the past. The memory literature of recent years is connected most intimately with traumatic events — the dispossession or taking of people — such as the Holocaust or the Cultural Revolution in China, and in Australia, that of the Stolen Generations. Witness such publishing phenomenon as Thomas Keneally's *Schindler's Ark* (1982), and its film version, *Schindler's List* (1993), directed by Steven Spielberg. The boom in memory literature is concomitant with the rising tide of the new postcolonial and postmodernist historiography (explained later in this chapter), which has engendered memory with a greater status.

Continuing this theme, not surprisingly, authors such as Dirlik write that 'in its most recent appearance memory has emerged as a competitor with history, in opposition to the latter' (2002a, p. 76). He goes on to state that 'memory may serve different purposes under different circumstances for different groups' (p. 76). Quoting from Hayden White (1996), Dirlik contends and event like the Holocaust 'may "escape the grasp of any language even to describe it and of any medium — verbal, visual, oral, or gestural — to represent ... it, much less of any historical account adequately to explain it"'. Consequently,

> memories of the experiences of traumatic events may in such cases well accomplish what history is unable to capture or explain. Memories may also serve to capture glimpses of the past for groups who have been erased from history. On the other hand, they add moral force to history in the case of groups ... seeking recognition of their grievances. (Dirlik, 2002a, p. 76)

A statement such as this may well resonate with the lived experiences of such groups as the Stolen Generations.

Publicly-stated memory serves to bolster the self-images of newly empowered groups seeking to overcome their images as victims in history. This is certainly the case with Indigenous memory literature, such as the film *Rabbit-Proof Fence* (2002), based on Doris Pilkinton's biography, *Follow the Rabbit-Proof Fence* (1996). For a more comprehensive understanding of Indigenous memory literature, readers are encouraged to consult Morris-Suzuki (1994).

Moving the discussion from biography to historical fiction, it should be noted that the publication of such works are associated with remembering what history forgets. Writing about the motives of the historical novelist, Bradley contends that 'Part of it is more explicitly political, seeking to recover something of the particularity of lives that have been obscured, whether by personal misfortune or by the political complexities that surrounds them' (2011a).

This connects with bringing forgotten, hidden or suppressed memories to the surface. The potency of these memories can be observed as the tears that were shed at then Prime Minister Kevin Rudd's apology in the Australian Parliament to the Stolen Generation on 13 February 2008 (see, for example, 'Wyatt Shares Stolen Generation Stories', 2010). But underlying this motive is a larger vision of the relationship between the individual and the historical, not just of the manner by which individual lives are shaped by history but of the way history too often elides the truth of the story it tells, failing to discern the accreditation of memory, loss and love that shape our lives and bind us to each other. To this end, Mitchell (2010) contends that Grenville's 'neo-Victorian narrative [in *The Secret River*] shapes Australia's present relationship to — and in terms of — a traumatic past' (p. 254). For Mitchell (2010), the narrative of the trauma in Grenville's novel is a reflection of contemporary national anxieties associated with Australia's stalled reconciliation process toward Indigenous Australians. As Kossew (2007) notes, relations between colonists and Indigenous Australians from the very early years of the settlement were based on mistrust. Indigenous Australians were seen as creatures of the forest, 'everywhere and ... only seen when they choose to be seen' (p. 16).

With national anxiety associated with much memory narrative, Mitchell (2010) draws on Toni Morrison's 1987 Nobel Prize-winning novel, *Beloved*. The novel is set in post-Civil War America. Morrison declared her novel was a '"memorial" to lives lost in slavery' (Mitchell, 2010, p. 270). Mitchell goes on to state in the tragic absence of any national memorials to slavery and suggests that 'Morrison implicitly positions historical fiction among other modes of historical recollection outside of academic history' (2010, p. 271). Indeed, this point has tragic poignancy — a point, perhaps, to which many History teachers are very sensitive — for many students, including those of Indigenous Australian groups and from immigrant groups. By 'positioning historical fictions as memory texts, alongside museums, monuments, and public commemorations, [this] foregrounds the ways historical novels seek to establish connections between past and present identities to interpret the past in and for the specific needs of the present, and to witness traumatic events long silenced and suppressed' (Mitchell, 2010, p. 271).

Yet, in reviewing three literary works, two of them memoirs, one a piece of historical fiction, Maria Tumarkin writes:

> Sooner or later all students of memory come across these words: 'There is nothing more invisible than a monument.' A monument is large,

> imposing, set apart, deemed sacred; yet somehow the eye doesn't quite see it.' (2012, p. 18)

For Tumarkin (2012), two of the works she reviewed moved her to tears, the memoir and the novel dancing in a tight embrace, novel and memoir achieving the same ends. For example, witness such works as the many Holocaust novels, many of which are drawn from memory, and dance in a tight embrace with the various Holocaust museums around the world.

With memory and the novel as a basis for their discourse with students, History curriculum lecturers in universities, and History teachers in schools and colleges, have an opportunity to consider with their students the special role some historical novels can play in revealing suppressed memories, in whatever form they may be.

The many meanings of historiography

As well as informing the reader about the past, the narratives of historical novels also connect with contemporary anxieties, many of which have surfaced in the wake of postmodernist theory. Since the late 1980s, theorists have been commenting on how postmodernist theory has shattered our old views of historiography. For example, Jenkins devoted a whole chapter to 'Doing history in the post-modernist world' (1991, pp. 59-70). Here, he noted that 'because post-modernists see nothing as fixed or solid this jeopardises the sorts of attempts they make to define what they see themselves as part of, whilst some commentators have doubted ... the very existence of the condition' (p. 59).

Twenty years later, Parkes (2011) pursued the fallout of how this has impacted on the meaning of historiography. Not surprisingly, historiography now had many different meanings for different people. Parkes notes:

> Sometimes it is used to refer to the study of the theories, methods and principles of historical research, the results of which are typically presented in the form of a historical narrative or typology that highlights

> changes and continuities in historical practice ... It even may be used to define that category of texts that provide advice on research methods for aspiring historians. More importantly, it refers to literature that comments on methodological issues related to the practice of history as a discipline. It also has been used to refer to texts that explore or argue for a specific approach to historical research. Historiography also has been used to define studies that examine the writings of particular historians or philosophers of history as they relate to each other, a particular methodology, or a specific period, or writings that debate the reliability of the work of a particular group of historians. (p. 105)

Likewise, Parkes (2011) writes 'the term may be used to refer to literature that attempts to describe or define the nature of historical research more generally' (p. 105).

However, Curthoys and Docker (2006) have written about evolutionary idealist views of history (see Chapter 10 of this book), noting that nonfiction may be categorised according to various criteria, often based on a particular methodological approach. Extending this line of enquiry, Parkes (2011) writes that the meaning of historiography may at times embrace:

> a discrete body of historical literature that focuses upon a particular topic — often using a common methodological approach — as in the use of a label such as 'the new Aboriginal historiography' ... Further, it may be used to refer to existing findings and interpretations on a particular topic, answering the question about what we know at this point about a particular person, period, event, idea, culture, and so on. Finally, it may refer to the actual practice of writing histories, based on available methodologies. (2011, p. 106)

Parkes concludes that these various meanings have in common 'a metatheoretical discourse that explores the changing forms and methods of historical representation' (2011, p. 106). Postmodernism, since the late 1960s 'has collapse[d] the distinction between history and historiography' (2011, p. 106).

Contextualizing the historical novel: what does literary and historical interpretation mean?

The historical novel has both contributed to these changes of the collective view of history and historiography, as well as mirroring the influence of postmodernism. Social norms and values change over the decades, as do readers' and critics' interpretation of historical novels written years ago. Davies (1996, p. 20) contends: 'if, as is so often demanded, the context of a literary work should be considered in interpreting it, which context is that? Is it the past context within which the work was created, or, rather, the different context in which the book and interpreter presently is located?'

The foundation of the rapport between author and audience — the shared memory of the past, if you like — is essentially contextual: 'In establishing the meanings of a work, the artist also fixes the identity. If the meaning of the work is unchanging, so is its identity' (Davies, 1996, p. 20). The meaning of the narrative is contextual in the sense the reader will interpret it in the context of generational changes in attitudes and values. Davies puts it this way: 'interpreters can explore what the work means to us in the *present*, taking account not only of the circumstances of its creation, but different social context, of discoveries and theories that post-date the work's origin' (Davies, 1996, p. 22, emphasis added).

For example, a reader of Kate Grenville's *The Lieutenant* will be required to make far different intellectual 'shifts' than when the same reader reads Mary Durack's *Keep Him My Country* (1955). The latter was written during Australia's era of literary colonialist mentality, while the former is a postcolonial work. There have been vast changes in Australian society since the 1950s when Durack wrote *Keep Him My Country*. It is a novel, inter alia, about non-Indigenous/Indigenous relations, and was written during a time when it was a criminal offence for a white person to cohabit with an Indigenous person (see, for example, Wyndham (1996)). Moreover, Davies explains that 'the meaning of a [literary] work is generated by hypothesising intentions authors might have had, given the *context* of the creation, rather than relying on their actual intentions' (1996, p. 21, emphasis added).

Author and reader, then, are united in a common bond of values and concepts, bringing them together in a mutual social experience. In the case of historical fiction, this is a shared memory of the past, an addressing of the social images binding a society. But the sensitive reader may condemn, for example, Durack for her colonial literary views of Indigenous Australians. The context in which the novel is written is of utmost importance. Davies contends that 'the original context theory is preferable to the modern context theory' (1996, p. 36). This is especially so because the former 'locates the object of interpretation in a fashion paying regard to those concerns without which literature would not be created and presented as it is, even if, once the artwork practiced is in place, subsidiary interpretative strategies come into play' (p. 36).

Moreover, 'the original context theory can also match the intuition that the meaning of a literary work lends itself to autonomous, multiple interpretations — even conflicting ones' (Davies, 1996, p. 36). It is precisely this that provides the many-layered meanings existing in the narrative form, providing multiple meanings in the communication between the author and reader over decades.

But does historical fiction have any special role in this narrative? Davies examines the need to pay 'homage to the efforts of the creators of the works, and the second showing the meaning the work presents to the critic's contemporary audience' (1996, p. 20). For example, how should we interpret nineteenth-century historical novels espousing Indigenous Australians in Social Darwinist terms as a fossil race, doomed to extinction according to the laws of the survival of the fittest? Clearly, it is anachronistic to condemn the author, because a strong currency of Social Darwinism existed during the late nineteenth century. But one would not expect such views to be espoused by characters in historical novels written in the late twentieth century. Thus, to return to Davies' (1996) point, he maintains there are two basic ways in which a work of fiction can be interpreted: either from the fixed point of view of the author at the time of writing, or from the point of view of the audience, which is subject to change with succeeding generations.

Student teachers and teachers generally may question whether historical fiction accurately captures the past when it purports to do so. However deeply a historical novel is set in the past, the question continues to loom: how could a historical novelist writing in 2010 ever *actually really know* what life was like in, say, the 1880s — a time when he or she could only have known through contemporary primary sources or through secondary sources. According to Davies, 'interpretation should concern itself with the meaning of the author's work. In discovering the meaning of the work, interpretations must refer and confine themselves to the conventions and practices, both of language and of literature, within or against which the author worked' (1996, p. 22). It follows that the 'meaning' of the historical novel is tied to what the author knows, and has experienced in his/her lifetime — through readings of historical sources — including contemporary interpretations of the past through secondary sources. As literary works, historical fiction is 'reshaped, renewed and reconstructed by their later reception and interpretation'. As with all 'cultural artefacts, the work is changed by its social environment'. Thus, because historical fiction is 'like a living thing, the work changes from time to time, while remaining self-identical' (Davies, 1996, p. 23) In Chapter 13, I will show how this applies, for example, to novels with strong Indigenous Australian themes such as Mary Durack's *Keep Him My Country* and Thomas Keneally's *Chant of Jimmie Blacksmith* (1972).

'the historian remains irrevocably tied to concrete evidence'

At the time of the writing of this book, the level of public discourse on the historicity of historical novels appeared to be gaining in momentum, almost at a parallel rate of the increase in the public's interest in the genre. For example, writing in *The Weekend Australian Review* on 14-15 November 2009, Cassandra

Pybus reviewed two historical novels: Kristin McKenzie's *A Swindler's Progress* (2009) and Gerald Stone's *Beautiful Bodies* (2009). Pybus asked 'why, with the option of historical fiction at their disposal, do writers present unfounded speculation as fact?' (Pybus, 2009b, p. 16). Pybus claimed 'the reading public seems to have an inexhaustible appetite for stories about the past, as long as they are told in an engaging and accessible style, with plenty of evocative description and a seamless narrative arc' (2009b, p. 16). She comments that both novels are 'intriguing stories that suggest potential material for a book to explain the current enthusiasm for popular history'. For Pybus, 'any publisher will tell you history [the historical fiction genre] is a much better publishing proposition than literary non-fiction' (2009b, p. 16).

Pybus argues that generally, the historical novelist has an enormous advantage over the historian: 'not even a master of the popular history genre, such as Simon Schama, can construct a past world as rich and satisfying as the parallel universe the novelist can imagine, nor create characters who are revealed to us in their intimate moments and private thoughts' (2009b, p. 16). For Pybus, this will nearly always be the case, because 'the historian remains irrevocably tied to concrete evidence, which is patchy at best and never allows access to the inner workings of the human psyche' (p. 16). Pybus claims 'the thrill of the historical novel is in the resurrection of the dead; the capacity to breathe vibrant life into the static characters frozen in the formal portrait, official documents, newspaper articles or court reports that are the staple evidence of the historian' (p. 16).

But how much latitude in the search for historicity should readers expect from the historical novelist? I always remember a private conversation with a prominent Tasmanian academic historian who was critical of his fellow Tasmanian author, Richard Flanagan, who had William Gould in *Gould's Book of Fish* (2001) doing things in nineteenth-century Tasmania that the historian considered ahistorical. This grated on the sensibility of this historian.

While commentators such as Pybus have spoken of the historical novelist seeking to breathe life into people and events in order to engage the audience in historical images and memory through the narrative in a manner normally beyond the license of the author of nonfiction, exactly how much license can the historical novelist take in this act? Here we enter the contested domain of recommending or choosing historical novels for students in History curriculum courses and teachers of History in schools.

* * *

This chapter has argued that the rise of the historical novel phenomena in Australia is associated with a similar upsurge in the publication of memory literature, such as Pilkington's *Follow the Rabbit Proof Fence*. The chapter then discussed some of the differences between memory and history. The latter is a disciplined enquiry dating back at least to Herodotus's histories written from the 450s to 420s BC. But memory is the grist to the mill for the historian, and in the twenty-first century is gaining massive attention from historians and other researchers. All of this activity serves to furnish the historical novel publication industry. Historical novels assist in ameliorating social and cultural groups who have suffered under officially sanctioned suppression of the tragic collective memories.

In 2012, students are able to read Australian historical novels, many written during the country's colonial past. During that time readers have read of such events as the glories of the pastoral industry, and the moral right of the European explorers and settlers over Indigenous Australians. Postcolonial and postmodern paradigms have brought these views into serious question. Within this context, this chapter has provided a brief opportunity to introduce ideas about the contextualising of the historical novel — what does literary interpretation mean?

How do we explain the rise in popularity of the historical novel? Perhaps it is because historians seek to write their histories based on primary sources, remaining irrevocably tied to concrete evidence. But this chapter has shown this may be very problematic, seldom allowing for the reader to access speculative accounts of the inner psyches of imagined people from the past. It is the way in which the historical novel provides access to the inner workings of the human psyche, I suggest, that furnishes its wide appeal, as well as its usefulness as a pedagogical device in the History curriculum.

6 'The plot against the plot': Page-turners for Students

When teachers or academics recommend a particular historical novel as a teaching/learning strategy for an undergraduate unit or classroom activity, they enter into a very problematic and contested domain. But most teachers or academics would agree that the first consideration should be meeting their students at their point of need. It is likely that many students will have been exposed to, or will have read, historical novels generally and/or Australian historical novels. Some may be aware of the changes that have come over the historical novel, and the Australian historical novel specifically, since the onset of the postmodernist and postcolonial paradigms.

At this point, teachers or academics might themselves that their principal concern here is not to teach literary criticism but rather to provide students with a potent teaching/learning strategy in their History curriculum. In short, I argue for the use of historical novels as a pedagogical device in the History classroom. That is not to say that if the opportunity arises, points of understanding of literary criticism cannot be developed from these opportunities. I argue, however, for the use of historical novels with a strong plot — a plot that will capture and sustain the attention of History students.

Rejecting the plot portraying an untidy reality

Recently, some literary commentators have begun to lament the loss of plot in many novels. Lev Grossman goes on to write that 'a good story is a dirty secret that we all share. It's what makes guilty pleasures so pleasurable, but it's also what makes them so guilty. A juicy tale reeks of crass commercialism and cheap thrills' (2010, p. 16). Indeed, he writes,

> we crave such entertainments, but we despise them. Plot makes perverts of us all. ... It's not easy to put your finger on what exactly is so disgraceful about our attachment to storyline. Sure, it's something to do with high and low genres and the canon and such. But what exactly? (p. 16)

In answering that question, Grossman is correct in suggesting 'part of the problem is that to find the reason you have to dig deep, down into the murky history of the novel' (2010, p. 16). Some readers will remember brilliant novels such as Alexander Dumas's *The Count of Monte Cristo* (1844-45) or such gripping movies as Zoltan Korda's *The Four Feathers* (1939), one of a number of adaptations of the 1902 novel of the same name by A.E.W. Mason. Along with strong characterisation, setting and so on, plot is vital to the novel. But in reality, life was not as portrayed by *The Count of Monte Cristo* (1844-45) and *The Four Feathers* and their ilk. Yes, there was once a reason for turning away from the plot, with artists recognising that society was murky and untidy, and should be portrayed as such. For me, many people recognised the appeal of the just-mentioned novels. But, still, 'to the modernists, stories don't tie up neatly. Events don't line up in a tidy sequence and mean the same thing for everybody. Ask a veteran of the Somme whether his tour of duty resembled the *Boy's Own* war stories he grew up on' (Grossman, 2010, p. 16). Yet, despite the heartfelt feelings of many readers, 'the modernists broke the clear straight lines of causality and perception and chronological sequence, to make them look more like life as it's actually lived. They took *The Mill on the Floss* and spat out *The Sound and the Fury*' (Grossman, 2010, p. 17).

Grossman (2010) notes that during the first two or three decades of the twentieth century, when modernist authors had abandoned the old neat and orderly worldview, the novel underwent rapid and mammoth change. He goes on to state: 'All the bad news of the modern era had just arrived more or less at the same time: mass media and propaganda, advertising, psychoanalysis, mechanised warfare' (p. 17). Instead, 'the rise of electric light and internal combustion had turned their world into a noisy, reeking travesty of the gas-lit, horse-drawn world in which they grew up' (p. 17). No longer would the 'orderly, complacent, optimistic Victorian novel' mirror the reality of the reader's world: 'They had nothing to say to them. Worse than nothing: it felt like a lie. The novel was a mirror the modernists needed to break [in order to] better reflect their broken world' (p. 17).

But to be fair to the modernists, the crop of novels they wrote set new benchmark literary standards: 'In the 1920s alone they gave us *The Age of Innocence* [Edith Wharton, 1920], *Ulysses* [James Joyce, 1922], *A Passage to India* [E.M. Forster, 1924], *Mrs Dalloway* [Virginia Woolf, 1925], *To the Lighthouse* [Virginia Woolf, 1927], *Lady Chatterley's Lover* [D.H. Lawrence, 1928], *The Sun Also Rises* [Ernest Hemingway, 1926] *A Farewell to Arms* [Ernest Hemingway, 1929] and *The Sound and the Fury* [William Faulkner, 1929]), not to mention most of *In Search of Lost Time* [Marcel Proust, 1913] and all of Kafka's novels' (Grossman, 2010, p. 17). For me, these were the halcyon years of the novel. In Grossman's (2010) words, 'I grant you, the [new writers were the] single greatest crop of writers the novel has seen. ... The 20th century had a full century's worth of masterpieces before it was half over' (p. 17). But, as Grossman insists, 'that rationale [of these novels] has outlived its usefulness', and increasingly people are turning to novels written with a strong plot (Grossman, 2010, p. 17).

The general novel-reading public has long recognised this, as have international best-selling popular authors such as Wilbur Smith, Geoffrey Archer, Stephen King and Ken Follett, and Australian authors such as Colleen McCulloch, at her best in *The Thorn Birds* (1977), Bryce Courtenay and Thomas Keneally. These are the kinds of novels that capture and sustain many readers' interest.

Choosing suitable historical novels

Groce and Groce (2005) describe some of the research in the US undertaken with teachers who 'expressed trepidation when choosing historical fiction for their students because they felt they lacked the necessary backgrounds needed to select accurate and well-written literature' (p. 103). They also note the research by another group (Apol et al., 2003) that 'actually presented their students (pre-service teachers) with substantial evidence the book they were reviewing, *Sadako*, (Coerr, 1993) contained several cultural and historical inaccuracies' (p. 103). According to Groce and Groce, Apol et al. report that 'in spite of this information, the students "chose to believe the truth of the story and based their choices about teaching this literature to children on their pre-existing assumptions' (2003, p. 429, as cited in Groce & Groce, 2005, p. 103). The values, skills and knowledge necessary in choosing appropriate historical fiction for school students need to be established in the first instance in pre-service curriculum units.

But what kind of advice do teachers and pre-service teachers need about choosing historical novels for the classroom? Groce and Groce (2005) suggest teachers should begin by collecting as many resources as possible around a particular theme, as expressed in a novel they have under study: for example, nonfiction books, biographies, primary sources, DVDs, and related historical fiction. In this way, teachers and student teachers are able to understand the various points of view associated with the particular topic or theme they have under study, enabling them to advice school students on the same practice.

Groce and Groce refer to Donelson and Nilsen, who note

> the best way to show young readers that there are different opinions and different ways of looking at history is to encourage the use of several books on the same subject. When a topic is to be discussed, instead of assigning all students to read the same book, bring in individual copies of various books, so that students can choose. (Donelson & Nilsen, 1997, p. 189, cited in Groce & Groce, 2005, p. 103)

This strategy encourages students to swap ideas, skim read sections and generally develop discourse in the classroom on the topic at hand.

Groce and Groce (2005, p. 104) especially urge teachers to use primary sources in conjunction with historical fiction. They remind readers of the many means by which this can be facilitated through the use of the Internet.

Certainly, for teachers and student teachers choosing which historical novel to use with their students, there exist excellent online services. As of 2012, simply Googling 'assisting teachers to choose books' will show such sites as the:

- NSW Premier's Reading Challenge 2011: Tips and Teaching Notes https://products.schools.nsw.edu.au/prc/teacherNotes.html
- Fiction Focus: http://www.det.wa.edu.au/education/cmis/eval/curriculum/publications/FictionFocus/anniversary.htm

I have found Chapter 10 of Levstik and Barton (2011) by far the most informative textbook account of the use of historical fiction in schools. The authors offer an excellent selection on 'selecting good narrative history', and suggest the following criteria to teachers in the selection of historical fiction suitable for the classroom:

- Does the book tell a good story? Scholarship is not enough to carry historical fiction. ...
- Is the story accurate and authentic in its historical detail, including the setting and the known events of history? ... this attention to accuracy and authenticity must not distract from the story.
- Is the language authentic to the times? ... Instead of striving for complete authenticity ... look for language that has the flavour of the times. ...
- Is the historical interpretation sound? ... Select several books representing the same topic from different perspectives and make sure that each perspective is supportable given what is currently known about the topic. Be sure characters act in accordance with these interpretations. ...

- Whose voices are missing? Because literature is so powerful, it is important to select as many different, historically sound perspectives as possible. ...
- Does the book provide insight and understanding into current issues as well as those of the past? ... history is not just about people in the past but also about the connections between the past and present. (pp. 118-19)

Satisfying the selection criteria: an example

Now let us see how this selection criteria works out in practice. Steven Saylor's *The Judgement of Caesar* (2004), a fantastic read, satisfies much of the above criteria, including telling a good story. Saylor, a graduate in history and classics from the University of Texas, is well-published, with 16 novels published in 22 languages, at the time of the writing of this book (Saylor Bibliography, n.d.).

Set in 48 B.C. amidst the contest for world domination between Pompey the Great and Gaius Julius Caesar, the main protagonist and equivalent of an ancient sleuth, Gordianus the Finder, finds himself in Alexandria attempting to cure his wife's mysterious illness. He witnesses the execution of Pompey by the boy king of Egypt, Ptolemy, and becomes privy to Caesar's romance with Queen Cleopatra. Because of a wicked plot, Gordianus must uncover the truth behind an attempted poisoning of Caesar whilst attempting to prove his once disowned son's innocence. As the novel unfolds, the audience sees behind the scenes to catch a glimpse of the decision-making, political corruption and racial prejudices of the antiquity.

The story in Sayloy's *Roma Sub Rosa* is accurate and authentic in its historical detail, including the setting and the known events of history, such as Caesar's relationship with Cleopatra. So this novel satisfies the second criterion listed above. Ancient Rome is most commonly included in the curriculum for Middle School, and it is here that this novel would be best suited. The work draws scrupulously on historical sources and forms a part of the *Roma*

Sub Rosa series, which covers most of Gordianus's life from 80 B.C. to 46 B.C. The *Roma Sub Rosa* — in Latin, 'Rome under the rose' — is the title of Sayloy's series of mystery novels set in, and populated by, noteworthy denizens of ancient Rome. If a matter was *sub rosa* — under the rose — it was a very confidential matter.

While dialogue in fiction is always constructed or contrived to some extent, the language is authentic to the times in Sayloy's *Roma Sub Rosa*. Through an erudite use of language, the personalities of Caesar and Cleopatra stay consistent with historical records. They remain powerful and politically shrewd, and at the same time very human to the reader. The presence of romance, battles, political intrigues, small family problems and everyday preoccupations provides a balanced view of antiquity and caters for a diverse audience.

Sayloy depicts the characters and their surroundings accurately and historically. The historical interpretation is sound. Sayloy rationalises and justifies Caesar's political and personal decisions, which reinforces the idea that human nature is constant, as well as assisting students to understand the role of motivation in decision making. Saylor's insertion of the 'good fortune' element into the ancient political intrigue also subtly introduces the idea that determinism has no place in history, a point I shall expand upon in Chapter 7 of this book.

Saylor preserves the values of Ancient Rome and includes them in his representations of religion, gender and slavery. He also contrasts the Roman views on these issues with traditional Ancient Egyptian beliefs, which provides an interesting comparison for the modern audience. Virtually no voices are missing from the novel: slaves, women and the great and mighty all have a voice in this novel. This serves not only as a tool for exploration of cultural and religious differences between the two cultures, but also demonstrates the irrationality behind prejudice, discrimination and racism at a safe distance. A well-constructed, credible and accurate historical fiction, such as *The Judgement*, is an effective pedagogical device in teaching empathy to its audience.

In order to understand the current political and economic climate, one must understand its origins, using the more ancient past as a map that guides us to think about the present. Contextualisation is crucial in history, as well as a firm grasp on chronology, facts and figures, important events and their causes and effects. All this is abundantly present in *The Judgement*. In my view, the book clearly provides insight and understanding into current issues as well as those of the past.

With teacher guidance, this novel is an ideal medium for developing deep historical understanding, thereby avoiding the debate over the dichotomy of historical understanding and factual knowledge. *The Judgement* achieves this by providing a comprehensive economic, cultural and political context of the fall of the Roman Republic and its aftermath on the Romans and the people of the then known world. It also explores the events that shaped historical climate in detail, thereby providing its audience with a chronology, names and personalities of the 'history-makers', as well as facts and figures. Moreover, it offers insights into the decision-making processes of those historical figures, and, in doing so, provides readers with an understanding of the cause-and-effect relationships of those events.

In *The Judgement*, the motivations of a middle-class Roman, an esteemed patrician, a Roman soldier, an ambitious and politically brutal Roman general, an Egyptian Queen down to those of the Egyptian peasants are all laid at the feet of the reader. The novel also asks its audience to evaluate the actions of these various participants, the validity of their motivation and their impact. Gordianus's lightly philosophical ponderings ask the readers to identify with those motivations, reflect on whether the readers themselves would be able to act differently were they in the same position and ask themselves how would life be different if these actions had never taken place. Indeed, all these 'by-products' of the book are somewhat subconscious, and it is possible for a student not to overtly perceive those various messages. There is also a plausible risk that students may accept historical fiction as truth, against which they measure all else. Nevertheless, a little teacher guidance can overcome this.

Good teaching in History should not solely comprise historical fiction reading, but the use of the historical novel ought to be used to supplement the learning process in a meaningful way. Therefore, historical fiction looms as an effective tool in producing critical thinkers, and by extension, proactive citizens.

To return to this chapter's initial topic, in order to develop empathy, historical understanding and critical thinking skills, students need to be engaged with the subject. Historical fiction successfully facilitates that. As Newrot (1996, p. 343) states, students become 'hooked' to historical personalities, and once their interest is piqued, it motivates them to ask more questions. I argue that Saylor's *Roma Sub Rosa* series achieves that.

* * *

While there were a vast number of modernist novels published in the twentieth century, many readers, as with Grossman (2010), appear to have welcomed the return of novels with engaging plots. Clearly, if teachers intend to use historical novels as a pedagogical device in the teaching of History, the novels should have a strong appeal with their storyline, that is, something that will grip and hold the attention of young readers. When a student finishes reading a novel, he/she ought to be able to say, 'Hey, that was great! I want to read something else, another historical novel, possibly around the same topic.'

Teachers may choose various ways to introduce historical novels to students in their History curriculum. All students may read the same title, or students may be able to select their own title. Teachers have an important role to play in guiding students towards selecting historical novels: Levstik and Barton (2011, p. 118-19) have provided a very thoughtful and comprehensive selection criteria to assist teachers in this regard. This chapter has used a recently published historical novel to elaborate on the way teachers might use this selection criteria.

Steven Saylor's *The Judgement of Caesar*, from the *Roma Sub Rosa* series, provides a wonderful entre to the use of the historical novel in the teaching of history: it is an engaging read and it also ticks all of the boxes of the Levstik and Barton's (2011) selection criteria. I would be very surprised that when students have finished reading this novel, and it has done its work in the rich discourse it will likely generate in the classroom, that many students will not be looking to read other novels in the *Roma Sub Rosa* series.

7 Counterfactual Histories and the Nature of History

Consider this historical account: the setting is the Cocos Islands in the Indian Ocean; the date is 7 November 1914; the author is Stuart Macintyre, the Ernest Scott Professor of History at the University of Melbourne, and, since 2002 a Laureate Professor of the University of Melbourne. He writes:

> The German raiders stood off till nightfall. Under the cover of darkness the Scharnhorst came alongside the Melbourne on the port station and opened fire. The sudden bombardment at close range crippled the Australian ship. Meanwhile the two German light cruisers engaged the Sydney on the starboard station and soon put it out of action. The raiders then cut into the troopships and raked one after another. The British cruiser, which had been leading the flotilla, steamed back into the carnage, and put up desperate resistance before it too listed helplessly out of action.
>
> The defenceless transport vessels scattered like sheep as the wolves bore in on their quarry. One after another, the troopships were overtaken and sunk. Horses and men perished in the darkness. When the British escort ships that had been waiting at the Cocos Islands reached the flotilla, dawn was breaking and the Germans broke off to steam east. Only eighteen troopships survived the disaster and the death toll exceeded 15 000. (Macintyre, 2006, p. 119)

Clearly, this must have been the greatest single tragedy in Australian military history. Why has not more been made of it in Australian historical research and teaching? The answer is simple: it never happened.

Counterfactual history, also sometimes referred to as virtual history (though not in the online sense), is a form of historiography that attempts to answer 'what if', questions known as counterfactuals (Bunzl, 2004, p. 845). The above quote by Macintyre is a sample of counterfactual history, the meaning of which becomes increasingly apparent as the reader proceeds through the chapter. Among other things, the Macintyre (2006) chapter goes on to describe how the territorially ambitious Japanese deceived Australia and Britain, and went on to conquer South East Asian and Pacific territory, as they did during 1941-42. Of course, readers may well ask why one of Australia's most respected historians, and a man considered an architect of the ACARA National History Curriculum, is writing such material?

For the purposes of this book, I distinguish between counterfactual and alternate histories, the subject for Chapter 8. Simply stated, counterfactual history is represented by the genre that the extract from Macintyre's writing exemplifies. Alternate history is more closely connected to popular culture, and typically written as a novel or presented as a film (see Schmunk, 2010, as discussed in Chapter 8).

What is counterfactual history?

To understand what counterfactual history is, it is first necessary to clarify the meaning of history. In his alluringly titled *What is History?*, the renowned historiographical authority E.H. Carr (1961/1987, pp. 44f, 90, 96, 105) referred to counterfactual history as a mere 'parlour game', a simple 'red herring' (as cited in Ferguson, 1997a, p. 4). I first studied Carr's *What is History* as a History 1 student at the University of Tasmania in 1968, and was fascinated by it. The fiftieth anniversary of Carr's famous historiography was celebrated with a series of five 15-minute broadcasts on the BBC.

Carr was born in 1892 and died in 1982. According to the BBC webpage advertising the celebratory lectures, Carr was well-known for his multi-volume history of the USSR, as well as for his writings on international relations.

What is History? remains his most famous work. Strangely, despite his denial of the value of counterfactual history in the book, it remains a landmark for the understanding not only of history but also of counterfactual history. In the words of the BBC webpage: 'when *What is History?* was published it became arguably the most influential text to examine the role of the historian for a whole generation of budding historians, asking them to scrutinize the way they shaped the past'. Indeed, 'today, the book remains a key text for many historians who came of age in the 1960s and is still widely read by the present generation of History undergraduates' (*The Essay*).

In the first essay in the BBC series on Carr, Richard Evans, Regius Professor of History at the University of Cambridge, 'delve[d] deep into questions about how the historian chooses which facts to present as history and place[d] *What is History?* in the context of the academic world of the 1960s, a world into which he was entering at the time'. As with me, for Evans reading Carr was a revelation. As the BBC puts it, Carr offered the new generation of academics, like Evans, 'the freedom to assess history in a wider-reaching, more interdisciplinary fashion' (*The Essay*). This, then, was what the book set out to achieve; this is also, I suggest, exactly what counterfactual history attempts to achieve, but in a more dramatic and unorthodox way — by challenging the facts.

However, Carr wrote these words well before many historians had began to doubt the veracity of traditional deterministic history, and well before the advent of chaos theory. Perhaps it is not surprising that in 2006 one of Australia's most respected and influential historians — Stuart Macintyre — committed himself to the genre. For him, there must be some academic worth in speculating in this way, as this chapter will later discuss.

The attraction of counterfactual history is evidenced by the research literature cited below. There is a growing number of historians who see counterfactual history in positive terms, putting contingency back into history, and serving as a 'necessary antidote to traditional deterministic tendencies' (Mordhorst, 2008, p. 5). Moreover, its development marks a growing acceptance of 'experimental elements into academic approaches to history' (Mordhorst, 2008, p. 5).

As the Macintyre (2006) chapter illustrates, counterfactual history seeks to explore history and historical incidents by extrapolating a timeline based on certain key historical events which did not happen or which produced an outcome which was different from what actually occurred.

Scalmer (2006) has described some of the attractions, or features, of counterfactual history for the serious historian:

- 'Historians study change. The key is causation: what made things turn out this way? Counterfactual thought offers one means of establishing an answer. ... The counterfactual helps us trace the limits of the possibility, and thereby the making of the world that is' (p. 3).
- 'The theoretical minded prefer to move from the abstract to the actual. Theories suggest hypotheses, and hypotheses must be tested. ... [counterfactual] history can provide a useful resource' (p. 4).
- 'Counterfactual scenarios can test the robustness of a theory' (p. 4).
- 'Evidence is a historian's best friend ... [but sometimes] evidence is scarce' (p. 4).
- 'Counterfactuals are fun' (p. 4).

As I shall argue in a later chapter, all these attractions make counterfactual history a valuable and potent teaching/learning strategy for primary, middle school and senior History students.

Other than constructing a whole new historical scenario, as does Macintyre (2006), and before then proceeding to develop a counterfactual ramification of this event, a central purpose of counterfactual history is to ascertain the relative importance of the event, incident or person where the counterfactual hypothesis is negating. Key figures in history are often featured in counterfactual scenarios. For instance, consider the counterfactual claim of 'what if Hannibal had decided to proceed to attack the walled city of Rome following his massive victory over the legions of Republican Rome at the Battle of Cannae on 2 August 216 BC, and was successful in wholly conquering Rome?' Another popular counterfactual is 'what if Hitler was killed in the July 1944 assassination attempt?' In both these counterfactuals all sorts of possibilities become readily apparent. In the case of Hannibal, the issue is what would European history have been like without a Roman influence? In the case of Hitler, there is the reasonable assumption that the German generals would have in all likelihood sued for peace, bringing an early end to the Second World War, at least in the European Theatre. In this case, the counterfactual brings into sharp relief the question of how important Hitler was as an individual and how his personal fate shaped the course of the war and, ultimately, of world history (Bunzl, 2004).

Moreover, traditional histories, particularly those dealing with powerful and far-reaching events such as the Second World War, make full use of counterfactuals — what if ... questions. In reviewing Max Hastings's *All Hell Let Loose: the world at war 1939-1945* (2011), Loosley writes of Hastings's erudite use of asking these questions and exploring possible scenarios. For example, with respect to the German's folly of attempting to subdue the British with the Luftwaffe, 'what if the Germans had simply ignored the British?' (Loosley, 2011, p. 23) All of this embodies much wonderful pseudo-historical speculation, which excites our imaginations. No wonder that there is a rising tide of interest in counterfactual history.

Popularising counterfactual history

Ferguson (1997a, p. 8) shows that the publication of Charles Renouvier's *Uchronie* in 1876 marked a significant development in the evolution of counterfactual history, popularising it in Europe. Then in 1907 'the most self-consciously literate of Edwardian historians, G.M. Trevelyan, wrote (at the suggestion of the editor of the *Westminster Gazette*) an essay entitled: "If Napoleon had won the Battle of Waterloo"' (Ferguson, 1997a, p. 9). This counterfactual history concluded Napoleon eventually died in 1836, '"the enemy alike of the ancient regime and of democratic liberty". In short, no Waterloo, no Whig history'. (p. 9). As Ferguson shows, during the following decades 'a motley crew, mainly composed of novelists and journalists' wrote and published forms of counterfactual history, such as the contributors to J.C. Squire (ed.) *If it Had Happened Otherwise* in 1932 (Ferguson, 1997a, pp. 9-20). By 1984, with the publication of John Merriman's *For the Want of a Horse*, counterfactual history became more professional in research and tone (Ferguson, 1997a, p. 15). Later, as many people began to ponder the difficulties of deterministic history, historiographers began to recognise counterfactual history's potential contribution to their discipline. Neill Ferguson's edited collection, *Virtual History*, was a landmark publication.

A central motivation of writing counterfactual history, according to Ferguson, is to provide an antidote to determinism, which is the idea that there is no free will in history, and that everything is the inevitable result of antecedent causes. For Ferguson (1997a & b), counterfactual history seeks to unmask traditional historiography as a construction that has created a deterministic view about the past. To demonstrate this, his edited work includes chapters by internationally acclaimed historians:

1. England Without Cromwell: what if Charles 1 had avoided the Civil War? (John Adamson)
2. British America: what if there had been no American Revolution? (J.C.D. Clark)
3. British Ireland: what if Home Rule had been enacted in 1912? (Alvin Jackson)
4. The Kaiser's European Union: what if Britain had 'stood aside' in August 1914? (Niall Ferguson)
5. Hitler's England: what if Germany had invaded Britain in May 1940? (Andrew Roberts)
6. Nazi Europe: what if Nazi Germany had defeated the Soviet Union? (Michael Burleigh)
7. Stalin's War on Peace: what if the Cold War had been avoided? (Jonathan Haslam)

8. Camelot Continued: what if John F. Kennedy had lived? (Diane Kunz)
9. 1989 Without Gorbachev: what if Communism had not collapsed? (Mark Almond)

Macintyre and Scalmer (2006) published their edited work *What If?* nine years after Ferguson's 1997 work. They included chapters on:

1. What if Tasmania had become French? (Jim Davidson)
2. What if Alfred Deakin had made a declaration of Australian independence? (Marilyn Lake)
3. What if Federation had failed in 1900? (Helen Irving)
4. What if the federal government had created a model Aboriginal state? (Tim Rowse)
5. What if Australia's baptism of fire had occurred at the Cocos Islands? (Stuart Macintyre)
6. What if Whitlam had won another opportunity to implement his program? (James Walter)
7. What if there had been a school of figure painting in colonial Sydney? (Virginia Spate)
8. What if Aborigines had never been assimilated? (Peter Read)
9. What if the attempted assassination of Arthur Caldwell had been successful? (Sean Scalmer)
10. What if the northern rivers had been turned inland? (Tom Griffith and Tim Sherratt)
11. What if a man's movement had triumphed in the 1970s? (Ann Curthoys)

In his Afterword, Niall Ferguson (1997b) wrote: 'it is the great error of historical determinism to imagine that their [James III and Charles I] achievements were in any sense predestined. We should never underestimate the role of contingency, of chance — of what the mathematicians call "stochastic behavior"' (p. 416). Indeed, the common thread of deflating a belief in determinist history runs through both publications.

What difference does it make when professional or academic historians write counterfactual history? Erudite readers will note that specialist historians have written the chapters. Indeed, some commentators on counterfactual history have stressed the quality of disciplined imagination that makes the difference between good and poor counterfactual history. As Bunzl (2004) writes, 'when it comes to examining the consequences of historical counterfactual, like most historians, Ferguson implicitly embraces the view that what is involved is always and only an act of imagination' (p. 848). Indeed, Bunzl goes on to argue that 'the difference between plausible and implausible counterfactuals might be thought of as a function of the degree to which we are able to discipline our imagination, and there is a case to be made that one of the effects of being a good (and specialised) historian is that one's imagination is just as disciplined' (2004, p. 848).

While not attempting to detail any pedagogical strategies for the use of counterfactual/alternate histories in schools, Lebow (2007) seeks to establish counterfactual thought experiments as a necessary teaching tool. He begins by arguing that 'counterfactuals are routinely used in physical and biological sciences to develop and evaluate sophisticated, non-linear models' (p. 154). In particular, 'they have been used with telling effect in the study of economic history and American politics' (p. 154). He does concede that 'for some historians, counterfactual arguments have no scholarly standing. They consider them flights of fancy, fun over a beer or two in the faculty club, but not the stuff of serious research' (p. 153). Lebow (2007) attributes this negative attitude to the rapidly rising popularity of alternate histories — that is, counterfactuals produced as novels, films or some other format for popular culture. That aside, for Lebow (2007), 'nevertheless, counterfactuals are an effective research tool, but comprehending this requires a clear understanding of their nature, the circumstances to which they are best suited, and robust protocols for conducting thought experiments' (p. 153).

Lebow's (2007) research and presentation is articulate and, I suggest, convincing. He begins 'by exploring the differences between counterfactual and so-called "factual" arguments and offer[s] the proposition that the difference between them is greatly exaggerated' (p. 153). For him, it 'is one of degree and not of kind' (p. 153). Users of counterfactuals need to be reasonable, and distinguish 'between miracle and plausible world and scholarly and folk counterfactuals, and their respective uses' (p. 153). Moreover, he proposes several 'criteria to guide plausible world counterfactuals' (p. 153). He then proposes 'special problems of applying counterfactual analysis to a problem as broad as the rise and success of the West' (p. 153).

Problems and tensions in counterfactual history

But does the specialist historian's writing of counterfactual history remove the problems and tensions that the counterfactuals might otherwise have? While acknowledging the achievements of counterfactual history, Mordhorst (2008) finds 'its theoretical foundations both speculative and incoherent' (p. 6). For Mordhorst, the obvious criticism of counterfactual history comes with verifying or falsifying its claims (p. 5). He points out that proponents of counterfactual history base their claims on the premise that the past is non-linear and chaotic, but then proceed to construct their own counterfactual history as linear and ordered in the historians' narrative. This is demonstrated with the Macintyre passage above.

Mordhorst (2008) then details what he argues are other significant problems and tensions with counterfactual history. The first tension relates to the way counterfactual history is 'built on the belief that there exists a real history written on the basis of historical facts'. This is demonstrated seperately in Macintyre's (2006) narrative above, wherein the initial setting is the mass movement of Australian and New Zealand troops across in the Indian Ocean in November 1914. Supporting this point, Mordhorst (2008) argues 'if you see your own narrative as counterfactual, there must be a factual narrative it has to be counter to' (p. 7).

While it may well be a fact that a large contingent of Australian and New Zealand troops were in a naval convoy sailing across the Indian Ocean in November 1914, the accepted deterministic historical narrative associated with the Gallipoli landings of 25 April 1915 is what Macintyre (2006) presumably is seeking to avoid in his counterfactual history. According to Mordhorst (2008, p. 7), this 'raises the issue of realism in counterfactual history and does so on the level where historical events are reconstructed to represent the past events and their causality in narrative validity'. Thus, for Mordhorst (2008, p. 7) 'the notion of factual history in counterfactual history implies that historians, through their methodological working-through of sources, are able to give valid and truthful descriptions that correspond with the events that have marked the passage of time'. Moreover, 'this is an incoherent construction because you cannot be right about "what happened" while being wrong about its "causality"' (p. 7). Indeed, 'these stories are causal chains, so any reassessment of the causal contingencies of history (in other words, any rejection of its determinism) must include a reassessment of its narrative contingencies (in other words, a rejection of its realism). In other words, counterfactual history only goes half way' (p. 7).

The second concern about counterfactual history for Mordhorst (2008) is that despite its drive to reject determinism, it in fact 'it reproduces determinism' (p. 7). For Mordhorst (2008), 'this problem is connected with the chaos-theoretical inspiration of modern counterfactual history, which it draws from the natural sciences'. Mordhorst reminds us that 'in the philosophy of science, chaos theory is often seen as the final step in the dissolution of the deterministic Newtonian view of the world as ordered, stable and linear' (2008, p. 8). Thus it is with the counterfactual historians who 'imagine that they are parting ways with the deterministic tradition in historiography that, they say, has ruled in history until today' (p. 8).

According to Mordhorst (2008), deeply seated in this assumption is the belief that 'only large events can have large effects'. But then he asks his readers to consider a seventeenth-century proverb:

> For want of a nail, the shoe was lost;
> For a want of a shoe, the horse was lost;
> For the want of a horse, the rider was lost;
> For the want of a rider, the battle was lost;
> For a want of a battle, the kingdom was lost!
> And all for the want of a nail! Mordhorst. (2008, p. 8)

For Mordhorst (2008, p. 8), 'the proverb follows a fully deterministic and mechanistic pattern'. In fact, for Mordhorst 'neither chaos theory nor counterfactual history can be said to be the antidote to determinism, it rather restores determinism at a different level' (p. 8). Mordhorst goes on to contend that 'it is by no means a coincidence that most physicists do not use the notion "chaos theory" but the extended notion "deterministic chaos theory" when they are describing their theory. By this means they stress there are short periods where chaos reigns, followed by long periods of deterministic development' (p. 8). Mordhorst concludes that 'likewise, it would perhaps be more precise if the counterfactual historians instead called themselves "deterministic counterfactual historians"' (Mordhorst, 2008, p. 8).

Mordhorst's third concern about counterfactual history is associated with his claim that for it to be plausible, 'it must develop in a bounded area where nobody or nothing can influence the process' (2008, p. 9). Consequently, Mordhorst argues that this means 'in order to reduce complexity and establish stability' (2008). Thus, the counterfactual historian 'has to presume that the historical context remains constant except for the changed events'. In other words, counterfactual history is construed in a *ceteris paribus* ('all other things being equal') framework; counterfactual historians can thereafter construct their narrative as a picture of a deterministic movement, in a bounded and well-ordered field where nothing can stop the process' (Mordhorst, 2008, p. 9).

In this context, I return to Macintyre's (2006) counterfactual history of the events in the Indian Ocean on that dramatic night of 7 November 1914. The great deceit by the territorially ambitious Japanese, who had one light cruiser in the escort, resulted in the near-complete deaths of the 30,000 Australians and New Zealanders. By 1915, Japan's ambitions were only too evident to the Australian government. Thus, Macintyre's counterfactual history runs:

> On 7 December 1916 the Japanese launched a naval assault on the American fortress of Corregidor in Manila Bay. Caught by surprise, the United States navy suffered serious losses. The [Japanese] South Seas Islands Defence Force quickly captured the American base of Guam in the Marianas, and then the American portion of Samoa ... A Japanese landing in the Bismarck Archipelago of New Guinea followed. (Macintyre, 2006, p. 127)

As Macintyre (2006) explains in his Coda:

> Some readers will note that I have Japan launch a naval attack on the United States base in the Philippines on 7 December 1916, exactly 25 years earlier than its air force attack on the Pearl Harbor base in Hawaii. The subsequent assaults on Guam, Samoa and Rabaul are all imaginary, and it will be apparent that I have superimposed key episodes of World War II onto World War I in order to anticipate their implications for Australian strategic policy. (Macintyre, 2006, p. 136)

Consequently, readers may want to know what were the various other ramifications of Macintyre's (2006) imaginary events in the Indian Ocean on the night of 7 November 1914. This precisely relates to Mordhorst's (2008) point about the counterfactual history being written in 'a bounded and well-ordered field where nothing can stop the process' (p. 9). Just to what extent does Macintyre (2006) need to go to contain his counterfactual narrative before it spins out of control? Perhaps Macintyre (2006) has made just too many alterations to 'the facts', offending Tetlock and Belkin's principle of changing as few historical facts as possible (1996, pp. 16-31, as cited in Bunzl, 2004, fn. 17).

For this reason, Mordhorst argues that 'it is no coincidence that counterfactual history has had it greatest success in economic history and among cliometric historians who primarily utilize models, statistics and *ceteris paribus* clauses' (2008, p. 9). In order to substantiate his point, he looks to R.W. Fogel's (1964) 'explicit use of a counterfactual model, which showed that the creation of the American railroads system was much less important for the economic development than assumed' (p. 9).

Mordhorst (2008) goes on to argue the only way out of this ontological mire, confronting the authors of counterfactual history, is to study their 'construction at least as closely as "the facts"? Instead of asking, "What if something different had happened?" the question should be asked, "What if other stories had been told?"' (Mordhorst (2008, p. 1). As with Fogel's example above, the great value of 'the counter-narrative method' it provides us with 'new insights into why some narratives attain hegemonic status, and how this can help us to understand the construction and function of historical consciousness' (Mordhorst (2008, p. 1). It is the hegemony of the story that needs to be evaluated. In the case of Fogel's US railways, the story of railways assumed a dominance it simply did not deserve.

But what might be the application of counterfactual history in historiography lesson in primary, middle school and senior History? Scott Roberts (2011) highlights the dearth of research on the use of counterfactual and alternate histories as a pedagogical device. At the time of the writing of this book, it seems that other than Roberts (2011) the only other work is Ragland (2007, p. 225), who briefly mentions its possibilities in the teaching of History. Roberts's enthusiasm for the use of counterfactual and alternate history as a pedagogical device rests on his commitment to have his students as 'active participants in their study of History and [to learn] history using hands-on approaches, sometimes described as "doing history", and not passively learning history by reading and answering questions found in textbooks, or listening to teacher-centred lectures' (Roberts, 2011, p. 119).

Research on teaching historiography in schools and senior colleges

Although there is no mention in any of the research literature that counterfactual history was ever intended for use in the school or secondary college History curriculum, has it a role therein? Not surprisingly, considering the dearth of History being taught in Australian schools for the three or four decades prior to the advent of the national History curriculum (see, for example, Critical Dialogue, 1997; Ryan, 1998), there is little Australian-based research on how historiography is actually being taught in schools and senior colleges. There is also an absence of research in Australia on how teachers might most effectively teach historiography in primary, middle school and senior school History. There may be a number of reasons for this, but certainly this points to the need for some national empirical research.

However, at the Australian History Teachers' Association of Australia (HTAA) 2010 annual conference there were two papers dealing explicitly with historiography, one of which was about 'historiography and the Chinese Revolution: perspectives of Mao and Mao's China' (Jenny McArthur, Victoria). Another paper dealt with 'teaching historiography through film' (Bruce Dennett, Macquarie University). Dennett wrote that 'historiography is as much a part of history as chronology and yet it is often neglected' (HTAA National History Conference, 2010).

Research on the teaching of historiography in schools and colleges is more developed in the United States. Seixas, for example, argues that disciplined or historical understanding involves 'not only a set of factual claims, but also an understanding of the warrant for those claims' (1999, p. 322). Of course, this statement looks to historiographical explanation.

Similarly, Bruce Van Sledright argues that teaching historical thinking involves closing the 'academic developmental distance between novices and experts' (2004, p. 230). More specifically, VanSledright defines historical thinking by including the ability to construct a reasonable narrative intertextually by comparing sources, accounting for bias and making reasonable explanations of the past based on the evidence. This touches on the use of counterfactual history. These are the intellectual skills that historians have but that school and college students do not. Counterfactual history primarily is historiographical explanation, and should be raised in History lessons whenever necessary, in the same way that a conscientious English teacher will continually look for issues regarding spelling or sentence structure with students.

On the other hand, Wineburg's (1991) research has shown that students, teachers and student teachers, who may be successful students of history if we use the criterion of memorising facts or retelling the narrative, do not necessarily have the ability to think historically. There needs to be an engaging pedagogy in assisting them to do so.

Fitting counterfactual history into the primary, middle and senior History curriculum

In the National Centre for History Education, Tony Taylor (n.d.) addressed the issue of developing 'historical literacy' in our school students. As Chapter 3 shows, he examined the question of what comprised 'historical literacy'. Although, Taylor's work is first intended for primary and middle school teachers, it has a strong relevancy for History teachers at all levels. The following elements are part of this literacy, and appear to have particular relevance to the use of counterfactual history in historiography work in History classes.

For example, if we consider the first two of Taylor's (n.d.) elements of historical literacy (events of the past; narratives of the past), it is apparent that this is one of the principal claims of counterfactual history, and one that is stated by Scalmer (2006): 'Historians study change. The key is causation: what made things turn out this way? Counterfactual thought offers one means of establishing an answer. ... The counterfactual helps us trace the limits of the possibility, and thereby the making of the world that is' (p. 3). Taking each of these elements of historical literacy and match it against counterfactual history as a pedagogical device, it is apparent, I suggest, that the use of counterfactual history in this manner enhances the development of historical literacy.

Where and how could counterfactual history fit in the History curriculum?

Clearly, counterfactual history requires a considerable degree of abstract thought from students. Teachers and students should first consider and use counterfactual history as a historiographical endeavour. Certainly, Parkes has argued for the 'teaching of History historiographically' (2009, p. 125). He contends that 'we must understand the act of teaching and learning history, as one of engaging in interpretive acts, as we read the histories that are made available to us' (p. 125).

Historiography, then, should be at the centre of the teaching and learning of history. But in respect to counterfactual texts, how is this best done? First, the History curriculum in all Australian education jurisdictions has scope for historiographical investigations. For example, the New South Wales History Extension course introduced in 2010 states that it,

> is designed to enable interested and capable students to build on the outcomes of the Stage 6 Ancient History and Modern History courses in relation to historiography and historical enquiry and communication.
> …
>
> The course builds on the knowledge and skills students are developing through the Stage 6 Ancient and Modern History courses, which in turn build from the students' study of History in Years 7-10. It extends student understanding of historiographical issues by exploring how historians work, and provides an opportunity for them to apply their learning by designing and conducting their own historical investigation. (NSW Board of Studies, History Extension, n.d.)

In this context, there is ample scope to have Years 11 and 12 History students engage in counterfactual history.

Counterfactuals, moreover, may be used in order to consolidate a unit of work where students could propose various counterfactuals. After an in-depth study involving the Anzac participation in the First World War, to conclude and to consolidate their enquiry, students could use Macintyre's (2006) counterfactual history of the Anzacs cited at the beginning of this chapter. Alternatively — and appealing to the need to develop creativity in historical thought, which often is cited in History curriculum documents (for example, SACE, 2012, p. 9) — students could write their own brief counterfactual histories, and then discuss the merits of each. This may help to ensure students begin to engage in discourse concerning deterministic history.

* * *

Counterfactual history can better inform the study of History, particularly the study of historiography. This chapter has shown that there is no clear understanding of how, and to what extent, historiography is taught in our Australian schools, so, at best it is likely its teaching is problematic. Therefore, to argue counterfactual history may assist in the teaching of historiography remains speculative. However, authors such as Macintyre (2006) and Ferguson (1997a & b) have demonstrated convincingly that counterfactual history plays a major role in our understanding of historiography.

Ferguson has demonstrated a central motivation of writing counterfactual history is to unmask traditional historiography as a construction that has created a deterministic view about the past. Thus, as Australian History teachers look more seriously to the teaching of historiography, they should do so in a manner that does not replicate any past narrow conceptions of history, imbedded in determinism. Students need to think of history as a chance affair, and asking 'what if?' is an important pedagogical step in their understanding of historiography. With regards to counterfactual history, its intrinsic appeal is well recognised.

Moreover, the elements of historical literacy, as developed by Taylor (n.d.), show that counterfactual history links directly with these aims of the teaching of History, and enhances their development. But the use of counterfactual History in the classroom not only achieves this, it does so in an engaging manner. As Scalmer declares, 'counterfactuals are fun' (2006, p. 4). Reading counterfactual histories excites our imaginations. And given that counterfactual history is imbedded deeply in historiography, it seems a logical pedagogical progression to make full use of this historical genre in the teaching of historiography to school History students. This response answers Clark's (2008) findings in her national survey of History teaching, which demonstrated how students look for variety in the pedagogy of the History classroom.

Not surprisingly, there is a growing number of historians and theorists who see counterfactual history in positive terms, as putting contingency back into history and as serving as a strong counterweight to traditional deterministic conceptualisations of history. Moreover, its development during the past few decades marks a growing acceptance of the great need to experiment in our approaches to history. Rightly, with counterfactual history, the History classroom becomes a wonderful and tantalising laboratory.

There are problems and tensions in counterfactual history. Having students discuss and debate these, however, can only increase their understanding of historiography and its central importance in the development of historical literacy, which is at the heart of the new imperatives in the teaching of Australian history in our schools and colleges.

8   Alternate Histories in the Classroom

> He certainly had no wish to be caught up in Dr Evatt's recent confrontation with the Royal Commission inquiring into Petrov's defection — an attack on ASIO involving accusations of fraud and conspiracy. Evatt's turbulent court appearances, the slanging matches initiated by the temperamental opposition leader, had filled the headlines over the past few days, foreshadowing worse to come. (Hasluck, 2011, pp. 20-21)

Throughout Australian States and territories, History students often study the 1954 Petrov affair in Australian history, as they do the 1975 Whitlam dismissal. How might teachers add some historiographical zest to these studies? How can alternate history, or allohistorical narratives, assist?

An Australian example

The recent publication of Nicholas Hasluck's *Dismissal* (2011) is timely in these regards. Alternate histories are usually set amidst the great events of world history — Napoleon, Hitler and Nazism, and so on. Indeed, as Croome (2011) has stated, in what might amount to a throwaway line, alternate history is 'a genre often undermined in Australia by the sense that nothing vital happens here, that nothing is at stake'. Indeed, for Croome, 'Hasluck is on the front foot in this respect, not least because his well-structured set piece hinges on the Whitlam dismissal, one of the handful of events in Australian history capable of stirring genuine emotion and debate'.

The central character in Hasluck's novel is Roy Temple, a romantic and a left-winger, but with a successful career at the Sydney bar. It's 1954, and Menzies's and Barwick's Petrov Commission is in full swing in Sydney. The Menzies Government's motives in establishing the royal commission are many (and indeed continue to this day as a source of speculation and conspiracy theories). But back in 1954, Hasluck's Roy Temple, who has had an earlier career with the Department of External Affairs, has left the department under a security cloud. However, he goes on to escape the clutches of the Australian Security Organisation (ASIO), who question him on matters of espionage during the 1954 Petrov Royal Commission inquisition. Unsurprisingly, when Temple is at the centre of events surrounding the Whitlam dismissal in 1975, Hasluck (the son of Sir Paul Hasluck, Sir John Kerr's predecessor as Governor-General) has him play a central role in this alternate history. This is, indeed, a fascinating and intriguing alternate history.

The central purpose of this chapter is to examine the rising cultural phenomena of alternate history, and how this connects with memory literature, a topic that I explored in some length in Chapter 5 of this book.

The rising phenomenon of alternate history

Rosenfeld describes the mushrooming phenomena of alternate history in Western popular culture, with a broad range of themes: 'the Nazis winning World War II, the American Revolution failing to occur, Jesus not being crucified, the South winning the Civil War, the atomic bomb not being dropped on Japan, Hitler escaping into postwar hiding, and many others' (2002, p. 90). But Rosenfeld draws our attention to just how extensively alternate history has manifested itself in literary forms: 'novels, short stories, films, television programs, comic books, historical monographs and essays, and internet web sites' (p. 90). This interest in the genre extends to 2013 Australia. Witness some of the present Australian-based web sites:

- *Alternatives: AH Directory* (n.d.) 'The Australian War of Independence (David Atwell) An independence crisis emerges in Australia in 1975'
- *Althistory Wiki* (n.d.) 'Commonwealth of Australia and New Zealand (1983-Doomsday)'
- *Club Troppo* (n.d.) 'Australian Alternate History Week'
- *Alternate History Discussion Board* (n.d.).

For a greater appreciation of alternate history, visit the *Uchronia* web site, which has 'a bibliography of 3100 novels, stories, essays and other printed material involving the "what ifs" of history' (*Uchronia*, n.d.).

This massive rising tide of cultural phenomena has prompted Rosenfeld (2002) to declare:

> So dramatic has the emergence of alternate history been that it has been reported on by the mass media and even grudgingly acknowledged by its most hostile critics — historians — some of whom have enthusiastically moved to legitimize the once-unwanted bastard child of their profession through collections of historical essays, inspired monographic defenses, and scholarly analyses. In short, as shown by this flurry of activity, alternate history has become a veritable phenomenon in contemporary Western culture. (pp. 90-92)

Rosenfeld (2002) has analysed the alternate history phenomena to show 'alternate histories lend themselves quite well to being studied as documents of memory' (p. 90), a proposition I will return to later.

Defining alternate history

Long considered to be a sub-genre of scientific fiction, alternate history has had a fascinating history as it emerged as a distinct element in our culture. Now academics, even historians, are taking it very seriously. Thus, it is now associated with a growing body of research literature. Witness the work by prominent Australian historian Stuart Macintyre (see discussion in Chapter 7, this book).

In defining historical fiction, the UK-based Historical Novel Society includes alternate history as a part of the broad genre of historical fiction (*Historical Novel Society*, n.d.). Alternate history differs from mainstream historical fiction in that it is premised on a conscious departure from historical fact. Thus, this definition would deem Hasluck's *Dismissal* an alternate history. This novel has a small number of fictitious characters alongside historical characters participating in historical events, and is based on considerable research. It consciously builds its narrative on the following question: what if the controversial events of 11 November 1975 in Canberra had been different?

Bunzl (2004) contends alternate history is related to, but distinct from, counterfactual history or virtual history — the terms used by some professional historians when using thoroughly researched and carefully reasoned speculations on 'what might have happened if ...' as a tool of academic historical research and historiography (see Chapter 7). Thus, Macintyre and Scalmer's *What If* (2006) is an example of a volume of counterfactual histories, all written by highly regarded scholars seeking to search out historiographical understanding of various events in Australia's history. On the other hand, alternate history, as I have described above, belongs more to popular culture; it is interested precisely in the hypothetical scenarios that flow from the negated incident or event. A fiction writer is thus free to invent very specific events and characters in the imagined history, as does Hasluck in *Dismissal*. Moreover, it can be presented in many different forms of media, as described above. It is not a purposeful exercise in historiography, as is counterfactual history. Yet, as this chapter will attempt to demonstrate, the genre raises many interesting historiographical perspectives and applications in the classroom.

In particular, alternate history sheds considerable light on the way in which memory literature contributes to historical understanding. Through examples, this chapter considers this proposition. From here, it provides some examples of how it might be used as a device to enhance historiographical understanding.

A brief history of alternate history

By 2005, so extensive had been the publications of alternate histories of various aspects of Nazism, Rosenfeld (2005) had published a book on this element of popular culture. His Introduction teases out the principal elements of alternate history. According to Rosenfeld, 'As a genre of narrative representation, alternate history is an age-old phenomena' (p. 5), tracing its origins back at least to the Greek historian Herodotus, who speculated on a Persian victory at Marathon, and the Roman historian Livy, who likewise pondered a hypothetical attack by Alexander the Great upon the legions of Republican Rome. But, for me, all of that may be more appropriately conceived of as an attempt at historiography.

The alternate history of recent popular culture is more often described and classified as science fiction, because that is the principal genre base from which it has grown. Indeed, as Rosenfeld states, 'up through the first half of the early twentieth century, both fictional and analytical alternate histories appeared largely in scattered pulp science fiction magazines and scholarly anthologies' (2005, p. 5). And so it continued through until the advent of Nazism and the Second World War provided more subject matter for the authors interested in the genre.

Since the 1960s, publication of alternate history has increased vastly, moving from the realms of scientific fiction (Rosenfeld, 2005, p. 5). Increasingly, it has become the product of the mass media, as well as the subject matter for the increasing number of websites (to which this chapter already has made reference), collectively indicating an increasing acceptance by the broad society. As Rosenfeld (2005) puts it: 'the best evidence for the increased acceptance of alternate history has been its embrace by the academic community, which has demonstrated a growing interest in the subject with a variety of recent publications' (p. 5). Moreover, 'especially as the most sceptical academics of all — historians — have slowly begun to set aside their long-time reservations about the field, it is likely alternate history will continue to gain in prominence and respectability' (p. 6).

Before we can consider how this rising phenomena can be utilised in the History classroom, attention should be paid to an important publication in Australian historiography. The publication in 2006 of Ann Curthoys and John Docker's *Is History Fiction?* was an important event, with regards to the purposes of this present chapter, as well as the unfolding of historiography in Australia. In answering the question that constitutes the title of their book, the authors ask further questions concerning the 'problems of historical truth, the relationship between historians and the past, and questions of fact, value, and interpretation' (p. 2). Moreover, their concern is with 'history's literary aspects — constituted through language, metaphor, rhetoric, and allegory — and the connections [they] see between questions of literary form and the desire for historical truth' (p. 2).

The book found immediate interest amongst History teachers. In March 2006 Curthoys delivered a keynote address to the NSW HTA's Extension History Forum, using *Is History Fiction?* as a focal point of her paper. Here she explored the relationship between history and fiction, contending that this relationship has always been a controversial one. She asked the critical question of can we ever know that a historical narrative is giving us a true account of what actually happened? Subsequently, the Queensland History Teachers' Association published the paper in its annual journal (Curthoys, 2006, pp. 10-17).

Historical interpretation, Curthoys and Docker (2010) affirm, is chancy and problematic: 'the historian navigates a perilous passage between fact and interpretation and problems like relations between particular and general, the empirical and the theoretical, the objective and subjective, by reflecting there is no definitive answer' (p. 133). So, that is the case by historians who seek to make some interpretation of past events. But what of authors who seek to write an alternate — a fictional — history? Just as is evidenced by the publication of Curthoy and Docker's (2006/2010) book, the flurry of publications of alternate history during the past few decades reflects more profound cultural developments away from traditional views on history.

Rosenfeld (2005) has reflected on 'the progressive discrediting of political ideologies in the West since 1945. In insisting everything in the past could have been different, in stressing the role of contingency in history, and in emphasising the open-endedness of historical change, alternate history is inherently anti-deterministic' (p. 6). He has shown the rise of popularity of alternate history coincided with the end of the Cold War and its deterministic ideologies: 'by declaring liberalism victorious, the end of ideological struggle initially gave many in the West the security to reconsider whether our present-day world was indeed inevitable or whether other outcomes — once thought too frightful to consider — were ever possible' (p. 6).

'Closely tied to the death of political ideologies in promoting the upsurge of alternate history is the emergence of the cultural movement of postmodernism', writes Rosenfeld (2005, p. 6). While alternate history clearly predates the rise of postmodernism, the latter movement has certainly assisted the former to move into the mainstream culture in Western societies. Postmodernism has had a distinct relationship with history. Witness works by Michel Foucault such as *Discipline and Punish* (1975). In particular, seminal works such as this have helped to encourage the acceptance of allohistorical thinking, particularly in the way in which these works challenge old ideas about determinism in history.

Moreover, Rosenfeld contends that 'postmodernism's playfully ironic relationship to history ... has found expression in alternate history's playful rearranging of the narratives of real history' (2005, p. 7). Indeed, Rosenfeld goes on to state that 'the blurring of fact and fiction so intrinsic to the field of alternate history mirrors postmodernism's tendency to blur the once-rigid boundaries that separated different realms of culture' (p. 7). Indeed, 'at the same time, the postmodern movement's general valorization of "the other" and its attempt to resurrect suppressed or alternative voices dovetails with alternative history's promotion of unconventional views of the past' (p. 8). Surely, it is the successful attainment of this ideal that makes Foucault's *Discipline and Punish* (1975) such a thought-provoking work. For example, the reader is left deeply empathising with those faceless souls in the hideous panopticon, that system of incarceration that has become a metaphor for control, power and surveillance.

This last point made by Rosenfeld (2005) connects with postmodernism's drive to encourage 'the rise of a more subjective and relativistic variety of historical consciousness so necessary for allohistorical speculation' (p. 8). Given that most historians now recognise that 'history is not about discovering a single "truth" about the past but understanding how diverse contingent factors determine its varying representations, it is no wonder accounts of the past that diverge from the accepted historical record have begun to proliferate as never before' (Rosenfeld, 2005 p. 9).

As this chapter has already suggested, virtual reality (as defined earlier in this chapter) has assisted the proliferation of alternate history in the same manner as it has with counterfactual history. And the internet has also assisted. Now, through powerful search engines, people have instant contact with like-minded others.

This has coincided with another profound cultural change. The new interest in alternate histories connects with the growing presence of what might be called a speculative sensibility within contemporary popular culture. Instead of mirroring reality, recent works of film and fiction explore alternatives to it. J.R.R. Tolkien's epic *The Lord of the Rings* (1954/1955), and J.K. Rowling's *Harry Potter* series (1997-2007) are hallmark developments in this regard, portraying fantasy and alternative worlds far removed from contemporary reality.

Rosenfeld (2005) shows that alternative history has entertainment as its primary motive. It is inherently presentist: 'It explores the past less for its own sake than to utilize it instrumentally to comment upon the state of the contemporary world' (pp. 92-3). For Rosenfeld, 'when authors speculate on the past they are really passing comment about how they perceive the present' (2005, p. 93). Alternate histories that play out, for example, nightmare scenarios, can also be making a statement about how the author perceives the existing society and culture. On the other hand, alternate histories that play out utopian-like societies and cultures are an escapist variant of the author's perception of a nightmarish present. In this manner, as I will discuss in greater detail below, alternate histories connect with the memory industry, which includes biographies, with online museums, re-enactments, celebratory days (for example, Australia Day), commemorative days (for example, Anzac Day) and so on. The memory industry includes not only literature associated with the event, but the event itself.

But as a proposed tool for students' historiographical study, what are the tensions and problems with alternate history? First, let us return to the genre's cousin, counterfactual history. While acknowledging the achievements of counterfactual history (see Chapter 7), Mordhorst (2008) finds considerable problems with it. Clearly, these issues must also apply to alternate history. But alternate history is written in the genre of historical fiction, long associated with science fiction. Using alternate history as a pedagogical device to stimulate historiographical enquiry and enquiries into memory literature begins with the assumption that the genre is 'speculative and incoherent'. After all, the genre does not confess to be anything else other than fiction. But how does it connect to memory literature?

Alternate history and 'memory' literature

Perhaps — associated with the baby-boomers and imbedded in the rising tide of electronic media — there has been a general proliferation of 'memory' literature, a genre discussed in Chapter 5. This has occurred since the 1980s. That said, historians long have taken memory as the raw material for history, as a means to getting at the truth of the past. The memory literature of recent years is connected most intimately with traumatic events such as the Holocaust or the Cultural Revolution in China. Witness such publishing phenomenon as Thomas Keneally's *Schindler's Ark* (1982) and its movie version, *Schindler's List* (1993). The boom in memory literature is concomitant with the rising tide of the new postcolonial and postmodernist historiography and has afforded memory a greater status.

Continuing this theme, we are reminded of what Arif Dirlik's point that 'memory has emerged as a competitor with history (2002b, p. 76, see discussion in Chapter 5, this book). Connected to this is the point Rosenfeld (2002, pp. 92-3) makes concerning alternate history. He insists that at a personal level, when we speculate about what might have been in our lives, if certain events had, or had not occurred, we are really expressing our feelings about the present.

The release of Nicholas Hasluck's Australian novel, *Dismissal* occurred at about the same time as more media speculation concerning Evatt and the Petrov affair. The opening pages of the alternate history are full of references to the alleged link between Evatt and Moscow in regard to the infamous Document J of the Petrov affair, where Menzies and Barwick had ASIO attempt to embarrass Evatt and the Labor Party for their own political gain. Today, many Australians remember this by the slogan of 'reds under the beds'.

But all of this resurfaced in 2011. For example, *The Australian* ran the following story:

> Today we reveal how the then prime minister, Robert Menzies, so distrusted Labor leader Herbert Evatt that he secretly ordered ASIO to hand top-secret files to Britain and the US for safe keeping ahead of the 1958 election that he feared Labor would win. It is a vital reminder of the fears of communist infiltration at the highest levels in Canberra in this volatile Cold War period. Some, like security expert Des Ball, believe the M15 files suggest Evatt was not just erratic but almost certainly a Soviet agent. Others give the Labor leader the benefit of the doubt. But the material, along with other revelations that ASIO chief Charles Spry warned M15 during the 1954 Petrov affair that Britain should consider withholding intelligence information from a Labor government, confirm the complete breakdown of the normal bonds of trust between political leaders and bureaucrats in this period. (*The Australian*, 2011)

The publisher of *Dismissal* is the Murdoch-owned Fourth Estate, also owner of *The Australian*. The concurrent release of the 'new' material on Evatt and Petrov affair and of *Dismissal* had distinct marketing implications for the novel. Taken together, there can be no doubt the 'new' media attention to Evatt and the Petrov affair, along with the publication of *Dismissal* were collectively an appeal to the Australia's memory industry, a term that I loosely refer to as covering the mass of historical re-enactments, museums, public historical displays, and so on (discussed earlier in this chapter). Moreover, it occurred during a time of intense political turmoil in Canberra, when the minority Gillard Labor Government was introducing major legislation, intensely opposed by the vast network of the Murdoch media. This point adds validity to Rosenfeld's (2002) point about the connection between the subject matter of alternate history and the times in which they are written.

Perhaps some readers of *Dismissal* (depending on their political viewpoint) will be left with a sense of regret, an intense feeling of what might have been in Australian history if Whitlam had not been dismissed in 1975. According to Elisabeth Wesseling (1991) this sense of regret is often at the core of alternate history:

> alternate histories are inspired by the notion that any given historical situation implies a plethora of divergent possibilities that far exceed the possibilities which happened to have been realized … [Moreover,] from this point of view, the progress of history appears as a tragic waste, not merely of human lives, but of options and opportunities in general, as a single possibility is often realized by the forceful suppression of alternatives … [Indeed,] alternate histories can be regarded as attempted to recuperate some of these losses. (p. 100)

This is a sentiment many Australians continue to reflect upon with regard to their memory of what some consider to be the untimely dismissal of the Whitlam government — and a sentiment that *Dismissal* may evoke in some readers.

Some examples of Australian alternate history

There is a considerable range of Australian alternate history that teachers may wish to use in various programs. For example, Australian immigration is a topic often included in the History curriculum. How might Australian alternate history deal with issues regarding China and Japan?

Anybody who has researched the Australian historical icons of *The Bulletin* and the *Lone Hand* for the decades from the 1890s through to the First World War could not but be impressed by the vast number of short stories depicting a Japanese or Chinese invasion of Australia. Ouyang Yu (1995) addressed the issues associated with this Chinese invasion literature, following through to Australia's bicentenary. Yu describes the paranoia contained in this early fiction regarding the Chinese in Australia: 'because of their cultural, religious and racial differences, the Chinese were deeply feared and hated as an undesirable Other' (1995, p. 5). There was also a deep eugenic fear of miscegenation from these invading Asian hordes: 'This obsession with racial purity would seem abnormal today but it was a genuine concern in those days when Chinese were believed to possess enormous power of corrupting the white blood with their inferior qualities' (p. 5). But these old fears were not easily forgotten. Several generations on, following the communist takeover of China in 1946, they reappear in alternate history. Now the Yellow Peril combined with the Red Menace.

Yu (1995) looks to several alternate histories, mostly published during the late 1960s, a period when the domino theory of communist and Asian invasion of Australia, assisted in dragging Australia into the Vietnam War. Again, alternate history can be read as a commentary of contemporary fears and anxieties. The alternate novels Yu (1995) writes of are: Kap Potham's *A Time to Die* (1967), John Hay's *Invasion* (1968) and Geoff Taylor's *Day of the Republic* (1968). Another alternate history described by Yu (1995) is P.L. Lyon's *The China Tape* (1981). With the domino theory now largely discredited, this latter alternate history, Yu (1995) suggests, should be seen as a response to

Australia's rapidly increased rate of Vietnamese 'boat people', Asian migration and the general anxiety concerning multicultural Australia, expressed through the public discourse by people such as the historian Geoffrey Blainey (p. 9).

With teachers discussing and having their students research various historiographical implications of the above connections with the history of Australian immigration, associated literature. for example, students may search 'Boat People' through *Trove*, (the comprehensive online search tool) and historiography students' engagement and consequent understanding of the topic ought greatly to be increased.

The strange case of Ned Kelly: merging alternate history with historiographic metafiction

Bertram Chandler was a prolific author of science fiction. His novels include *Rendezvous on a Lost World* (1961), *Beyond the Galactic Rim* (1963) and *The Broken Cycle* (1975). But it is his *Kelly Country* (1983) that is pertinent here. In this alternate history, as Wilde, Hooten and Andrews put it, Chandler 'considers what might have happened if Ned Kelly had won the siege of Glenrowan' (1994, p. 675). For Chandler's alternate history, the end result was an Irish Republic in Australia — the Australian revolution. But all this could have been very different. Chandler has one of his characters ask: 'what if the course of history was changed way back in 1880 [the beginning of the Australian Revolution]? What if the special train [bringing the police] had not been derailed outside Glenrowan? What if the police party had cleaned up the Kelly Gang, as they were then called?' (Chandler, 1983, p. 333).

But how does this alternate history connect with a better-known historical fiction of the Kelly Gang? Readers will naturally ask how seriously should historical novelists adhere to 'true' history, that is, history as perhaps perceived by the general populace? Can history be made into a farce, in the name of art and creative enterprise? And how does any such historical fiction connect with a declared alternate history, long classified as science fiction, such as Chandler's *Kelly Country*?

As if to remind his readers of the fickleness of historical 'truth', Peter Carey's self-reflective account of the Ned Kelly legend, *True History of the Kelly Gang* (2000), is one such work in which historical truth is subjugated in the interests of other artistic pursuits. As Huggan puts it: 'throughout Carey's novel, history slides imperceptibly into the more distant recesses of folk memory, while the documented discoveries of archival research converge with the fabrications of the adventure tale' (p. 64). Moreover, 'this structural ambivalence is reinforced by the remarkable act of sustained ventriloquism by which Carey is able to give voice to [Ned] Kelly's memories of his ancestral Irish, as well as his more immediate Australian past' (Huggan, 2007, p. 64). Thus, 'the narrative is consistently doubled, as the subjective recounting of Australian colonial history encounters half-buried memories of an Irish ancestry — an ancestry that clearly causes Kelly as much pain as pride, and through which the repetitive patterns of a larger [historic memory of unfairness] can be seen inexorably to emerge' (Huggan, 2007, p. 64). Set against the commodified status, Carey has created his own history of the Kelly Gang.

But what do we mean by Kelly's commodified status? In answering this question, note Tom Gillin's (2012) review of Ian W. Shaw's *Glenrowan: the legend of Ned Kelly* and the siege that shaped a nation. Gilling writes:

> Anyone who sets out to write another history of Ned Kelly — or Gallipoli, Kokoda, or the First Fleet, for that matter — can expect to have to answer the question: why? These subjects, the low-hanging fruit of Australian popular history, have all been covered so often, so thoroughly and so well that it seems reasonable to ask what any new author can offer. (p. 22)

Indeed, the publications regarding Ned Kelly have been many and varied. Witness Robert Drewe's *Our Sunshine* (1991), shortlisted for the 1992 Miles Franklin Literary Award. Peter Carey heaped praise on the work nine years before the publication of his own *True History of the Kelly Gang* (2000)

(Funnell, 2012). The reason for this sustained publication on Ned Kelly is because books on the subject sell, as will testify the many tourists who flock to Glenrowan annually, or buy the souvenir items. This is the essence of commodified history.

Historiographic metafiction 'also has the potential to challenge the national/global memory industries from which it draws increasing sustenance' (Huggan, 2007, p. 61). For Huggan, this is 'the commodification of memory', which 'is the function of a globalized late capitalist society in which historical consciousness has been eroded by nostalgia — a society of the souvenir as much as of the spectacle, in which an ever-growing number of commercially viable memorabilia and pseudo-historical constructions have granted the illusion of access to, while effectively substituting for, the lived experiences of the past' (Huggan, 2007, p. 61). So when does historiographic metafiction end and alternate history begin? The boundaries, I suggest, are increasingly blurred.

Connecting with film: the meeting point of counterfactual inquiry and historical methodology

There are a vast number of counterfactual films that could be used to connect with a study of a work of alternate history in a History classroom. *They Looked Away* (2003) [about Auschwitz] could be used in this way, also as a teaching strategy to consolidate a Second World War/Holocaust unit. The documentary film focuses on how history might have turned out had the Allies bombed Auschwitz in 1944. Miller (2004), a consultant for the film, explains that 'every holocaust survivor we spoke to wished that the Allies had bombed the camp. Some innocent people certainly would have been killed, but some would have been saved, not because the Nazis would have stopped killing Jews, but because their highly evolved and efficient system for doing so would have been disrupted' (Miller, 2004, p. 100). *They Looked Away* attempts to resolve the issue through comparative history, the meeting point of counterfactual inquiry and historical methodology.

Miller (2004) explains 'we thought of sources for the film differently from written history. We knew that having the squadron leader for the Buchenwald Raid explain how he had destroyed the weapons plant and avoided Auschwitz would be far more compelling than scholarly deliberation over whether the term "precision bombing" applies to World War II' (Miller, 2004, p. 109).

Thus, an example of connecting film and text in an exercise in alternate history in the classroom may involve first viewing *They Looked Away*, then having students read selective chapters from related histories, for example Tami Davis Biddle's contribution to M.J. Nuffield and M. Berenbaum's edited collection *The Bombing of Auschwitz: should the Allies have attempted it?* (2000). This engages students in a form of comparative history — comparing the real with the 'what if …?'.

But we know the Allies did not bomb Auschwitz. Miller concludes by stating:

> comparative history represents a sound methodological compromise to problems of counterfactual enquiry. As long as one is dealing with an event that never happened, there is always the possibility of asking about a similar event that did [such as the Buchenwald Raid]. …
>
> Whenever you ask a question about something that never took place you have to analyse all possible reasons why it did not take place, including those given by the very people who had the power to make history turn out differently. …
>
> Of course, conventional history is hardly unfaultable either. Nevertheless, it seems more acceptable to criticize the flaws and prejudices in explanations of historical outcomes, than to gauge why one factor is more likely to have obstructed a certain ending than another. (2004, p. 109)

Certainly, when History Curriculum and Methodology graduates have developed this level of historiographical thinking, they will be better prepared to engage their future students in learning experiences that encourage them to realise the vagaries of history.

* * *

As a cultural phenomenon, alternate history is now very prominent, and potentially attractive to History teachers. As it emerges from its categorisation as a sub-genre of science fiction, gaining the respect as an object of serious study by academic historians, its potential in History classes should, I argue, be obvious.

While alternate history may date back to Herodotus, the rising phenomena of alternate history in our popular culture may have many causes, not the least being the rising popularity of the electronic media and the insatiable demands it places on the production of new material. Now alternate history is presented in a vast array of media, including DVD, books and comics. The primary motive of alternate history is entertainment. Here, fantasy and alternative worlds are far removed from contemporary reality, and these works enjoy massive appeal with the public-at-large. Thus, as Rosenfeld (2005) suggests, alternative history, apart from being fun, is inherently presentist.

It is the presentist nature of alternate history that distinguishes it from counterfactual history. Chapter 7 showed the latter to be a much more serious attempt at historiography, mostly written by historians who seek to promote a greater historiographical understanding of a particular pivotal event in history. An example of this would be Macintyre's (2006) account of Australia's baptism of fire in November 1914 (see Chapter 7). Most alternate history, in contrast, is written in the form of a novel, and its primary purpose is mostly entertainment.

The brief history of alternate history given in this chapter largely has shown that since the 1960s, publication of alternate history has increased vastly, moving from the realms of scientific fiction. Typically, with subject matters such as Nazism and the postwar speculations on Hitler surviving his Berlin bunker, increasingly it has become the domain of the mass media. It is moving to being a distinct genre, separate from its traditional location of science fiction.

Like any good 'lie' or mistruth, alternate history usually contains an element of (possible) truth. An example of this was Hasluck's (2011) novel, *Dismissal*. This occurred at about the same time as wider media speculation concerning Evatt and the Petrov affair. Thus, alternate history often explores subject matter held in the collective beliefs of society concerning some form of conspiracy: in a sense it is in the realms of collective 'marginal' memory. For many readers, as in the issues explored in Hasluck's (2011) *Dismissal*, there is an appeal to conspiracy theory.

During the twentieth century there was a mass of published material in Australia exploring the themes of some form of Asian invasion of Australia. This provides examples of Australian alternate history, and how these works might be used to assist student understanding of memory literature, and as a device to their enhanced historiographical understanding of such topics as Australia's twentieth-century defence and foreign policy.

9 'Caught in time's cruel machinery': Time-slip Novels in the History Lesson

'But when it comes to the river of history, the watershed moments most susceptible to change are assassinations — the ones that succeeded and the ones that failed. Archduke Franz Ferdinand of Austria gets shot by a mentally unstable pipsqueak named Gavrilo Princip and there's your kickoff to World War 1. On the other hand, after Claus von Stauffenberg failed to kill Hitler in 1944 — close, but no cigar — the war continued and millions of people died.'

I had seen that before, too.

Al said, 'There's nothing we can do about Archduke Ferdinand or Adolf Hitler. They're out of our reach.'

I thought of accusing him of making pronounal assumptions and kept my mouth shut. I felt a little like a man reading a very grim book. A Thomas Hardy, novel, say. You know how it's going to end, but instead of spoiling things, that somehow increases your fascination. It's like watching a kid run his electric train faster and faster and waiting for it to derail on one of the curves.

'As for 9.11 if you wanted to fix that one, you'd have to wait around for forty-three years. You'd be pushing eighty, if you made it at all.'

Now the lone-star flag the gnome had been holding made sense. It was a souvenir of Al's last jaunt into the past. 'You couldn't even make it to '63, could you?'

> To this he didn't reply, just watched me. His eyes, which had looked rheumy and vague when he let me into the diner that afternoon, now looked bright. Almost young.
>
> 'Because that's what you're talking about, right? Dallas in 1963?'
>
> 'That's right', he said. 'I had to opt out. But you're not sick, buddy. You're healthy and in the prime of life. You can go back, and you can stop it.'
>
> He leaned forward, his eyes not just bright; they were blazing.
>
> 'You can change history, Jake. Do you understand that? John Kennedy can live.' (King, 2011, pp. 51-52)

Jake and his mate, Al, have just stepped from a storeroom in Al's diner in the year 2011 back to the 1950s. Al has set Jake the great challenge of saving JFK from the sniper's rifle, and thus altering the course of history. Stephen King's time-slip novel *22.11.63* makes fascinating reading, and from my experience, many secondary History students find it extremely appealing.

What is the time-slip genre?

As Chapter 4 showed, the UK-based Historical Novel Society (n.d.) defined historical novels to include time-slip novels. Apart from being arguably a legitimate member of the genre, there are excellent commercial reasons for this. Walk through many upper-primary school or middle school classrooms and it's highly likely you will see students reading time-slip novels. Sometimes referred to as historical fantasy, time-warp fantasy, time-travel or past-time fantasy, the genre is very popular with younger adolescents, as it is with many older readers.

Time-slips have been popular at least since the publication of H.G. Wells's *The Time Machine* (1895). As Bradley (2011, p. 22) puts it, this genre has become one of the 'most fertile tropes of science fiction, spawning not just a small library of short stories, novels and comics, but films, television shows, including the *Dr Who* series, running periodically since 1963. Also included is a host of subgenres, from the dizzying possibilities of Stephen Baxter's *XeeLee* stories to semi sci-fi fictional tearjerkers such as Audrey Niffenegger's *The Time Traveller's Wife*. Daphne du Maurier's *The House on the Strand* (1969) is a classic in the time-slip genre.

Erlandson and Bainsbridge explain that the genre's popularity 'lies partly in the fact that it crosses three distinct genres (fantasy, historical fiction and contemporary realism) and takes the reader to a time that is quite distinct from current time, one that might be perceived as being less complex than today' (2001, p. 1). Indeed, 'it enables the reader to step back from contemporary life and see the struggles of human existence from a more distanced, reflective perspective' (p. 2.). Time-slips mostly are pure escapism, providing the reader with a bridge to a past perceived as more accommodating and pleasant. For this reason, Erlandson and Bainsbridge observe 'contemporary readers in the "middle years" can certainly identify with the need to get away from the routines of life when they grapple with issues that are beyond their control; issues such as body image, bullying, anxiety, divorce, death, and adolescence itself' (p. 2).

Erlandson and Bainsbridge go on to contend that it is the author's ability to convince readers to 'suspend disbelief' that has made the study of fantasy literature controversial in some schools. But, for me, it need not be controversial in the History curriculum. Erlandson and Bainsbridge state that 'some adults do not consider children capable of distinguishing between reality and fantasy even though school curricula often state middle years students should be able to make the distinction' (p. 3). Is it not the teacher's role when using this genre in the History lesson, simply to explain that the time-slip is a literary device to engage the reader, and get students to consider 'what if …?'. Apart from engaging the students with the history of the period, the purpose here is principally historiographical. As Erlandson and Bainsbridge put it: 'Time slip fantasy, however, is generally regarded as the most conservative of all fantasy literature. It does not deal with supernatural events, but uses a literary mechanism which allows young readers to imaginatively move through time' (2001, p. 2).

A recent time-slip novel in the History classroom

In reviewing international best-selling author Stephen King's *11.22.63*, Bradley (2011) explains this sense of escapism provided by time-slip novels in another fashion: 'running through most [time-slip novels] is a desire as simple as it is profound, a desire not to explore the future but escape to the past. After all, what is the wish to travel back in time but a fantasy about the possibility of changing it, of undoing the damage of our failures?' (p. 22).

In King's *11.22.63*, Bradley suggests, Al believes 'stopping the assassination will prevent the bloody cascade of events that followed it: the killings of Martin Luther King and Robert Kennedy, the Detroit riots, Vietnam' (2011, p. 22). However, is it simply a matter of stopping Lee Harvey Oswald? Or is the whole thing part of a much larger conspiracy, involving multiple players? In his afterword, King declares he is '98 or 99 per cent certain' that Oswald was not the agent of dark and sinister forces, but a 'dangerous little fame junkie who found himself in just the right place to get lucky' (King, 2011, p. 22).

For me, the appeal and value of this time-slip for History students exists on at least three levels. First, there is the intrinsic appeal of the plot. When Jake departs 2011 America for the year 1958, he needs to spend five years waiting to know if they have been successful in preventing the assassination of JFK. But Jake finds much that is fascinating in his country in 1958. Many younger readers of this novel will likely engage strongly with the socio-cultural differences of America in the 1950s compared with 2011.

Then there is the captivating attention to the socio-cultural differences between the two eras portrayed in the novel. Through Jake we learn there is much appeal in America of the late 1950s. He dallies in this period. After a diversion to Derry (the fictional Maine town that appears in several of King's works), Jake, now known as George, relocates to Texas, where he meets a woman and falls in love. As Bradley puts it, 'These early sections of the novel are most irresistibly entertaining, enlivened not just by King's supreme control of the form but by his sardonic wit and usual generosity of spirit and expansiveness' (2011, p. 22).

But this leads to what I consider an important historiographical reason as to why History students should read this particular novel. Bradley (2011, p. 22) puts it this way: 'beneath the reassuring glow of King's portrait of an earlier, simpler time moves a darker and less comfortable vision, a glimpse of the terrifying machinery moving below the surface of human history, and which stands as a stark, chilling rejoinder to the fantasies of escape embodied in so many time travel stories. Don't we all secretly know this?' Or, as King puts it, 'Men with hammers, men with knives, men with guns. A universe of horror surrounding a single lighted stage where mortals dance in defiance of the dark (King, 2011, p. 195, as cited in Bradley, 2011, p. 22). There is a connection here with many earlier statements in this book concerning the special role this genre can have to counter students' deterministic views of history.

Time-slip histories and changing interpretations of the Great Depression in Australia

There are, however, other time-slip novels that serve to explore other issues connected with the teaching of History in our schools. Consider this question: do Australians have a balanced view of Australian society during the Great Depression or have the old views associated with the Australian Legend and the Aussie Battler (see Chapter 13) prevailed? Over the last two generations, as revisionist historians have examined the period, interpretations of the Depression have shown important changes. Consider Sparrow's review of David Potts's study, *The Myth of the Great Depression* (2006):

> Throughout the '60s and '70s, Potts interviewed survivors of the Depression and noticed that, alongside deprivation and misery, many recalled moments of joy and pleasure. It's in this sense he decries the 'myth' of the Depression. Most of us think of the era only in terms of wretched victims rotting on the dole when, actually, the struggle to survive provided many with a sense of purpose, even a happiness, absent from more prosperous times.
>
> Yet, by pushing this idea to the limit and then beyond, Potts has transformed an interesting thesis into a polemic far more unbalanced than the orthodoxy he seeks to correct. (Sparrow, 2006)

Revisionist histories often have difficulty in first claiming recognition by the general public. To a large extent, Potts's study dealt with memory (see especially Chapter 10). Sparrow's critique of Potts may have benefitted from a more considered appreciation of Potts's research on memory. Among other things, he wrote how 'the hurts imposed by the economic Depression were usually salient — dramatic and immediate in impact (such as sackings, evictions or job rejections) or significant changes in conditions (such as people being forced to life in a slum or changing to a demeaning type of work)' (Potts, 2006, p. 202). Indeed, for Potts, 'these sudden and important changes encouraged encoding, and allow recall and evaluation. The good things are often about holding the line in old ways: supportive family relationships, entertainment, self-help (like home gardening) and community cooperation, all of which respondents often regarded as less presentable as a "Depression" experience' (p. 202).

Clearly, many people who had lived through the Depression as children had positive views of their childhood. McLaren's (1999) study of childhood during the Depression in country Australia certainly supports Potts's (2006) research. So, too, do autobiographies and novels such as Catherine Edmonds's *Caddie* (1953/1977), later a motion picture that appeared in Australia the year after the International Year of Women (1975), having received support from the International Women's Year Secretariat. The autobiography — with some embellishments — describes the life of a woman, with her children, who is forced out of her middle-class home during the Great Depression in Sydney. Edited and introduced by the well-established Australian author, Daphne Cusack, the book was first published by Constable & Co. Ltd in London in May 1953.

Many of the myths of the Depression were embellished in *Caddie*, in its book and film version. Richie (1996), in his notes on Edmonds life, writes: 'to some degree, *Caddie* embellished the truth and fabricated a legend. Cusack regarded its factual discrepancies as relatively unimportant: she saw her late protégée as an archetypal battler, a woman imbued with resilience and humanity'. Richie notes that the book was 'eventually published in Australia in 1966, the book was reprinted in 1975 and 1976 (seven times). That year *Caddie* was adapted as a feature film'. The film underscores the battler image of working-class women during the period (see, for example, *Caddie, 1976*, n.d.)

In many respects, recent later interpretations of the Depression challenged the Australian Legend, myths associated with 'a fair go' and a land of opportunity, while underscoring the myth associated with the Australian Legend and the Aussie Battler. Despite the negative effect that the Depression had on the Australian Legend during the 1930s (R. White, 1981, pp. 145-7), by the 1980s, apparently, the views of people who had their childhood during the Depression were changing to more positive memories. Museums began to make collections of the era.

Jackie French's novel *Somewhere Around the Corner* (1994) draws on many of these nostalgic memories of childhood in the Depression. And it does so through time-slip. Barbara, a runaway in contemporary Australia, is 'pulled around the corner' backward in time — drawn into a timeslip. Awakening in the year of 1932 in the middle of the Great Depression, the confused girl meets a kindly boy named Jim, who brings her home to Poverty Gully, a relief camp for the unemployed. While Jim's parents view their strange visitor as neglected and delusional, they are quick to accept Barbara as one of the family. Their run-down shack has no floor nor beds, but there Barbara finds the love and compassion denied her in her 'other world' (French, 1994). Through Barbara's eyes, French describes Poverty Gulley:

> The strangeness descended all over again. Dirt floors and hessian sack windows were tolerable in summer. What would it be like to huddle there when the winds blew through the cracks? The gully was a world where there were no antibiotics when you were sick, where people died of a sore tooth, with no electric light or heaters or stoves indoors when it was cold and dark. (1994, p. 149)

And again:

> 'What are you looking for?'
>
> 'The seat belt.'
>
> 'The seat what?'
>
> 'The seat belt. You know.'
>
> Young Jim shook his head. 'Never heard of it. What does a seat belt do when it's at home?'
>
> 'It stops you flinging forward when you stop suddenly or when you crash.'
>
> Sergeant Ryan look amused. 'Funny lot of drivers you've been riding with, love. You won't need one of those things while I'm at the wheel.' (French, 1994, p. 31)

In the novel, French describes what it was like in Australia during the Depression. She uses a teenage girl as the main character, something that will appeals to the target audience (years 6, 7, 8). This enables the students to identify with Barbara, imagining what they themselves would think if they were in a similar position to the main character.

The novel goes into detail about what the Depression was like from a teenager's perspective. The main character is amazed at the type of clothes people wear, their hairstyles, what they eat and what their homes look like. French also describes the horrible things that occurred throughout the

Depression years in Australia, such as the rapid increase in homelessness, the forced relocation of families, and children being forced to new locations away from their schools. These types of descriptions, I suggest, appeal to students.

French's *Somewhere Around the Corner* (1994) follows on from another highly regarded New Zealand/Australian author of children's novels, Ruth Park (1917-2010). Other than *Playing Beatie Bow* (1980), her best known works are the novels *The Harp in the South* (1948) and the *Muddle-Headed Wombat* (1962-82). Winner of the Australian Children's Book of the Year Award in 1981, *Playing Beatie Bow* is about a group of children in the trendy Rocks District of Sydney. A member of the group — Abigail — is transported back to the same district in Victorian times, engaging in wonderful time-slip adventures. Written for upper primary and middle school students, the novel provides a fascinating insight into the Rocks District when it was not so trendy, in fact when it was what one historian has described as the cesspool of the Pacific region. The Rocks website captures the change from goal to port to tourist attraction:

> Its colourful history-filled with tales of 'shanghaied' sailors, rough gangs, and gritty life can still be traced in the many surviving buildings from the last two centuries. But today the renovated former warehouses, sailors' homes, and dens of iniquity house a unique mixture of fine restaurants, one-of-a-kind shops, and galleries showcasing both established and emerging talent (*Heritage & History*, n.d., n.p.).

* * *

The emerging plethora of timeslip history is pertinent for teachers of History as they seek to engage their students in History, and in particular to develop their historical literacy in respect to the historiography of their subject matter. As with adults, many school students find the genre wonderfully engaging, with marvellous intrinsic appeal. The examples of timeslips this chapter has revealed show enormous potential to provide historiographical opportunities, illustrating what Stephen King has his hero claim: 'It's a perfectly balanced mechanism of shouts and echoes pretending to be wheels and cogs, a dreamclock chiming beneath a mystery-glass we call life. Behind it? Below it and around it? Chaos, storms' (2011, p. 195). Indeed, when students come to understand this to be the essence of history, they have claimed much historiographical ground.

PART III

DECONSTRUCTING THE HISTORICAL NOVEL

10 Whose History? Historical Fiction and the Discipline of History in the Classroom: Varying Views of the Past

Alert students will often tell teachers and university lecturers that there is sometimes a significant discrepancy between the same historical characters, settings or incidents in historical fiction and nonfiction. An illustration of this point arises with hugely successful author Bryce Courtenay's work of historical fiction, *The Potato Factory* (1995), and a subsequent work of nonfiction, which sought to put the record straight on Isaac (Ikey) Solomon, one of the principal characters in Courtenay's novel. Judith Sackville-O'Donnell, a Melbourne author, challenged Courtenay's depiction of Ikey Solomon, who was also believed to be the model for Charles Dickens's fictional villain Fagin.

Sackville-O'Donnell's *The First Fagin: The True Story of Ikey Solomon* (2002) sold about 1500 copies. While a commendable publishing feat, this fares very poorly in comparison with Courtenay's *The Potato Factory*, whose sales exceeded manyfold that of *The First Fagin*: '*The Potato Factory* was last year [2003] listed by Angus & Robertson as 17th on Australia's 100 favourite books. Gold Logie-winner Lisa McCune was among the stars in a TV mini-series based on the novel' (Schwartz, 2004).

This is just one example of where a dedicated and motivated professional historian can take issue with the historicity of a piece of historical fiction. Clearly, if the sales of *The Potato Factory* are an index to the success of the novel then the demonstrated warping of historical fact does little to offend the reading public. Do people prefer the 'history' they read in historical fiction? Apparently many do. But can they trust it for its historical veracity?

Truth and deception in the writing of history

To begin, a short narrative of the changes in points of view. For example, during the 1950s and 1960s British and American points of view in history dominated the content in the school curriculum: for example, the causes of the Second World War. For me, as a secondary school student in New South Wales during the 1960s, a dominant and influential text was Winston Churchill's *The Second World War* (1953). In his six-volume history of the conflict that appeared between 1948 and 1953, Churchill established the accepted interpretation of the origins of the Second World War: that Hitler launched a war of conquest. Rossi states that, 'In 1950, *Time* magazine, then at the height of its power and influence, named Winston Churchill "Man of the Half Century". His reputation was at a peak because of his leadership of the Allied cause in World War II and his role in alerting the Free World to the threat of Communism by his "Iron Curtain" speech in early 1946' (Rossi, 2002).

But what did *Time* magazine write about Churchill sixty years later? In a review article headed, 'The ugly Briton: a scholarly account of Churchill's role in the Bengal Famine leaves his reputation in tatters', Shashi Tharoor reviewed Madhustree Mukerjee's new book, *Churchill's Secret War* (*Time*, 29 November 2010, p. 43.) The review article is an enlightening account of many things to do with literature and history, not least, of the changing attitudes of *Time* magazine to India.

Why the change? For one thing, the global balance of economic power has moved decidedly in India's favour during the past several decades. India's role as a prominent trading partner with the US, and that country's emerging economic power, is now significant. Tharoor writes that 'Churchill said that history would judge him kindly because he intended to write it himself'. After all, Churchill coined the phrase, 'history is written by the victors'. But Tharoor (2010) is far less enthusiastic about Churchill's multi-volume history of the Second World War than were my History teachers back in the 1960s. She writes: 'the self-serving but elegant volumes he authoured ... led to the Nobel committee, unable in all conscience to bestow him an award for peace, to give him, astonishingly, the Nobel prize for literature — an unwitting tribute to the fictional qualities inherent in Churchill's self-justifying embellishments' (Tharoor, 2010).

Many people recognise the prestige and authority a Nobel Prize bestows, notwithstanding the complex and contested effects and legacies of the Prizes in a broader context. Tharoor goes on to argue that 'few statesmen of the 20th century have reputations as outsize as Winston Churchill's, and yet his assiduously self-promoted image ... rests primarily on his World War II rhetoric, rather than his actions as the head of a government that ruled the biggest empire the world has ever known' (Tharoor, 2010).

Churchill wrote in his history of the Second World War: 'no great portion of the world population was so effectively protected from the horrors and perils of the world war as were the people of Hinduism' (quoted in Tharoor, 2010). In turn, Tharoor wrote that 'few people during the immediate post-war decades, reading this last paragraph would have doubted this being the truth. We were continually told in schools and in the media the British Empire — later the British Commonwealth — existed in order to improve the lives of the people of the empire'. According to Tharoor,

> British imperialism had long justified itself with the pretense that it was conducted for the benefit of the governed. Churchill's conduct in the summer and fall of 1943 gave the lie to this myth' ... 'I hate Indians,' he told the Secretary of State for India, Leopold Amery. 'They are a beastly people with a beastly religion. The [Bengal] Famine was their own fault', he declared at a war cabinet meeting, for 'breeding like rabbits'.

Tharoor, goes on to suggest that 'Churchill's only response to a telegram from the government in Delhi about people perishing in the [Bengali] famine was to ask why Ghandi hadn't yet died' (2010). Tharoor goes on to say that 'in 1943, some 3 million brown-skinned subjects of the Raj died in the Bengal famine, one of history's worst'. As part of the war effort, Churchill ordered the diversion of food from the starving Indians to already well-supplied British soldiers, and to stockpiles in Britain and elsewhere in Europe, including Greece and Yugoslavia: 'And he did so with a churlishness that cannot be excused on grounds of policy' (Tharoor, 2010).

Tharoor writes: 'Some of India's grain was also exported to Ceylon (now Sri Lanka) to meet needs there, even though the island wasn't experiencing the same hardships'. Tharoor asked what did Churchill care about starving Bengalis? 'Australian wheat,' he wrote, 'sailed past Indian cities (where the bodies of those who had died of starvation littered the streets) to depots in the Mediterranean and Balkans; and offers of American and Canadian food aid were turned down' (Tharoor, 2010). Unimaginable today was the control Britain had over the lives of everyday Indians: 'India was not permitted to use its own sterling reserves, or indeed, its own ships to import food' (Tharoor, 2010). Tharoor (2010) makes a strong case against Churchill's treatment of this topic. It is almost as if his treatment belongs to the realms of historical fiction.

MacMillan's assessment offers corroboration to Tharoor's slightly later work, showing how Churchill created 'a sweeping and magisterial account which glossed over many awkward issues' (MacMillan, 2009, p. 40). From these accounts, it seems that Churchill's history of the Second World War may well suffer for want of 'truth', the very point which some critics have condemned historical novels.

Indeed, the discrediting of Churchill's work — his grand narrative — supports Hayden White's views about the writing of history. In reviewing White's *Fiction of Narrative: essays on history, literature and theory 1957-2007* (2010), Inga Clendinnen writes:

> For all its wistful aspirations, history was not, never had been and never could be a science. It was an art, and its closest kin was poetry. …

> There is no such thing as a real story. Stories are told or written, not found. And as to the notion of a true story, this is virtually a contradiction in terms. All stories are fictions. Which means, of course, that they can be true only in a metaphorical sense and in the sense in which a figure of speech can be true. (2011)

Clendinnen concludes — in words that resonate for the above discussion about Churchill's history of the Second World War — that:

> White's recognition of the covert seductions of narratives created to sustain nation to the fantasies of special destiny shaping individual biographies (and, alas, autobiographies) remains essential knowledge, especially in view of the advice being given to younger historians by older ones that if they want to challenge the market dominance of the historical novelist, they had better get back to storytelling. (p. 28)

Most politicians are aware that histories are essential in nation-building.

'History as fiction'

'If the past is another country, historical novels are forged passports,' wrote Frank Campbell in *The Australian* in 2008. Campbell began his critical article on historical fiction by pointing out the debate on the veracity of historical fiction has been in the public discourse for at least a century. He writes that the 'perceptive American critic, Brander Matthews, said in 1897: "the historical novel is aureoled with a pseudo-sanctity in that it purports to be more instructive than a mere story. It claims ... it is teaching History". But it is not history: we cannot reproduce what has passed' (Campbell, 2008). Campbell added:

> 'How can we know the past?... After all, psychology 101 suggests that even simple events are reported inaccurately. Aren't there as many realities as witnesses? If present matters of fact are opaque, how can we possibly re-create the culture of a Manchester police station of 1973, or 19th-century naval life, let alone the world of Claudius or Spartacus? (Campbell, 2008)

But we have uncertainty of the present, also, Campbell counters. Indeed, 'How do we know we exist at all? ... I might exist, but the evidence for you is unconvincing. One more drink and we'll all be phenomenological postmodernists, whose grip on reality depends entirely on the next coffee' (Campbell, 2008).

Campbell reiterates the argument that 'historical fiction is said to tell us more about the present than the past'. Historical novels are really scenarios or dramas — Campbell refers to them as 'lectures' — about how the present sees the past. He uses the example of *Gone With The Wind* (1936), and how it stereotyped 'the antebellum American south and still shapes perceptions' (Campbell, 2008). But while the historical novel often has been dispatched to the rubbish pile, for me it re-emerges, as is evident in the vigour and popularity the genre enjoys today.

But how does this debate affect children's appreciation of history? I argue that History teachers should seek for our students to develop multiple viewpoints, and to become critical readers of history. Groce and Groce (2005, p. 101) show not only that children's reading of historical novels enhances their appreciation of novels generally, but also enhances development of the values underpinning an understanding of history. The researchers suggest students may benefit from understanding multiple viewpoints in history in two ways: they may exhibit increased tolerance for others in contemporary society as well as an increased ability to evaluate our own culture. For Groce and Groce, historical fiction helps to achieve this because, as Nawrot (1996) argues, it depicts life beyond the context of the student's own lives and time.

Thus, with the enhancing of children's understanding of historical developments, their reading of historical fiction often requires teacher guidance. And this is particularly so with historical fiction portrayed through film. As far as the pedagogical use of film in the History curriculum is concerned, most commentators will argue there usually are very different approaches (see Marcus, ed., 2003). What of classics such as C.S Forester's *Hornblower* series (1938-67) or Patrick O'Brian's *Master and Commander* (1970), or Robert

Graves's *I Claudius* (1934), all of which went on to become classics of cinema and television? Erudite teachers have long used clips from the DVD versions of these much-acclaimed productions to use as key components in their teaching/learning strategies for their History lessons. So for Campbell, and for me, all is not lost. At its best, historical fiction is 'a delicate arrangement of lies designed to spell truth. Historical fiction, the most elaborate embroidery of all, can illumine the past rather than traduce it, but requires detachment from the present as much as immersion in the past. Journeymen and propagandists need not apply' (Campbell, 2008).

A deficit model of historical writing?

But what motivates authors of historical fiction to write their work? There exists the suggestion that some do so to 'fill in the blanks' left by authors of nonfiction histories. For example, what motivated Tolstoy to write *War and Peace* and structure it in the manner he did? The work is, in my view, one of the most sublime creative literary efforts ever produced. There is every reason to believe Tolstoy wrote from a deficit model of historical writing. In his *Some Words about War and Peace*, published in 1868, he wrote that one motivation in writing *War and Peace* came from common misinterpretations of the social and cultural characteristics in Russia of the period covered by the novel (1805-20):

> If we have come to believe in the perversity and coarse violence of the period, that is only because of the traditions, memoirs, stories, and novels that have been handed to us, record for the most part exceptional cases of violence and brutality. To suppose that the predominant characteristic of that period was turbulence, is as unjust as it would be for a man, seeing nothing but the tops of trees beyond a hill, to conclude that there was nothing in the locality but trees. (Tolstoy, 1868, trans. A. Mandelker, 2010, p. 1310)

Hence, Tolstoy structured his novel with narratives about war and peace, through the fortunes of four Russian families. For readers of the novel, characters from the Bezúkhovs, the Rostóvs, the Bolkónskys and the Kurágins provide some of the most memorable literary characters readers ever encountered.

Indeed, in the case of the search for historical truth, whatever that may be, in some instances historical novelists have sought to improve upon extant historical accounts. Mandelker shows that in the case of *War and Peace*, Aylmer and Louise Maude, in their centenary edition of Tolstoy's complete works (*Centenary Edition of Tolstoy's Works*, Oxford, 1928-37) write that 'Tolstoy consulted many other authorities and private letters, diaries, and memoirs of the members of his own and other families that had engaged in the [1806 French/Russian and Austrian] war. These private sources sometimes enabled him to correct mistakes he judged that the historians had made' (cited in Mandelker, 2010, p. 1325).

Often, the deficit motivation for writing historical novels continues into the present-day. Speaking at a University of Technology, Sydney (UTS) seminar on history and writing, academic Paula Hamilton discussed what she label the 'deficit' model of history writing. Here, she refers to historical novelists who contend that they have turned to fiction because of a perceived 'gap' in the historical record they feel driven to fill. Hamilton argues it is the apparent limits of history that make writing possible; the role of the writer is to fill in the blanks left unattended by the writers of nonfiction histories (Hamilton, 2003). Nelson states that 'in practice, the "deficit" argument takes various forms in which the writer supplies the interiority or atmosphere deemed to be missing from history, or manufactures actual historical events that lack the necessary proofs to count as history' (Nelson 2007).

Writers of nonfictional history, and some serious professional historians, may rail at this approach to their craft. As Nelson contends, 'One of the central problems with the "deficit" argument is that it speaks to a very naturalised theory of history, in which historians labour altruistically in archives to unearth relics of the past, which are converted into an historical record conceived as truth' (Nelson, 2007). Indeed, 'in this sense, it is merely the writer's job to extend the edifice, to make it more "perfect", more "complete" — without "gaps"'(Nelson, 2007). In short, this model entails fictionalising the unknown detail in the archival sources, as developed in the narrative: for example, types of clothes being worn by various characters.

Inga Clendinnen is one such historian who declares this model to be anathema to the craft of the serious historian. While she admits the need to be close and personal with her readers in her narrative, the larger 'difference between History and Fiction is the moral relationships each establishes between writer and subjects, and writer and reader'. The historian of nonfiction has a moral obligation to be strictly 'nonfictional' (Clendinnen, 1996). For Nelson, the fictionalising of the detail should not be an issue with the historical novelist: 'the factual events of the story could be altered and improved, but the period details had to be as realistic as possible' (Hamilton, 2003, cited in Nelson, 2007).

'Mining' and 'pillaging' historical knowledge

Kate Grenville once quipped that 'as a [historical] novelist, my relationship to history has always been pretty much the same relationship the Goths had to Rome. History for a greedy novelist like me is just one more place to pillage' (Grenville, 2005). She is not suggesting there is a recklessness about her historical research, or a general disregard for convention. Do the spoils of that 'pillage' — the historical knowledge gained from reading her historical novels — offer any general worth? Or to put it another way, how much can the knowledge gained from historical novels be of value to the general populace, or indeed, a History curriculum?

Grenville — far from endorsing recklessness — confessed to an abiding regard for historical truth: 'When Jill Roe said of history "Getting it right means you can't make it up", it was a reminder to novelists like me that, although we might use history, we also have to respect it'. Indeed, 'it's all very well to play fast and loose with historical truths, but there comes a point when we have to get it right, or try at least' (Grenville, 2005). Here Grenville is addressing an important issue in the writing of history, an issue historiographers for decades have been addressing. The historical novelist need not be 'playing' with history any more than does the professional historian, notwithstanding the novelist's obligation to storytelling.

Generally, historians take their craft very seriously. They even have gone to 'war' over substantial issues in what they perceive to be appropriate recording and interpretation of history. Many students will be aware of the term 'history wars'. The term was coined in the United States in 1994 to describe the argument between those who favoured a triumphalist account of American achievement and those urging a more muted and critical stance. Australia had its own 'history wars' beginning sometime around 2000 (Windschuttle, 2002). In considerable part, this had to do with debates over so-called 'three cheers' versus 'black armband versions of history. Part of the debate involved the relative veracity of historical nonfiction and historical fiction. What could historical fiction add to the debate?

When Grenville claimed *The Secret River* (2005) would rise above the parochial squabbles of the then raging history wars by getting 'inside the experience' of the past, she provoked a strong response from some academic and professional historians. For Collins (2008), 'this ire was particularly surprising in the case of Mark McKenna and Inga Clendinnen, two leading historians noted for the eloquent reflective, literary quality of their respective books on the intimacy between Indigenous and settler Australians' (Collins, 2008).

Clendinnen (2003) and McKenna (2002) strongly questioned Grenville's views on the role of her historical novel with regards to her claims to historical truth over that of their own profession. Indeed, it is this very jousting over the province of historians and historical novelists to historical truth that has led Gay Lynch to assert 'historians would be better placed to study King Canute than attempt to prevent fiction writers working in their field' (Lynch, 2007, p. 2).

Nevertheless, serious professional historians do feel aggrieved about the various raiding parties of historical novelists into their perceived traditional territory. Clendinnen claimed 'novelists have been doing their best to bump historians off the track' (Clendinnen, 2006, p. 23, cited in Lynch, 2007, p. 2). She contended that she was on the lookout for historical fiction writers who show attitude ('exuberant confidence', 'insouciant exploitation of fragments of the past'), 'lack historical professionalism (the collapsing of time, opportunistic transpositions, and elisions) and show off their subjective petticoats' (Clendinnen, p. 23, cited in Lynch, 2007, p. 2).

All of this public literary jousting prompts Lynch to ask whether 'the battered protagonists in the history wars tried to throw off the cheerful trailing historical fiction writers doing business in their own way?' (2007, p. 3). Lynch notes what was said at the close of a 2007 Sydney Writers' Festival panel ('Making a Fiction of History'). Here, according to Lynch (2007, p. 4), Clendinnen conceded some 'fictional truths'. For Lynch, Clendinnen's 'consistent message might be: stay behind your lines and you won't get hurt' (p. 4).

However, clearly Grenville's *Secret River* has invited comments about the relationship between history, literature, and public ethics in contemporary Australia. While it attracted praise and criticism for its representation of early Australian frontier history, McKenna has decried the positive reviews of the book as symptomatic of '[a] cultural space [that] has opened up into which writers of fiction are now more commonly seen as the most trustworthy purveyors of the past' (Lynch, 2007, p. 5). Similarly, John Hirst considered the book was an expression of a misguided and ill-informed contemporary liberal imagination (Hirst, 2007, p. 36).

In my view, the developing public stoush seemed to be as much about professional territory as anything else. Had writers of historical fiction any right to trespass onto the domain of historians? In reviewing Grenville's next novel, *The Lieutenant*, Stella Clarke reminded readers of what McKenna had said about Grenville 'of getting above herself, of thinking she was doing history better than the professionals'. As Clarke wrote, 'it was fine for novelists and historians to jog along on their separate tracks, on either side of the ravine (this is tough terrain) that separates truth from untruth, but Clendinnen thought Grenville had somehow moved over and tried to 'bump historians off the track' (Clarke, 2008).

Clarke continued: 'Undaunted, Grenville struck back … with a strong defence of her approach, saying she really did not think of *The Secret River* as history' (Clarke, 2008). Grenville may have been more interested in perfecting her craft as a historical novelist than competing with historians. In Clarke's words, 'with historians pushing to cleave publicly to unmodish virtues of precision, her more contemporary emphasis on nuance threatened to push them beyond credibility' (Clarke, 2008). According to critic and novelist Jane Sullivan (writing at that time in *The Age*), Clendinnen remained implacable, even after the publication of Grenville's persuasive explanatory account of her approach, *Searching for the Secret River* (2006) (Clarke, 2008).

Some historical novelists seemed to have watched closely the Grenville versus historians spat. For example, Richard Flanagan seems to have been careful not to have ventured into this imbroglio when talking about his novel, *Wanting* (2008). Don Anderson comments: 'Keeping in mind, however, the great Kate Grenville v. Inga Clendinnen bout regarding rival claims of history and poetry in *The Secret River*, Flanagan is understandably cautious in denying history to be his "true subject"' (Anderson, D., 2008). Anderson concluded: 'Though surely Aristotle said something in his Poetics about poetry being superior to history?' (2008).

But the public debate of historical fiction versus history continued to grow during the first decade of the twenty-first century, and Grenville's novels were at the centre of the public debate. For example, Clarke (2011) writes, 'in recent years, a forest of journalistic and academic work has rehearsed and extended the original spat' (p. 19). Other Australian researchers, however, see the relationship between history and historical fiction in more conciliatory terms. Sutherland and Gibbons conclude that 'Historical fiction and history reflect a symbiotic rather than a parasitic relationship. Each gives to the other, from their respective strengths' (Sutherland & Gibbons, 2009). They continue:

> Even so the common elements between literature and history, especially through the use of narrative, the recreation of an historical era and the attempts to establish a link between the past and the present remain. … Inevitably there are differences between the work of historians and writers of historical fiction, but these differences may be thought of … in terms of family resemblances. Bearing this analogy in mind historical fiction should never be thought of as the poor relation. Historical fiction can take its place at the family table in equal company with History. (Sutherland & Gibbons, 2009)

Sutherland and Gibbons also insist it is 'appropriate to also acknowledge the significance of the reader' (2009). The authors refer to Bird (2009), who depicts a reader of historical fiction as being 'in a position of privilege, [who] to a degree becomes a player in the history' (Bird, 2009, p. 20, cited in Sutherland & Gibbons, 2009).

In reviewing Hilary Mantel's *Wolf Hall* (2009), Bird added: 'Historical fiction does what all fiction does: creates a world in which characters live and die' (Bird, 2009, p. 20). Moreover, 'But the historical novelist takes over your musings and engages your senses, setting the scene, painting the landscape, animating the bodies, minds and souls of the characters' (p. 20). Thus, in highlighting the effects produced by the writer's craft — effects that allow the reader to identify more completely with the experiences and emotions of the historical characters and their world — Bird is in fact drawing attention to how historical fiction might enhance teaching and learning in the History curriculum.

Clarke (2011) looked to the publication of Kate Mitchell's *Australia's 'Other' History Wars: Trauma and the Work of Cultural Memory in Kate Grenville's* The Secret River (2010) as being evidence of this growing interest in the historical fiction and history debate. Moreover, for Clarke, *The Secret*

River, 'with associated commentary, turned up on educational curriculums. In the history v fiction debate, Grenville is totemic' (p. 19).

In her acknowledgments for *Sarah Thornhill* (2011), Grenville notes history has become a dangerous word for her to utter. She emphatically states that *Sarah Thornhill* is is a novel — fiction — not history. 'Yet', Clarke asks, 'is it that simple?' (2011, p. 19). Clarke continues: 'this novel revisits the fascinating, troubling territory of the history wars. It rows out on to the secret river of contemporary Australian anxiety [concerning Indigenous/non-Indigenous relationships] … and navigates a fictional tributary' (p. 19).

Clarke reminds readers that 'Grenville's three novels have been deluged by commentary on her treatment of the Australian past, over and above discussion of their [relative literary] merits'. So, why continue to inflame the debate? 'Why go back, then, to the ambitious ruthless emancipist, William Thornhill, and the horns of his prickly dilemma? Why not just cut the history out of the fiction?' (Clarke, 2011, p. 19). For Clarke, 'Grenville's range extends well beyond historical fiction, as in [her] … Orange award-winning *The Idea of Perfection* (1999)' (Clarke, 2011, p. 19). Clarke (2011) considers that Grenville 'is, apparently, driven by the same compulsion that gnaws at other commanding writers, such as Flanagan, Pulitzer prize-winner Geraldine Brooks, and recent Miles Franklin winner, Kim Scott (*That Deadman Dance, 2011*)'. (p. 19).

Clarke contends that for these notable contemporary authors of Australian historical fiction, their chosen genre 'is not just about dramatising the past but about tackling a contemporary "culture of forgetting", acknowledging history's "secret river of blood" (terms used in *Australia's 'Other' History Wars*)' (2011, p. 19). Moreover, 'it is histories that are Grenville's concern. Sarah's [Grenville's principal character in *Sarah Thornhill*] story shows how unknown individual stories fill the past and create the present' (p. 19). Indeed, the present mostly is not far from the historical novelists' fundamental drive: 'Stricken, Sarah appalled by knowledge of her father's inhumanity, believes "there is no cure for the bite of the past". However, the act of storytelling offers hope for a fuller understanding [of the present]' (Clarke, 2011, p. 19). Indeed, 'Scott, in response to his Miles Franklin win, said: "There is a lot of reconciling — particularly reconciling ourselves to a shared history — that is yet to happen"' (p. 19). For Clarke 'Grenville's vivid fiction performs as testimony, memory and mourning, within this collective, postcolonial narrative' (2011, p. 19).

Superior to history? But whose history?

With all this stoushing between writers of historical fiction and professional historians, exactly what type of historical knowledge is at stake here? How does the knowledge gained from reading historical novels fit with the kind of knowledge then Australian Prime Minister John Howard yearned for on the eve of Australia Day 2006 when addressing the National Press Club? Howard said:

> Too often, [history] is taught without any sense of structured narrative, replaced by a fragmented stew of 'themes' and 'issues'. And too often, history, along with other subjects in the humanities, has succumbed to a postmodern culture of relativism where any objective record of achievement is questioned and repudiated. (Howard, 2006)

Here Howard desires a history that advances a kind of eulogy of Australia's past, one in which there is a steady advancement of the nation, highlighting the triumph of progress. This is often labelled evolutionary idealism.

This was a message which he sustained through to September 2012 (when he was no longer Prime Minister). When delivering the Sir Paul Hasluck memorial lecture in Perth, he 'slammed' (as Elks and Packham described it) the proposed new ACARA Senior History Curriculum as being 'unbalanced' and 'bizarre' (Elks & Packham, 2012). In an editorial, *The Weekend Australian* responded by declaring,

> compared with the hodgepodge of social justice, feminist, ecological and peace studies foisted on students of history and its feeble cousin SOSE ... in recent decades, the new national curriculum is a significant

step forward for teachers and students. Provided it is well-taught — and this will be a challenge because well-qualified history teachers are in short supply — students should gain a broad overview and some in-depth knowledge of the events, political movements and individuals who shaped the ancient and modern worlds, including Australia. ...

Mr Howard also raised important questions about the lack of focus on Australian federation, lack of balance in the draft senior 'workers' rights' unit and the omission of liberalism and conservatism, egalitarianism, Darwinism, imperialism and Chartism as key ideas of the late 19th and early 20th centuries. (*The Weekend Australian*, 2012)

To be fair to John Howard and *The Weekend Australian*, adopting an evolutionary idealist approach does not necessarily mean excluding those vital elements of the late nineteenth and early twentieth century history from a History curriculum. It is all a matter of balance, as John Howard and *The Weekend Australian* suggest, and the triumph of one over another should not, I suggest, be labelled progress.

Curthoys and Docker (2006) draw attention to the work done by Butterfield (1931) in raising criticism of evolutionary idealism, or a Whig interpretation of history: 'history should not be written as a story of progress. Butterfield not only argued against triumphalist tendencies in historical writing, but also raised doubts about the possibility of objective history itself' (Curthoys & Docker, 2006, p. 98).

But how does this triumphalist-cum-evolutionary-idealist view of history translate to authors of historical fiction? The very sort of sentiment Howard made in such an influential national forum regarding Australian's understanding of our nation's past has also captured the attention of writers such as Louise Wakeling, who, in regard to the writing of historical fiction, has stated:

New Historicists, in particular, have questioned the kind of totalising, transcendent and coherent narratives which have given meaning to (or rather imposed meaning on) past events, and hence their arguments are of considerable relevance to any writer who aims to recreate some aspect of the past in fictional mode, as in the historical novel. The question at issue here, for the writer of fiction, as for the historiographer, is not so much the truth or falsity of one view of history or another, but rather 'Whose history is it anyway?' (Wakeling, 1998, pp. 16-17)

It is the very question of evolutionary idealists' interpretation of history — historiography — that has motivated Wakeling to look to Hayden White (H. White, 1982, pp. 17-18, as cited in Wakeling, p. 17). More than most scholars in postcolonial history, White has been influential in persuading writers of history, in both fictional and nonfictional forms, to question their values in interpreting history. First, writers need to recognise history is chaos. According to White, 'the chaos of phenomena in the past that constitutes the most meaning of "history" is, in its very ordering and setting down, made meaningful within the particular non-contradictory, unitary world-view or ideology' of the evolutionary idealist. For Wakeling, reflecting on White's work, 'this is true for both factual and fictional history. Historical discourses derive their form from whatever moral, political, social or aesthetic values have in society, and sometimes in opposition to them'. There can be no agnostic, innocent view of historical interpretation — all writers of history are bound in an ideology of one form or other: 'there can be no "history" without ideology' (Wakeling, 1998, p. 18).

Providing insights into the work of the writer of historical fiction

By the beginning of the twenty-first century, Australian historical fiction was being marketed in styles never before imagined. First, Australia's best-selling author of historical fiction, Bryce Courtenay, chose to add a 'Note on Sources' to his published work, *The Potato Factory*, and to confirm that he had consulted 'the wonderful resources of the State Libraries of Victoria and New South Wales, and also of those of the Australian War Memorial' (Courtenay, 1999, pp. 657-59). For the public-at-large, the presence of such a bibliographical note may serve to legitimise the historicity of his work.

Other Australian historical novelists, however, have gone further. The year following the publication of her *The Secret River*, Grenville published *Searching for the Secret River* (2006), which was in fact based on her exegesis for her doctorate in Creative Arts at UTS. The publication of this work, in a sense acting as a preface to Grenville's original novel, provoked Gay Lynch's (2007) research extensively cited already in this book. Moreover, the very popularity of the two works suggested to Lynch there was an emerging genre at hand, one in which there is a published background to a historical novel, much in the same manner as DVD producers produce a Director's Cut to background material to a popular DVD. Only the success of future publications will tell if exegetical works continue to gain public interest. They may well serve an important function in the classroom.

In the classroom: changing interpretations of history, and the changing nature of historical fiction

Historical writings in their various guises have undergone massive changes in the past several decades. A wonderful new realism is now expressed in the pages of written history, not the least historical novels written for younger readers. Groce and Groce (2005, p. 110) refer to the work of Jacobs and Tunnell (2004), who write of this new realism in children's literature as bringing 'a great depth of honesty for younger readers'.

Groce and Groce (2005, p. 110) go on to write, quoting MacLeod, who comments further on this topic: 'Children's literature, historical as well as contemporary, has been politicized over the past thirty years; new social sensibilities have changed the way Americans view the past' (1998, p. 27).

Given these new paradigms in children's historical fiction, what are some essential criteria for evaluating historical novels written for younger readers? In attempting to answer this question, Groce and Groce (2005) look to Donelson and Nilsen (1997), who argue a good historical novel features 'an authentic rendition of time, place and people being featured' (p. 190, as cited in Groce

& Groce, 2005, p. 110). Moreover, historical fiction should write history as it was, and 'no attempt should be made to shelter the reader from the realities of the time period' (Hancock, 2004, p. 147, as cited in Groce & Groce, 2005, p. 110). Most emphatically, 'history should not be sugarcoated' (Jacobs and Tunnell, 2004, p. 119, as cited in Groce & Groce, 2005, p. 110). This has not always been so — and historical novels such as Ernestine Hill's *My Love Must Wait* (1948) come to mind. Hill's novel glorified the life of Matthew Flinders, particularly his six-year detention in Mauritius during the Napoleonic Wars.

Changes in historical fiction and implications for school History teaching

How has historical fiction changed over the years, and how does this affect pedagogical and curriculum decisions made by teachers? This question has a direct impact on what decisions teacher educators make for their undergraduates in respect to content. It is not surprising to learn the changes in the interpretation and writing of history are mirrored in the changes in historical fiction written for young readers.

The revisionist women's history movement dating from the 1970s is one example of how broader historical interpretation has been reflected in historical fiction written for younger readers. Groce and Groce (2005, p. 109) refer readers to how Hickman (2001) approaches this reality with younger readers. She often searches for a balanced point of view in the novels she asks her students to read: 'when I am reading in my critical-theory mode, I might look for a character who is not only true to the record but who embodies qualities that would be useful against injustices of our time as well as her own' (p. 97, cited in Groce & Groce, 2005, p. 109).

Groce and Groce (2005) make one other very important point about the criteria for choosing suitable historical novels for the classroom. They insist that 'readers of historical fiction should be aware of overgeneralizations such as grouping all Native Americans into a homogeneous group with similar characteristics and cultures' (p. 110). This is in accord with Galda and Cullinan, who observe 'noteworthy historical novels do not *overgeneralize*; they do not lead the reader to believe, for example, that all Native Americans are like those portrayed in any one story. Each character is unique, just as each of us is, and while the novelist focuses on one person in a group, it should be clear that the character is only a person, and not a stereotype' (Galda & Cullinan, 2002, p. 208, as cited in Groce & Groce, 2005, p. 110, emphasis in original).

* * *

In considering this debate between the relative historical truths contained in historical fiction and nonfiction, it is, I suggest, an error to think that the facts of the nonfiction are any more complete than those contained in historical fiction. Churchill's *History of the Second World War* is an example of histories that can be written to suit the political agendas of people and, indeed, nations. But, as was the case here, readers can only trust that revisionists will eventually recast the historical record with some credence to all voices contained in the history. But not all commentators agree on the relative historical insights provided by historical fiction. For example, Campbell (2008) laments the weight given to historical novels in their contested historical veracity. Some might consider it is simply wrong that Bryce Courtenay's work of historical fiction on the life of Ikey Solomon far outsells serious nonfiction on the same topic, such as Sackville-O'Donnell's *The First Fagin*.

Some commentators might allege historical novels are written to fill in the gaps left by historical nonfiction. This is a deficit model of historical writing, and brings into focus the purpose for which historical fiction is written. Most authors of historical fiction, for example Grenville, would argue that they write novels not to compete with historians but do so for the sake of their chosen art form. While they may 'pillage' historical facts, they do so for a different purpose than do historians.

Another problem facing those who argue for the greater veracity of nonfiction histories over historical fiction, comes with the question of exactly whose histories are being referred to. There are those who contend evolutionary idealist, whiggish histories, as eulogised by former Prime Minister John Howard in his address to the National Press Club on the eve of Australia Day 2006, affords a tragic example of how nonfiction history can serve political agenda, while masquerading as objective histories.

The writing of children's historical fiction during recent years has reflected these same developments. Increasingly, this genre now encompasses an open honesty, pulling few punches. Rather than avoiding sugarcoated treatment of difficult topics that authors might once have avoided, issues such as gender, race and so on, are now written about openly and portrayed transparently.

11 Understanding the Past through Historical Fiction

Many students undertaking teacher-preparation courses in Australian universities, and/or teachers are likely to be avid readers of Australian historical novels. This chapter is written with the object of deepening their appreciation of the rich tapestry of the Australian historical novel. It does so in order that they might increase their understanding of the way that historical novels can fully engage students in an appreciation and understanding of Australian history, particularly the different ways in which generations of Australian historians as compared to writers of historical fiction have perceived the past.

Historical novels versus History textbooks in the classroom

Although textbooks have not always been used in significant numbers for SOSE/HSIE/History in Australian classrooms, their use may increase with the advent of the national History curriculum. But that is unclear at the time of the writing of this book. It is clear, however, that in New South Wales secondary schools, where history continues as a mandatory subject in grades 7-10, that History textbooks are used widely. My own experience is of crates of class sets of three or four different textbooks being available for any class, often dominating all of class time, the lesson being little more than reading comprehension.

What advantages do historical novels have over traditional-style textbooks? Groce and Groce (2005) remind us of the fact textbook publishers are faced with massive challenges in attempting to present a huge amount of knowledge and skills to students at a particular grade level: 'There will routinely be criticism of how material is presented or of information that has been omitted for various reasons' (p. 101). Few academic/teacher educators or teachers would argue historical novels should entirely replace textbooks in the classroom of university teacher education unit in History curriculum, but I argue that the the historical novel does have a special role here. As Groce and Groce comment 'historical fiction offers teachers a classroom complement to the text that can be examined for viewpoints either absent or minimized within the textbook. Researchers espousing the benefits of trade books [historical fiction] due to the limitations of texts are plentiful' (2005, p. 101). In order to support their argument Groce and Groce (2005, p. 100) point to the reasons Lindquist advances for the use of historical fiction in her classroom, and which I have referred to in Chapter 3.

But in the case of conflicting accounts in textbooks and historical novels, what should teachers have their students believe? In answering this highly vexed issue, Groce and Groce (2005) concur with Lasky, who contends 'the textbooks have been telling us partial truths and then telling it as a slant' (Lasky, 1990, p. 161, as cited in Groce & Groce, 2005, p. 100). Sipe, writing back in 1997, applauded the abundance of 'quality historical and nonfiction trade books' available to schools, teachers and students. In his view, they represent a 'vast improvement over the representations imbedded within school textbooks in their presentation of material and the regency of research presented' (Sipe, 1997, as cited in Groce & Groce, p. 110).

Groce and Groce remind us that any History teacher who has used texts and themselves read historical novels or used them as a teaching/learning strategy in their History programs can advance another powerful reason why historical novels are a powerful partner to textbooks, supplementing and complementing what textbooks have to offer (2005, p. 102). Historical fiction offers, as Tomlinson, Tunnell, and Richgels state, 'human motives, human problems, and the consequences of human actions. In historical literature, facts, names, and dates are woven into the story as part of the setting' (1993, p. 52). Moreover, 'when facts are an integral part of a compelling story, they are much more interesting and of more immediate consequences to a young reader than when presented in lists and pseudo-prose collections, as in a textbook' (p. 52). This stands in sharp contrast with textbooks which are 'repositories of information that students read and memorize [or read in order to answer set questions in the textbook] without developing judgement or perspective' (p. 52, as cited in Groce & Groce, 2005, p. 101).

But Groce and Groce advance another reason why children's reading of historical novels will have other advantages over their reading of textbooks (2005, p. 102). Indeed, the value in historical novels as revealing human motives, and the 'consequences of character actions better than textbooks' is again stressed by Tomlinson, Tunnell and Richgels (1993). This provides enormous opportunities for teachers to discuss with students.

Historical novels also tend to have richer language and structure than textbooks: 'results ... revealed that the samples of tradebooks [fiction as well as nonfiction] contained more complex sentence structures, more extensive word choices, and deeper topic exploration than the textbook. And despite the more advanced language structures imbedded within the historical novels, children found them easier to comprehend than the textbook accounts' (Tomlinson, Tunnell & Richgels, 1993, p. 54, as cited in Groce & Groce, 2005, p. 111).

My own experience is that many History teachers will confess to one another significant missing elements in textbooks. To illustrate this point, I recall my teaching a year 7 class in a New South Wales high school, where I was using a particular textbook in a unit on comparative Indigenous cultures and the effect of colonisation on these cultures. The textbook used graphics from the 1970 movie, *A Man Called Horse*, staring Richard Harris. The film was itself an adaptation from a short story in *Collier's Magazine* of 7 January 1950, and was reprinted in 1968 as a short story in a book called *Indian Country* by Dorothy M. Johnson. In 1958 it was made into an episode in the television series *Wagon Train*.

Once, when I was teaching a group of year 7 students, I wanted to add to an illustration from *A Man Called Horse* by showing clips from the actual film. I wanted to impress upon the students the personality of the main character in the film, and to provide them with a feeling for what it was like to be a Native American on the American plains as the European colonising powers approached them. Now I realise that I was prompted to do this because of the one vital thing missing for History teachers: people. Jacobs and Tunnell emphatically state why they believe History textbooks are inadequate: 'The people are missing! The best one-word definition of history is, in fact, "people"' (2004, p. 117, as cited in Groce & Groce, 2005, p. 102). Without human beings, whose emotion and actions influence the times, there is no history. And many readers will attest, one way that we remember grand historical novels from the strength of characters portrayed in them.

But are History textbooks *closer to the truth* than historical novels? Note that Chapter 12 of this book will advance many arguments to show that historical truth mostly is a very relative thing. Groce and Groce develop this line of argument with regards to the relative historical truths contained in historical fiction with the argument that 'a common concern when using historical fiction is that it may contain information that is misleading, outdated, or simply wrong' (2005, pp. 102-03). Groce and Groce were following Levstik and Barton, who had claimed that some recent historical fiction was 'blatantly inaccurate, cursed with tunnel vision, and mired in romanticism … historical events are rearranged or facts omitted to avoid controversy' (2001, p. 110, as cited in Groce & Groce, p. 102-03).

Certainly, different historical novelists abide by the different standards of research. Indeed, the use of a novel may not be enough to present the facts completely. In fact, some authors may manipulate historical facts in order to fulfil their own writing agendas (as cited in Groce & Groce, p. 103). During a discussion session following a paper delivered at the HTAA Annual Conference held in Adelaide from 3-5 October 2011, it was generally agreed amongst History teachers that when using historical novels in the classroom it is useful for an authentication process be provided for novel studies. Here, students have the opportunity to engage in the act of determining the historical accuracy of the narrative. Including this early in the learning process associated with any particular historical novel encourages students to identify the facts that may have been inserted to enhance plot development or sensationalise the story.

Exploring sensitive and controversial issues

Compared with the use of traditional textbooks, the belief in the capacity for historical novels to build empathy in students for individuals or groups in history by now is well established. But often these people or groups are associated with very sensitive issues, as is the case with a study of refugees into Australia. When I was writing this book there was much political controversy regarding refugees seeking asylum in Australia.

Paul Bracey, Alison Gove-Humphries and Darius Jackson have researched how the use of historical novels as a teaching/learning strategy might be a preferred approach with regards to issues that are challenging and/or controversial. They write of their strong belief in 'exploring the experiences of refugees and evacuees' through the use of historical novels. For them, this 'clearly has resonance with contemporary issues'. The use of historical novels in 'addressing the needs of specific children who have faced the trauma of displacement, or providing an informed and balanced means of exploring the experiences of newly arrived citizens, beyond the often negative headlines in the media' has an obvious advantage (2006, Bracey, Gove-Humphries & Jackson, p. 103)

Reflecting on Irish schools, Bracey et al. wrote that 'in 2002, most of the arriving children came from Iraq, Afghanistan, Zimbabwe and Somalia' (Bracey et al., p. 103). This statement will likely resonate for many Australian teachers in 2013. Sensitive to the needs of many recently arrived children in Irish schools, and seeking to explore the lived experiences of refugee children, Bracey et al. chose two historical novels set in Ireland and telling the story of evacuees during the Second World War. They show that some authors have taken an historical perspective in order to distance their studies from the trauma of the recently arrived children. Clearly, this has many similarities with the concerns of many Australian teachers. Where can Australian teachers look to replicate what Bracey et al. have done in Ireland?

Students in my graduate diploma History Curriculum Methods course in 2012 at the University of Adelaide started by googling 'historical fiction, Australia refugees'. One website they encountered was HistoricalNovelsinfo (http://www.historicalnovels.info/Australasia.html), a US-based site. This listed major Australian adult historical novels. It was not difficult to select suitable Australian historical novels dealing with displaced persons, or forced migration. These included (amongst many others):

> Belinda Alexandra, *Silver Wattle*, about two sisters who flee Prague for Australia in the 1920s and work in the Australian film industry …

> Christopher Koch, *Out of Ireland*, a literary novel in the form of a journal kept by an Irish rebel convicted of sedition and transported to Van Diemen's Land (now Tasmania) …

> John Lewis, *Savage Exile*, about two nineteenth century English girls imprisoned on false charges and transported to Australia where they must struggle for survival …

Following a close review of the novel, the students were now able to commence developing units of work dealing with 'displaced persons and refugees in Australia' using historical novels as a major teaching/learning strategy.

The challenge: understanding the past through the Australian historical novel

Many of the nation's best-known novels and romances have a strong historical component or background. This holds true from Marcus Clarke's convict novel, *For the Term of His Natural Life* (1882) to Henry Handel Richardson's epic gold-rush trilogy *The Fortunes of Richard Mahony* (1917-29). Then there are the popular outlaw/bushranger romances, like 'Rolf Boldrewood's *Robbery Under Arms* (1888) and Rosa Praed's *Outlaw and Lawmaker* (1893). However, just as historians' views of the past have undergone massive changes from colonialist to postmodernist and postcolonial views, so too have writers of historical novels and their interpretations.

Pierce (1992) observes, 'some of the historical novels written in the century from 1850 to 1950 were less self-conscious and formally inventive than others'. There were the 'avowed costume dramas', for example Ernestine Hill's retelling of the romantic exploits of Matthew Flinders in *My Love Must Wait* (1941); and other works 'incidentally given to hero-worship, among them J.H.M. Abbott's depiction of Governor Arthur Phillip in *Castle Vane* (1930), one of his several novels of early Sydney' (Pierce, 1992, p. 305). Of course, we know these as historical novels, yet underpinned by a triumphalist, or evolutionary idealist, view of history. No doubt this view of history dominated many of the historical novels written during the 1850s through to the 1950s, and even through to the 1980s. However, it had a particular dominance during the second half of the nineteenth century.

H.P. Heseltine has shown during the second half of the nineteenth century Australian fiction was dominated by 'the saga, the picaresque and the documentary'. These were novels conceived 'primarily in terms of time'. They were sagas, in their 'purest form', but often approaching the documentary in form. According to Heseltine 'the classic pioneering novel which charters the course of an Australian family from its (usually humble) beginnings through a whole range of good and evil fortune, and against a background of assorted natural phenomena — the inevitable floods, fires and draughts' (Heseltine, 1964, p. 200, as cited in Pierce, 1992, p. 307). Of course, this is in accord with popular notions of the Australian Legend — the Aussie Battler winning through against the elements. For Heseltine, the paradigm for this is Brian Penton's *Landtakers* (1934), the first part of an unfinished trilogy, dealing with pioneering life in Queensland in the middle of the nineteenth century (Heseltine, 1964, p. 200, as cited in Pierce, 1992, p. 307).

Commonly considered a landmark in nineteenth-century Australian historical fiction, was Clarke's *His Natural Life* (1874), later published as *For the Term of his Natural Life* (1882). Postmodernists interested in the history of Australian law and punishment have enjoyed a resurgence in attention as a record of prison life in Van Diemen's Land (see, for example, Tourism Tasmania, n.d.). The architecture of Tasmania's Port Arthur penitentiary offers much in this regard. According to Pierce, Clarke's novel 'addresses themes pertinent to recent theoretical inquiry, especially as pertains to Foucauldian investigations into criminology and examinations of the impact of globalization upon literary production'. Moreover, his 'critique of colonial institutions is accompanied by a challenge to the inevitability of those institutions that nonetheless does not settle for an easy or moralistic recuperation' (Pierce, 2007, p. 157). The novel was first published in serial form between 1870 and 1872 in the *Australian Journal* as *His Natural Life*.

His Natural Life 'demonstrates, beyond the mere frisson of new geographical settings, what can be appreciated as genuinely "new" about the new literatures in English' (Birns, 2005, p. 127). And for Birns, the novel 'presents a dilemma virtually endemic to the body of Australian literature of which he is in an early manifestation: does Australia literature put new content into old forms, or does it do something more radical to the inherited tradition of the English novel?' (p. 128). The novel's continued popularity is also likely due to the considerable attention through tourism to Tasmania's Port Arthur, the setting for much of the novel. In the popular mind it provides a literary history of the period.

According to Robert Dixon, Rolf Boldrewood[3] and Sir Walter Scott share some common literary ground: apparently, both had a very limited understanding of their time, but this did not prevent them from writing 'deeply significant portraits' of their respective country's history — in Boldrewood's

---

[3] Rolf Boldrewood was the pen-name of Thomas Alexander Browne (1826-1915), failed squatter in colonial Victoria and New South Wales, then police magistrate, goldfields commissioner and part-time writer of serialised novels. See Eggert & Webby (n.d.).

case of 'Australian society in the years before Federation' (Dixon 1986, p. 324). Yet, by any standard, it is an engaging novel. Written in the first person, present tense, Boldrewood's *Robbery Under Arms* (1882) has a dramatic and charming opening paragraph:

> My name's Dick Marston, Sydney-side native. I'm twenty-nine years old, six feet in my stocking soles, and thirteen stone weight. Pretty strong and active with it, so they say. I don't want to blow — not here, any road — but it takes a good man to put me on my back, or stand up to me with the gloves, or the naked mauleys. I can ride anything — anything that ever was lapped in horsehide — swim like a musk-duck, and track like a Myall blackfellow. Most things that a man can do I'm up to, and that's all about it. As I lift myself now I can feel the muscle swell on my arm like a cricket ball, in spite of the — well, in spite of everything. (Boldrewood, 2005, p. 1)

First appearing in serialised form in the *Sydney Mail* between 1882 and 1883, Boldrewood's *Robbery Under Arms* is 'the quintessential bushranging adventure tale' (Eggert & Webby, n.d.). The serialised version of the novel was an instant success. Hailed as an Australian classic only a few years after it first appeared in book form in 1888, it has remained in print ever since and has frequently been adapted for stage, radio, film and television (Eggert & Webby, n.d.).

Eggert and Webby (n.d.) state that 'many cultural meanings have been claimed in its name [and] … while praised by its first readers for its excitement, romance and the historical authenticity of its pictures of the 1850s in Australia, *Robbery Under Arms* was, by the 1950s, being heralded for its pioneering use of the Australian vernacular' (Eggert & Webby, n.d.). According to these authors, 'earlier writers had produced some journalistic sketches in this style, but Boldrewood appears to have been the first to attempt a long narrative in the voice of an uneducated Australian bushman'. However, due to the boost of postcolonialism during 'the 1980s and 1990s this response had become overshadowed by exposure of the stress fractures of masculinist and colonial discourse that the novel gingerly bridges' (Eggert & Webby, n.d.).

Henry Lawson was inspired by this style (Eggert & Webby, n.d.). So, too, were later writers. For example, also written in the first person, present tense, in the voice of the uneducated Australian ex-convict Jewish colonial, is Bryce Courtney's novel *The Potato Factory* (1995). However, the historical accuracy of Boldrewood's novel was not brought into public question, as was the case with *The Potato Factory*, an issue discussed in Chapter 10.

By the mid-twentieth century Australian historical novelists began to manifest a more conscious view of the relationship between their craft and Australian history. For example, Eleanor Dark once defined what history meant to her. It was 'in the community what memory is to the individual. Without memory we should be unable to learn from our past experiences, and knowledge of its history is in the same way indispensable to a nation' (Dutton, 1985, cited in Pierce, 1992, p. 306).

Dark was author of a trilogy of Australian historical novels: *The Timeless Land* (1941), *Storm of Time* (1945) and *No Barrier* (1953). These dealt with the first decades of European settlement in Australia. These works, according to Pierce, 'took an uncomplicated, socially responsible and moralising view of the utility history of their history for Australians. Her high-minded reflection was less problematic than her procedures as an historical novelist' (Pierce, 1992, p. 309). Indeed, as Pierce goes on to state 'it might have reinforced a dismissive notion of the historical fiction that was produced before and soon after the Second World War' (Pierce, 1992, p. 309).

According to Pierce, the literary successor to Eleanor Dark and her ilk took a much 'more anxious' and self-conscious view of Australia's past and what 'knowledge of its history' might mean for an Australian historical novelist. David Malouf once remarked: 'I have no particular interest in the past. It seems interesting only in that it is inside the present; it's also going to be inside whatever future there is' (Willbanks, 1992, cited in Pierce, 1992, p. 310).

Yet, as revealed in his novel *The Great World* (1990), Malouf is very much concerned with understanding the past. This novel works back from the stock market crash of 1987 to Australian experiences in the Second World War. Its central character, Digger Keen, hammer in hand, is driving a nail when he remarks:

> Even the least event had lines, all tangled, going back into the past, and beyond that into the *unknown* past, and other lines leading out, also tangled, into the future. Every movement was dense with causes, possibilities, consequences; too many, even in the simplest case, to grasp. (Malouf, 1990, cited in Pierce, p. 311, emphasis in original)

Employing a similar metaphor, Thomas Keneally in *Gossip From the Forest* also emphasised the complex but certain continuities between the present and the past. Willbanks writes: 'There is a direct fuse, a fuse that is still burning between the past and present, and the fuse that runs from the railway carriage at Compiègne where the delegates made the armistice at the end of World War One [described in his novel, *Gossip From the Forest*, 1975] is still burning in Australia' (Willbanks, 1992, cited in Pierce, 1992, p. 310).

Indeed, Pierce suggests, an understanding of the past is precious to both Malouf and Keneally. They do not wish 'to simplify temporal connections. Each urges against the cultural malaise of historical amnesia'. For both, their historical fiction 'seeks to reanimate the national past in the present' (Pierce, 1992, p. 312). But how does the art of the historical novelist connect with the past? What role does the narrative play in connecting with the past?

Andrew Taylor noted concerns that certain poets held with the past. For Kenneth Slessor, R.D. FitzGerald, James McAuley, Francis Webb, as well as for novelists such as Patrick White and Thomas Keneally, 'the past and narrative go hand in hand'. For Taylor this 'narrativization of the past' acts not as a crude attempt to establish a national identity, or link with some supposed Australian Legend, but rather 'as a manoeuvre to keep the past apparently accessible to the present'. Thus, 'by asserting a metonymic continuity of the past with the present, the moment of origin that the past is sensed to contain may be touched by narrative travel along the diachronicity of history. And this is, after all, the nature of tradition' (Taylor, 1987, cited in Pierce, 1992, p. 313).

Statement such as Taylor's suggest further questions about the Australian historical novelists' relationship with the past, and their motives. Pierce puts it thus: 'Is this yearning for "origin", the search for roots, the establishment of provenance, a keen business in the historical fiction of a postcolonial culture such as Australia?' (1992, p. 313). Indeed, 'More contentiously still, which narratives of the past, or rather whose stories, have writers preferred? These are matters which overtly and implicitly have occupied recent authors of historical fiction in Australia' (p. 313).

For Pierce, the period of the late 1800s through to the Second World War was marked by 'a qualified pride' in the country's perceived history, but also 'what it might become' (1992, p. 313). But with the decolonisation of Australian written history following the Second World War, vast changes were afoot: 'From the 1950s ... historical fiction is rarely the vehicle for unconstrained and idealistic affirmations about Australia's future. Instead the past becomes a treasure-trove of guilt, amply satisfying cultural death wishes. For numbers of authors, expiation is the preferred mode of operation' (Pierce, 1992, p. 313).

These changes were evidenced by 'a roll call for "marginalised" figures in the historical landscape; attempts at empathy with the victims of imperialism, patriarchy, racism, capitalism [and] efforts to refuse historical interpretations that work *de haut en bas*' (p. 313). For Pierce, one of the first victims of these changes was the conception of the Australian Legend. But also the period marked the emergence of writers of history who wrote in a number of genres.

One of the first of these was Mary Durack (1913-1994). For Wilde et al. (1994), her 'most significant literary works' are the novel *Keep Him My Country* and the nonfiction work, *Kings in Grass Castles* (1959). She also wrote biographies, plays, children's nonfiction, and a variety of historical writings (Wilde et al., 1994, p. 245).

Nancy Cato (1917-2000), a fifth-generation Australian, was of much the same generation as Durack. In 1950, Cato edited the *Jindyworobak Anthology*. Arguably, she is best known for her historical sagas. *All the Rivers Run* (1958), is a novel of the Australian saga of life along the Murray River. This book, which became a television series made her modestly rich and famous and popularised Australia overseas (Zinn, 2000). The novel was especially popular in the United States, enabling Cato to give up journalism — she had been the Queensland correspondent of the *Canberra Times* — and focus on her writing and love of conservation. The book became the first of a trilogy — with *Time, Flow Softly* (1959) and *But Still The Stream* (1962) — which, when published in a single volume, became popular around the world. In all, Cato wrote more than ten large novels. She also produced volumes of poetry and short stories (Zinn, 2000).

Cato had strong concerns for Indigenous Australians. A major work was *Mister Maloga* (1976), the story of Daniel Mathews and his Maloga Mission to Indigenous people on the Murray River in Victoria. She also wrote three books about Tasmania, one about the woman who was once considered to be the last Indigenous woman on the island, *Queen Truganini* (1976). In her much-loved home, Noosa in Northern Queensland, she was a devoted environmentalist. *The Noosa Story: A Study In Unplanned Development* (1979) was an environmental work about her adopted Queensland home. She was a devout environmentalist, feminist, and workers' advocate. *Brown Sugar* (1974), a novel about Queensland and the trade in indentured workers from the South Pacific, was another international success. *The Heart Of The Continent* (1989) is about two generations of outback and wartime nurses (Zinn, 2000). Environmental, feminist, Indigenous Australian themes and themes concerning workers' rights pervade her novels. These themes are best represented in *Forefathers* (1983), and provide History students with various and relevant perspectives to their studies.

As Durack and Cato were crafting their historical novels and histories, Patrick White (1912-1990) stood as a colossus on the Australian literary scene. John Boston states that White — winner of the 1973 Nobel Prize for Literature — is not singularly a historical novelist, although three of his more famous novels may be rightly claimed as that.

> It is as a historical novelist, in *The Tree of Man* [1955], *Voss* [1957], and *A Fringe of Leaves* [1976], that White most securely establishes his reputation. Once he returned to Australia in 1946 with the intention of remaining there, Australia and its history were in his blood again. His family, after all, had been here for four generations. *The Tree of Man*, his first novel written in Australia, tells the story of a young couple, the first settlers in a rural area near Sydney. … The novel ends in the early forties, but neither the Second World War nor the rapid industrialization of Australia at that time is mentioned: White wanted to keep the illusion of a pre-industrial country.
>
> *Voss* is set in the late 1840s, the expedition that it describes being modelled upon that of Ludwig Leichardt in 1848; but White was less in the story of exploration than in the theme of an overreacher who, like himself, was bent on moulding Australia according to his own will. The novel reflects both White's own ambition and his fear of that ambition. (Beston, 2007, pp. 252-53)

For White, Australia provided a sublime natural environment for his immense creativity.

In the tradition of Durack and Cato as writers of both historical fiction and nonfiction, Thomas Keneally has been a much more prolific writer of history and historical fiction. Taylor wrote:

> Launching the first volume of Thomas Keneally's history of Australia on Thursday, Kevin Rudd gave an eloquent speech in praise of Keneally's work and the need for a nation to understand itself through its past.
>
> 'Our national story is still very much a work in progress,' said the Prime Minister. (Taylor, L. 2009, p. 13)

In reviewing Keneally's nonfiction work, Pybus wrote:

> When it comes to writing page-turning narrative, be it fiction or nonfiction, no one does it better than Thomas Keneally. This astonishingly prolific writer, who has more than forty books to his name, has produced two books this winter ...
>
> We boast a number of historians who are fine stylists ... but Keneally leaves us all for dead.
>
> With the novelist's eye for small, revealing detail, Keneally pays particular detail to two little-known colonists ... (Pybus, 2009, p. 11)

Keneally also had published in 2009, *The People's Train*, a book of historical fiction about a Bolshevik in Brisbane before the October Revolution. Thus, by 2009 Keneally arguably represented the high-water mark of historian and writer of historical fiction.

But even the best can stumble, drop a pass, or forget their lines. And for the highly regarded, and, for many, a master historian, Geoffrey Blainey (2011), Keneally did just that with his nonfiction work *Australians: from Eureka to the Diggers* (2011). Blainey (2011) writes that 'it is exciting but also a bit hazardous when Keneally the novelist pushes aside Keneally the historian' (p. 18). When comparing adventures of Ned Kelly with the Melbourne banking establishment of the time, Blainey insists: 'here the historian has gone into hiding. The talented novelist has taken over the story, his sense of drama intervening, his imagination soaring' (p. 18). And for Blainey (2011), this is not the only instance of factual error in *Australians*. A reading of Keneally's *Australians* and Blainey's review provides History teachers with opportunities for discussions with students on what they consider to be an appropriate use of historical evidence, and the conclusions that can be determined from that evidence.

But what of Peter Carey's work — the four-times winner of the Miles Franklin Award, and heir to Patrick White (Gaile, 2005, p. xxiv) — as historical novels? How can we summarise in several paragraphs his place in the history of Australian historical fiction? First, here Carey is set squarely in postcolonial conceptions of the past. In reviewing Carey's *Parrot and Olivier in America* (2009), James Bradley writes:

> Carey may be a republican, and a passionate believer in the possibilities of Australia and Australian culture, but the spirit of his fiction is too restless, too contrarian to have much truck with the sentimental pieties of Australian nationalism. Like Kate Kelly in *The True History of the Kelly Gang* (2000) dismissing Ned's and Joe's stories about the brave fight against the English back in Ireland as sentimental nonsense about brutal murderers, Carey's fiction repeatedly evinces a profound ambivalence about the self-deceptions of colonial culture, about the dishonesty at its core, and the celebration of its mediocrities as virtues. (Bradley, 2009, pp. 22-3)

For Gaile, Carey's work should also be thought of as being linked to myth:

> In the critical reception of his writings, myth is one of the most frequently mentioned concepts, perhaps next to the 'posist' discourses, his flights of fancy (variously dubbed 'fantasy' or 'magical realism' or fabulation'), and his predilection for narrative trickery and showmanship. There is, in fact, hardly an essay or review article on Carey that fails to mention the word 'myth' or one of its lexical relatives. (Gaile, 2005, p. 37)

Faking the past? Historiographic metafiction and neo-historical fiction

How is this linkage to myth manifest in Peter Carey's novels? Is there any literary advantage in a novel reworking the past in order to whip up public discourse concerning a potentially divisive view held in Australian society — for example, the 'true' story of Ned Kelly and his rightful place in Australian history. How seriously should historical novelists adhere to 'true' history, that is, history as perhaps perceived by the general populace? Can history be made a farce of, in the name of art and creative enterprise? In a sense, this is what the 'history wars' did at the beginning of this century.

As Graham Huggan has argued, the history wars in Australia have provoked various accounts of how history has served to divide the nation

(Huggan, 2007). He refers to Stuart Macintyre and Anna Clark's *The History Wars* (2003), a study showing how the history in Australia has been subject to intense controversy and public scrutiny by various social commentators who accuse its practitioners of rewriting and falsifying the history of European settlement in Australia. In this respect, Huggan (2007) claims that not least of these are 'a large number of creative writers, especially novelists, whose primary concern is perhaps less to recover than to re-imagine the past' (p. 61). This has led to the boom during the last three decades in what Pierce has termed 'neo-historical fiction' (Pierce, 1992, p. 305). This is essentially a part of 'a much wider attempt to counteract the perceived cultural malaise of historical amnesia', and to 'reanimate the past in the present' by treating public and private, fact and fiction, as intersecting, mutually invigorating spheres (Pierce, 1992, p. 305).

Huggan (2007, p. 62) also draws our attention to another aspect of this attempt to 'reanimate the past in the present' by some writers. This is an emphasis on what Pierce calls 'the partiality and unreliability of the sources from which formal and fictitious histories are constructed' (Pierce, 1992, p. 310). Moreover, related to this has been the global emergence of 'an identifiable kind of self-consciously hybrid historical fiction' (Huggan, 2007, p. 62), what Linda Hutcheon awkwardly calls 'historiographic metafiction', (Hutcheon, 1984-5, cited in Huggan, 2007, p. 63), which, according to Huggan, seeks to 'combine genuine and fake historical sources and, blurring the line between them, to produce ironic commentary on the ideologies of veracity and authenticity that govern official representations of the past' (Huggan, 2007, p. 63).

As if to remind his readers of the fickleness of historical 'truth', Carey's self-reflective account of the Ned Kelly legend, *True History of the Kelly Gang* (2000), is one such work where historical truth is subjugated in the interests of other artistic pursuits. As Huggan puts it, 'Throughout Carey's novel, history slides imperceptibly into the more distant recesses of folk memory, while the documented discoveries of archival research converge with the fabrications of the adventure tale' (2007, p. 64). Skilfully, Carey consistently unfolds the narrative 'as the subjective recounting of Australian colonial history encounters half-buried memories of an Irish ancestry — an ancestry that clearly causes Kelly as much pain as pride, and through which the repetitive patterns of a larger [historic memory of unfairness] can be seen inexorably to emerge' (Huggan, 2007, p. 64).

Carey consequently 'creates' a history of the Kelly Gang that is juxtaposed to the 'commodified status of Ned Kelly as national icon and anti-imperial resource', deliberately dissolving 'the boundary between oral and written, fictional and nonfictional sources, thereby maintaining a dynamic balance between competing versions of the historical past' (Huggan, 2007, p. 64). I find with my teacher education students that a reading of Carey's *True History of the Kelly Gang*, amongst other things, provides an opportunity to introduce the notion of commodified history, and challenge many aspects of it, while at the same time looking for other examples, for example Anzac.

For Huggan, 'historiographic metafiction, much like the postmodernism that inspired it, is now far less radical or transformative than it appeared, say, twenty years ago' (Huggan, 2007, p. 65). Indeed, 'sometimes it is merely dull or formulaic, provoking the suspicion it might now have reached its sell-by date. Still, at its best such fiction allows for a spirited re-engagement with the past that is both ethically responsible and aesthetically satisfying' (Huggan, 2007, p. 65).

Referring to Chris Healy, Huggan (2007) suggests historiographic metafiction 'also has the potential to challenge the national/global memory industries from which it draws increasing sustenance' (Healy 1997, as cited in Huggan, 2007, p. 61). For Huggan (2007) this is 'the commodification of memory', which 'is the function of a globalized late capitalist society in which historical consciousness has been eroded by nostalgia — a society of the souvenir as much as of the spectacle, in which an ever-growing number of commercially viable memorabilia and pseudo-historical constructions has granted the illusion of access to, while effectively substituting for, the lived experiences of the past' (p. 61). For me, much the same explanation applies to the contemporary rush for 'collectors and collectable' television programs.

By the beginning of the second decade of the twenty-first century, the writing of history engaging the audience in historical images and memory through the narrative the historical novel genre is demonstrably a highly ideologicalised and even a political activity, causing much angst between many novelists and the writers of nonfiction. The historical novel genre has undergone massive changes since appearing in Australian literature during the second half of the nineteenth century.

* * *

Few academic/teacher educators or teachers would argue that historical novels should entirely replace textbooks in the classroom or university teacher education units in History curriculum. However, I argue that the historical novel does have a special role here. Historical novels can 'put the personality into history', bring historical events and characters to life, and provide voice to characters in a way textbooks never can. And surely, without human beings, whose emotion and actions influence the times, there is no history.

Historical fiction effectively establishes opportunities for discussion central to historical literacy, and student empathy, while exploring sensitive and controversial issues. Examples of this are with teaching units of work associated with refugees and evacuees. For example, I argue that to teach an understanding of the current issues associated with refugees in Australia, a 'safe' approach is to study refugees and evacuees through historical fiction. For example, evacuees from war-torn London during the Blitz suffered many of the same anxieties of other evacuees and asylum seekers the world over.

Many of Australia's best-known novels and romances have a strong historical component. Australia's literature, especially as it is portrayed through the history of writing historical novels, portrays much of our aspirations and anxieties. For example, the Australian Legend is mirrored in many varied and interesting ways through the Australian historical novel. And this is no less with current anxieties concerning our understanding of Australian history.

While the history wars in Australia have provoked various accounts of how history has served to divide the nation, historiographic metafiction repeats this through challenging our understandings of a commodified history. Peter Carey's *True History of the Kelly Gang* achieves just that, and in doing so edges historical fiction ever closer to counterfactual history and alternate history.

12 Unpacking Historical Novels for their Historicity: Historical Facts and Historical Agency

Historical novels can tell us much about not only our past, but also what we collectively hold to be important about our past. Usually, they provide an insight into the past in many and varied ways, including ways that are, I suggest, simply impossible to present to students of history through textbooks. This chapter will show how the development of an appreciation of historical facts and historical agency can be achieved most fruitfully through the use of historical novels in the classroom.

The historical novelist and facts

Historical figures have become historical characters in this type of novel. But is their characterisation partly imaginary? Often the novelist will explain what he or she has done with their characters. Witness Ken Follett (2010) in the back page of his novel set in the Western Front of the First World War:

> Several real historical characters appear in these pages, and readers sometimes ask how I draw the line between history and fiction. It's a fair question, and here's the answer.
>
> In some cases, for example when Sir Edward Grey addresses the House of Commons, my fictional characters are witnessing an event that really happened. What Sir Edward says in this novel corresponds to the parliamentary record, except that I have shortened his speech, without I hope losing anything important.

> Sometimes a real person goes to a fictional location, as when Winston Churchill visits Tŷ Gwyn. In this case, I have made sure that it was not unusual for him to visit country houses, and that he would have done so at around that date.
>
> When real people have conversations with my fictional characters, they are usually saying things they did say at some point. Lloyd George's explanation to Fitz why he does not want to deport Lev Kamenev is based on what Lloyd George wrote, in a memo quoted in Peter Rowland's biography.
>
> My rule is either the scene did happen, or it might have; either these words were used, or they might have been. And if I find some reason why the scene could not have taken place in real life, or the words would not really have been said — if, for example, the character was in another country at that time — I leave it out. (Follett, 2010, p. 851)

The combined sales of Follett's books exceed 100 million. It is evident that people respond to his narrative and to the manner in which he interweaves facts into the historical novel, adding colour and meaning to his stories.

Compare Follett's approach to writing historical novels to that of Leo Tolstoy (1868, trans. A. Mandelker, 2010, p. 1314) when he was commenting in *Russian Archive* on his approach to his writing of *War and Peace* (1869):

> So the task of artist [*historical novelist*] and historian are quite different, and the reader should not be surprised when my book disagrees with an historian in the description of events or persons.
>
> But an artist [*historical novelist*] must not forget that the popular conception of historical persons and events is not based on fancy, but on historical documents in so far as the historians have been able to group them, and therefore, though he understands and presents them differently, the artist like the historian should be guided by historical material. *Whenever in my novel historical persons speak or act, I have invented nothing, but have used historical material of which I have*

> *accumulated a whole library during my work. I do not think it necessary to cite the title of these books here, but could cite them at any time in proof of what I say.* (emphasis in original)

The genre of historical fiction, however, has evolved in huge proportions since Tolstoy wrote *War and Peace*.

There are also standards that have been devised by Stephens (1992), including:

> the existence of the narrative must be historically authentic, and represented authoritatively. ... Characters must be credible and invite reader-identification ... Readers should feel they have learned more about a time and a place through the illusion that they have experienced them vicariously ... [and] The text should show that humans behave and feel in ways that remain constant in different periods. (1992, p. 72)

It is these historical fiction principles that distinguish a historical novel from a novel that contains merely elements of history. The genre has evolved in many ways during the last century.

Prior to the nineteenth century, history was written in the narrative story form that did not separate historical facts from the telling of morality tales. Historians whose style reflects this blending of historical fact and moral tale include ancient Greek writers such as Homer, Herodotus, Thucydides and Sophocles. A more recent historian who writes in this style is late nineteenth century American historian, Frederick Jackson Turner, who blended his facts on American westward expansion artfully with a moral tale about America's identity (Turner, 1906/1965).

In the late-nineteenth century, there was a change in historiography towards a more empirical, scientific, facts-based form of historical literature and the writing of morality tales came to be seen as a different literature form, separated from that of historical literature. But change came slowly: Shann (1930/1967) sought to reinforce his story of the virtues of the Australian pastoral industry with facts surrounding wool production and export.

Not surprisingly, then, within schools, the study of history most often has been associated with the both the study of historical facts and the values and morals of the school's local community. Ruth Reynolds (2006) asked 'how can [history as an empirical study] be used in the schools founded by the nation's states when what the state wants is a civic message to be told and a moral to be learned' (p. 28). She was responding to then Prime Minister John Howard's message to the National Press Club on the eve of Australia Day 2006, where, as discussed in Chapter 12, Howard yearned for a type of history taught in schools that would develop in students citizenship and a eulogy of 'Australian values', whatever they might be.

One answer to this problem of reconciling current empirical academic historical study and the model requested by educational institutions is a return to the use of story narrative and literature — historical fiction — to inform and educate readers about the past. Ruth Reynolds (2006) argues that history, as modelled by Herodotus and Thucydides, better suits a world that acknowledges and validates the multiple perspectives, each reflecting different cultural mores, than a historical study seeking empiricism and objectivity. But, certainly, that does not mean to say that the historical novelist does not abide by a strong regard for facts.

A well-written historical fiction, according to Herz, is both accurate in the historical details portrayed and a good story filled with excitement and adventure challenging their audience as well as engaging their interest. An author of historical fiction 'must not manipulate historical facts to make the novel more interesting or exciting' and they have an obligation to maintaining the integrity and accuracy of historical facts while 'creatively blending these facts with imagination to create a story that engages the reader on both the emotional and intellectual level' (Hertz, 1981, p. 2).

In *A Rose for the Anzac Boys* (2008), Jackie French has been able to remain truthful to the events that happened during the Great War while artfully crafting a narrative that is engaging to readers emotionally, as they experience the war as seen through the eyes of Midge, Anna and Ethel. At the same time, readers are extended intellectually, as they piece together, letter by letter, what happened on the frontlines of the war.

As R. Reynolds (2006) reminds us, historical fiction requires the inclusion of multiple perspectives, the chronological sequencing of events, and the demonstration of historical literacy skills. Lindquist (1995) reinforces this argument by stating that historical fiction promotes the idea that historical events can be told from multiple points of view. It seeks to achieve this by introducing readers to characters whose ideas and values vary from their own and whose response to situations and problems differ from character to character. French's *A Rose for the Anzac Boys* demonstrates this through the use of letters throughout the novel. These letters are written by soldiers on the front, Midge, servants, as well as relatives in England — people from all classes of society, whose lives had been affected by war in many different ways and who viewed the war from different perspectives.

A Rose for the Anzac Boys can be used to dramatise life in England during the Great War, and the all-pervading idea propagated by governments that everyone needed to do their part in the war effort. This notion is evident in Midge's eagerness to do something to help the soldiers. Even if it was just serving Cocoa at a canteen in France, at least 'she'd be *doing* something. Something grander and braver than studying irregular verbs. Something for King and country!' (French, 2008, p. 34, emphasis in original).

Historical agency and historical novels written for younger readers

John Boyne's *The Boy in the Striped Pyjamas* is an example of a novel that contains a great deal of potential to connect with students. It is also worth studying from the point of view of historical agency. It is written from the perspective of a young German boy whose family have to leave Berlin, as his father is put in charge of a concentration camp. It explores the Second World War, particularly from a German perspective, informing the reader considerably about the nature of the Holocaust.

As Rycik and Rosler remind us: 'reading historical fiction provides students with a vicarious experience for places and people they could otherwise know. Often, they are able to see history through a child's point of view and identify with their emotions' (2009, p. 163). *The Boy in the Striped Pyjamas* is a wonderful example of this, as the protagonist is a nine-year-old boy named Bruno. While something like the Holocaust may seem like a daunting topic for a teacher with a middle-school class, this novel makes it far more accessible by personally a child's story. Hence, students can begin to deal with such a large and devastating event.

The use of historical fiction has the potential to bridge the gap between historical knowledge and understanding. Nawrot explains the power of historical fiction: 'when reading historical fiction, students enter into the historical setting and live with the characters. They feel the characters' suffering and pain and exult in their triumphs. Names and events are given a background setting and context' (1996, p. 343). Hence, when reading *The Boy in the Striped Pyjamas*, a student will not be viewing history as a student reading a textbook would, as an outsider looking in on an unfamiliar place, but as an insider involved in the construction of history as it evolves. Instead of looking at facts and figures that try to describe the treatment of Jewish people, in *The Boy in the Striped Pyjamas* the student is positioned alongside a German boy looking at a Jew through a fence and trying to make sense of this in relation to his own understanding of the world, heavily influenced by the propaganda he has been exposed to. The historical novel gives the student a unique and far more engaging insight into how history is created: in short, it is historical agency from the ground upwards.

The historical novel brings an element of excitement to history and shows the personal and emotional elements, removing the sterile, academic label history often has. Using well-known historical novels as examples, Rycik and Rosler (2009) demonstrate this quality in Elizabeth Friedrich's *Leah's Pony*, observing 'they can experience the sadness Leah feels when she must sell her pony to provide money for her family during the Great Depression' (Polacco,

1998, p. 163). Indeed, readers 'can sense the fear that Monique has when her family hides a girl pretending to be her sister from the Nazis in *The Butterfly*' (Polacco, 2011, p. 163).

Boyne artfully teases out this emotional element of his historical novel, particularly in the final pages when Bruno is missing because he has been exterminated in the gas chambers: 'Gretel returned to Berlin with Mother and spent a lot of time alone in her room crying, not because she had thrown her dolls away and not because she had left all her maps behind at Out-With, but because she missed Bruno so much' (Boyne 2006, p. 215). In this example, the extermination of millions of people is represented by the pain of one family. This is much easier for a student to grasp and brings a different quality to history than could possibly be gained from a textbook.

Teachers have many other choices available when choosing historical fiction to tease out historical agency during the Holocaust. Jerry Spinelli's *Milkweed* (2003) tells of the adventures of a mischievous Gypsy orphan in a Warsaw ghetto during the Nazi occupation. *Milkweed* explains life on the streets, while the plight of Misha and his friends and their desperate fight for survival further illustrates the dangerous circumstances in which minorities, such as the disabled, homosexuals, non-white peoples and the elderly, found themselves during the era of Nazi occupation of Poland. The novel demonstrates that there is significant merit in focussing on single historical events through the eyes of character/s who are of a similar age to the students because they will learn about the event and more readily appreciate how it affected the people living during that time.

For that reason, Misha is an effective protagonist for students to identify with, as Spinelli takes pains to breathe life into his main character by developing his relationships with Uri and Janina, as well as his emotional and naïve personality, and his triumph over adversity. Misha's personalised and unique story further endorses the view that history is a series of interconnected and fluid personal problems to be solved, and often a search for personal identity.

At the beginning of *Milkweed*, Misha does not realise he is different, he does not understand what a Gypsy or a Jew is, and yet he is the victim of ethnic persecution. Through his friendship with a band of filthy street urchins and close encounters with 'Jackboots', Misha realises he is considered by many to be 'dirt' — and that there are special activities for the 'men in beards', which can include scrubbing the footpath with those beards. The simplicity of Misha's observations as he moves throughout Warsaw examine the changes in rules, attitudes, cultures and relationships that were characteristic of the Nazi period.

Historical fiction could have particular currency in the middle school where students find narratives easier to understand than expository writing. For students to engage with history it must be transmitted to them in an accessible mode. Nawrot explains: 'a story is more easily understood than is expository text ... As the facts find places within the broad framework provided by the story, they are retained in memory' (1996, p. 343). Hence, reading *The Boy in the Striped Pyjamas* and *Milkweed* offers a marvellous entrée into a unit of work on the Holocaust. Not only will it be a hook, engaging the interest of students from the outset of the unit, it will provide a framework for later learning on this topic. The facts and figures presented in a textbook are then likely to have some meaning for students who will otherwise be overwhelmed by such an unimaginable event and will struggle to feel any connection to it.

Historical agency

Knowing history — the development of historical literacy — involves more than simply knowing historical dates, events and personalities. Understanding history is an extremely complex and problematic process. Gaddis demonstrates how historians create patterns and relationships to give meaning to the ambiguities and complexities of the past, thus reducing the infinitely complex to a finite, understandable, frame of reference (2002, p. 32).

However, we know that primary school and middle school students tend to see history as a pageant of heroes and villains, faced with an array of stark moral choices, rather than appreciating how it usually was: historical characters being faced by difficult, confusing and morally ambiguous choices. Indeed, in order to capture their students' attention, I have seen many teachers teach history in this manner.

How, then, can teachers encourage their students to conceptualise history? First, teachers need to recognise how historians create historicity through invoking several second-order concepts (Lee & Ashby, 2000), such as historical significance, evidentiary warrant, continuity and change, progress and decline, empathy and moral judgment, and historical agency (Seixas, 1996). While these constructs are interrelated, following Damico, Baildon and Greenstone (2010) I focus here on historical agency, a concept central to understanding the past. What makes histories coherent and intelligible is the presence within them of human agents reasoning, making choices, and exercising their will (Roberts, G., 1997, p. 257). Teachers should begin by conceptualising historical agency as a complex relationship between structural forces and individual actions (Lewis, Enciso, & Moje, 2007; Seixas, 2003).

Damico, Baildon and Greenstone argue 'by situating sympathetic protagonists in complex historical situations, quality historical fiction can help students recognize history seldom offers straight-forward choices or easy answers' (2010, p. 1). The authors put this another way: 'good historical fiction can give middle grades students a port of entry into the important, but otherwise abstract concept of historical agency' (p. 1).

Seixas, Fomowitz and Hill argue for a more sophisticated understanding of historical agency, involving contexts such as 'economic, political, and social upheavals, along with the shaping influences of individual actors' (2005, p. 12), which point to the complex relationships among personal causes, effects, and structural forces. They 'define historical agency as *the relationship between structural forces that shape historical events and the ways people influence, shape, and are affected by these events.* That is, human beings are autonomous agents with abilities to affect change, yet there are social structures that constrain and limit what individuals can do' (Seixas, Fomowitz, & Hill, 2005, p. 120, emphasis added).

For the classroom teacher, Damico, Baildon and Greenstone have constructed four important questions which can be used to interrogate a historical novel for historical agency:

1. What key people/characters, events and issues, and settings/contexts are discussed in this novel?
2. What role do the main characters play in bringing about or shaping significant events or issues?
3. In what ways are the main characters affected or shaped by certain contexts or conditions?
4. How are key concepts in history — significance, change and continuity, progress and decline, perspective and judgement — portrayed in terms of agency? (Damico, Baildon & Greenstone, 2010, p. 4)

I endorse the usefulness of teachers framing discussions around these questions.

* * *

This chapter has afforded us an opportunity to dwell for a moment on issues relating to development of historical literacy, especially in relation to students understanding issues relating to historical facts and historical agency. Moreover, The novels written for younger readers I have referred to in this chapter provides an opportunity to lead students towards a better understanding of history from various points of view, particularly the way in which the historical novel can provide a voice for less dominant social groups, or for groups often referred to as 'the enemy', or 'the other'.

Developing an understanding of historical agency inevitably requires students to understand how historical novelists make use of facts. This chapter discussed how within schools the study of History most often has been associated with both the study of historical facts and the values and morals of the school's local community. The interpretation of historical facts by the historical novelist is closely connected to the manner in which he or she interprets history, and portrays historical agency. This chapter concluded by flagging how Damico, Baildon and Greenstone (2010) had constructed four important questions to interrogate a historical novel for historical agency.

13 Key themes in Australian History and their Reflection in Historical Novels

Australian historical fiction tends to fall into some dominant categories, reflecting perennial themes that are forever being reinterpreted: first settlement, European inland exploration, pastoralism, conflict with Indigenous Australians, patriotism and war are common themes of Australian historical fiction. In writing these novels and responding to these themes, among other things, novelists inform readers much about how Australians think of themselves and of how they perceive the Australian nation. Novels often challenge conventional values in these respects. Certainly, they offer engaging insights for students into Australian history.

National character and our convict heritage

For the most part, Australia's history is founded on the convict past. Only South Australia is excluded from this history. But even then, many South Australians continue to research their convict heritage. Not surprisingly, Australian convict history is enormously popular with the general public.

Here I am concerned with examining some of the ways in which historical fiction dealing with our convict past can shed new understanding on this aspect of our history in ways that fail nonfiction. Can fiction offer a dimension of understanding on this subject that nonfiction cannot? I first offer a brief survey and analysis of the nonfiction convict history, before proceeding to examine some examples of the fictional genre.

A casual stroll through any section of any reputable Australian bookseller will reveal the quantity of convict histories in fictional and nonfictional genres. The most notable of this nonfiction for 2008 alone included:

- Babette Smith's *Australia's Birthstain: The Startling Legacy of the Convict Era*
- Babette Smith's *A Cargo of Women: Susannah Watson and the Convicts of the* Princess Royal
- Brian Walsh's *Voices from Tocal: Convict Life on a Rural Estate*
- Hamish Maxwell-Stewart's *Closing Hell's Gates: The Death of a Convict Station*
- David Levell's *Tour to Hell: Convict Australia's Great Escape Myths*.

There is a mass of convict nonfiction published for any single year. Among other things, this chapter will demonstrate the appeal the subject in well-written form has to publishers.

Interpreting Australia's convict past: convicts and Australian nonfiction

Celebrated nationally on 26 January, Australia Day always generates a plethora of public discourse on our national character. Amongst other matters, usually the nation's convict heritage comes into the spotlight. During the weeks prior to Australia Day, there are often several books or films launched featuring Australia's convict heritage. Movies such as *Van Diemen's Land* (2008), based on the confronting and horrific confessions of Australia's most notorious convict, Alexander Pearce, invite horrified audiences to understand Australia's convict past. But a fresh approach was needed to an overdone subject. As Byrnes writes:

> This is the third film based on the story in two years and it solves the problem by elevating it, treating it as a spiritual journey. This is Pearce's descent by way of Dante's *Inferno*, a progression through the seven rings of the Tassie wilderness. (2009)

Another indication of the continued tourist appeal of convictism is the case of the Tasmanian tourist mecca of Campbell Town in the Northern Midlands. The street in the main thoroughfare is lined with red bricks, one for each individual convict sent to the state. Each brick details an individual's crime. Australia's convict heritage is big business.

Babette Smith is one of many Australian historians who find a ready audience in writing on Australia's convict heritage. Following on from her recently published work, *Australia's Birthstain*, Smith contributed a full-page article in *The Weekend Australian* on the eve of Australia Day 2010 on the subject of Australia's national character. She suggested that 'most Australians nominate egalitarianism as a key value of our society. We are sure it exists but struggle to describe what we mean by it' (Smith, 2010, p. 4). She claimed, however, that 'outsiders have not found it difficult. In the 1920s, visiting novelist D.H. Lawrence wrote, 'There was really no class distinction. There was a difference of money and of smartness.' However, for the great novelist, in Australia, Smith continued, 'nobody felt *better* than anybody else, or higher; only better off. And there is all the difference in the world between feeling *better* than your fellow man, and merely feeling better *off*' (Smith, 2010, p. 4, emphases in original).

For Smith, this pervading sense of egalitarianism and all its associated values has its roots in our convict past. Not surprisingly, convictism as a contributing factor to a national ethos has stimulated considerable research and debate over the decades. Smith contends: 'our ignorance was compounded by scorn that a penal colony could give rise to such distinctive equality' (Smith, 2010, p. 4). Moreover, 'in 1958, when Russell Ward, a historian of the old Left, made his claim of egalitarianism in his book, *The Australian Legend*, he was attacked by young historians of the new Left for whom class shaped everything' (Smith, 2010, p. 4). Indeed, 50 years on (during which time the new Left has aged somewhat) Smith goes on to assert that research in the convict archives has underscored Ward's belief in the influence of convictism on the national character (2010, p. 4).

Smith offers a highly readable account of the influence of the Australian convict heritage on our national character. Moreover, she highlights the fact Australians have viewed the nation's convict past in very different ways. As Marian Quartly writes, 'convict history is carried by Australia as a beloved burden' (1998, p. 154). But it has not always been so. As Smith writes, at one time in Australia's history its convict past was viewed as a 'birthstain'.

During the 1980s, Richard White's *Inventing Australia* (1982) influenced much of my research in Australian history. The work spends considerable space in analysing the influence of our convict past on our perceived national character. White shows how and why perceptions of our convict past have changed from the time of Australia's convict era, when to have been a convict, or to have convict parentage, was a birthstain of considerable proportions, a view advanced by some nineteenth-century evangelical protestants.

Quartly considers the example of John West, a Congregational minister who wrote the first historical assessment of the convict era. West's *History of Tasmania* (1852) was written 'during the heat of the campaign to end transportation' (Quartly, 1998, p. 154). West blamed Britain for the brutality of the convict system and the detrimental impact it had on colonial society. A generation later, literary identities such as Marcus Clarke continued the theme of the degrading influence of convictism. The result was a mass of Australians who sought to disown their convict ancestors.

But that attitude soon faded from our national psyche. According to Quartly, by the 1930s exceptional Australians — proud Australians — such as Mary Gilmore, condemned Australians generally, and Australian historians specifically, for 'excluding the convicts from the emerging national history' (1998, p. 154). Quartly reminds us that Gilmore wrote:

> Shame on the mouth
> That would deny
> The knotted hands
> That set us high. (quoted in Quartly, 1998, p. 154)

Quartly then writes of the great works of Australian historians which redresses the imbalance of our historical accounts of our convict history: Russell Ward's *The Australian Legend* (1958), L.L. Robinson's *The Convict Settlers of Australia* (1965), A.G.L. Shaw's *The Convicts and the Colonies* (1966) and Humphrey McQueen's *A New Britannia* (1970) (Quartly, 1998, p. 155).

All of this academic effort to rewrite the history of our convict past was reflective of a national change of mood. Quartly writes: 'the search for a useful convict past drove private history as well as the academic kind'. Indeed, 'before the 1960s in eastern Australia, and rather later in WA, a convict ancestor was a matter of shame and concealment. But members of the burgeoning genealogical societies have come to regard a convict in the family as a proud badge of Australian identity' (1998, p. 155).

Now associated with this national change of mood was a drive by professional historians to write gendered accounts of convicts. Quartly (1998) describes this development: 'the genealogical impulse fed back into formal history with publications such as Babette Smith's *A Cargo of Women* (1988), which presented the author's convict ancestors and her shipmates as capable, self-directed women, and Portia Robinson's several histories of convict women and their daughters, including *The Women of Botany Bay*' (1988) (p. 155). For Quartly, authors such as Smith and Robinson have argued convict women were good mothers, respectable citizens and important nation builders.

By the late 1980s, professional historians had assumed a normalist approach to convict history. One such work is Stephen Nicholas's collection of essays, *Convict Workers* (1988). According to Quartly, in the central essay for the book Nicholas concluded that '"The convicts transported to Australia were ordinary British and Irish working-class men and women", similarly skilled and better-educated than those they left behind, and they formed the basis of a highly efficient colonial workforce' (Quartly, 1998, p. 155).

But, as Quartly argues, 'the normalisers have not touched the popular imagination' (1998, p. 155). In particular, she singles out Robert Hughes's *The*

Fatal Shore (1987), 'the historical best-seller of the last decade', as an example of a book pandering to old stereotypes. She writes: 'Hughes energetically (if erratically) dismisses the rationalists. Botany Bay was no proto-capitalist workplace, it was a place of exile, privation and death — a gulag' (p. 155). Moreover, 'Hughes' central concern was to display the suffering of the convicts and the viciousness of their gaolers'. Indeed, as if for the market place, 'he revived the moral language and the pornographic detail of the nineteenth-century reformers and novelists to create a story as compelling and as partial as theirs' (p. 155). Despite the host of well-researched and well-argued works of professional historians whom Quartly (1998) referred to in the above paragraphs, Hughes's (1987) view of Australia's convict past had wide popular appeal. At the time of Hughes's death in August 2012, the influence of his *The Fatal Shore* (1988) was summarised by John McDonald, the *Sydney Morning Herald*'s art critic. McDonald suggested that Hughes showed he could go beyond the world of art criticism with *The Fatal Shore*: 'He is somebody who I think helped to put Australia on the map. People knew Australia often through Robert Hughes' ('Fatal Shore Author Robert Hughes Dies Aged 74', 2012).

The Fatal Shore was, I suggest, a product of astute market research in the lead-up to Australia's bicentenary. And there can be no doubting its success. But it provides a very good starting point for prospective authors of Australian historical novels on the subject of how to interpret convict history in order to meet popular demand, if would-be authors should choose such a cynical approach to their craft.

Convicts and Australian historical fiction

Wilde, Hooton and Andrews (2000, p. 185) write that in many respects the history of convict fiction written in Australia matches the writing of convict nonfiction. From the 1850s, there was a rush of fictional publication highlighting the evils of convict transportation to Australia. Clarke's *His Natural Life* was one such novel. Others included John Hebblethwaite's *Castle Hill* (1895) and E.W. Hornung's *The Rogue's March* (1896).

Then came the publication of perhaps more mature novels wherein the convict experience formed only an 'intrinsic or incidental part of the subject matter or themes of the work ... The novels forming part of such a tradition can be numbered not in dozens but in hundreds and include several multi-volume historical sagas ...' (Wilde, Hooton & Andrews, 2000, p. 185). Scenes featuring street life, courtroom scenes, prison hulks and the voyage to Australia feature in many Australian historical novels concerning convicts (Wilde, Hooton & Andrews, 2000, 'Convicts in Australian Literature', pp. 183, 186). Thomas Keneally's *Passenger* (1979) is one such novel, as is Patrick White's *A Fringe of Leaves*. Wilde, Hooton and Andrews consider even such literary notables as White 'in his own way is as opportunistic in his use of the convict experience as any NSW Bookstall novelist' (2000, p. 187).

L.T. Hergenhan, in his *Unnatural Lives: Studies in Australian Fiction About Convicts*, argues that 'of all the convict novels [Keneally's] earlier novel, *Bring Larks and Heroes* [1967] is the one most palpably about the author's present as well as the past. It speaks to us as "a contemporary novel" (Keneally's own term for it)' (1983/1993, p. 139).

Interestingly, as shown by an interview by Beston, 'Keneally said he did not think of *Bring Larks* and his *The Chant of Jimmie Blacksmith* "as historical novels. I had to do some research but they're essentially contemporary novels"' (Beston, 1973, p. 55, as cited in Hergenhan, 1983/1993, fn. 1, p. 193).

Hergenhan goes on to show how Keneally made use of his historical 'facts' to develop his narrative: 'all the convict novelists ... sought in different ways to transcend time and place but Keneally is the most consciously determined to do so' (1983/1993, p. 139). Moreover, according to Hergenhan 'he has also stated though the novelist who uses history must draw on facts — "how [his characters] lived, what they ate, what they washed their bodies with (and how often)" — he need not prove his reliability to other scholars and his readers, as an historian must' (p. 140).

Williamson places *Bring Larks and Heroes* above nonfiction works such as Hughes's *The Fatal Shore*:

Bring Larks and Heroes lays bare the horrors of the convict era two decades before ... *Fatal Shore*'s appearance, when there were few works on transportation in print. Only Marcus Clark's *For the Term of His Natural Life* and Jessica Anderson's *The Commandant* bear comparison with it as fictional explorations of the period. A notoriously exacting historian of the day, John Ritchie, made the novel compulsory reading for his first-year students at the Australian National University. 'Where else', he said, 'will students get a more vivid and truer idea of those early days?' (Williamson, 2012, p. 18)

The historical novelist, then, attempts to use his/her 'facts' in a very different way than the author of historical nonfiction: the former to engage the reader, the latter to explain history. Often the former can achieve both in a more compelling manner.

Convict novels as reflections of current anxieties concerning Australian history

Jean-François Vernay's (2009) history of the Australian novel provides an insight into convictism and the Australian historical novel post-1988, the bicentenary year. Because of the national discourse concerning the bicentenary, Australian historical novelists responded with works which reflected their own sensitivities to the place of convictism in Australian history. Vernay puts it this way: 'writers like Peter Carey, Kate Grenville, Colin Johnson, Christopher Koch, Richard Flanagan, David Malouf and Roger McDonald appropriated these colonial episodes according to their respective sensitivities and, in this way, gave an impetus to the publication of a huge number of historical novels' (2009, pp. 181-82).

Peter Carey's eponym character in *Jack Maggs* (1997) 'is an orphan driven to the brink of criminality by a merciless British system'. The novel 'evokes this weighty heritage by having an England haunted by its colonial past'. Moreover, 'Maggs is thrown into prison and transported to Australia in accordance with the tradition of convict literature and he returns to England full of illusions (which the metaphor of somnambulism perfectly conveys: as a sleepwalker, Maggs is imprisoned by his dream of an idealised mother country) and disillusioned'. Vernay goes on to observe 'written in the style of a Victorian melodrama, the novel is a postcolonial re-writing of Charles Dickens' *Great Expectations* (1860-1861) — Jack Maggs being a re-invented version of the convict Magwitch' (2009, p. 186).

In the vein of Geoffrey Blainey's *Tyranny of Distance* (1967), where Australia's geographical isolation was such a powerful determining force on the nation's history, Vernay writes that *Jack Maggs* 'takes up a common theme in Australian literature, the theme of loss lived out as a traumatic experience that gives rise to a feeling of abandonment'. Moreover, 'According to David Malouf, and *Jack Maggs* is a typical example, Australians like being seen as orphans in the Pacific abandoned by a wicked stepmother (i.e. Perfidious Albion)' (2009, p. 186).

Vernay conceives of Kate Grenville's *The Secret River* as being 'written in the tradition of colonial literature in vogue in the nineteenth century. It takes up the archetypical plot of the convict who is offered a new life in Australia at the end of his sentence'. Moreover, 'William Thornhill, destitute in London at the end of the eighteenth century, was, like Daniel Defoe's Moll Flanders, reduced to thieving in order to survive. His infamy does not go unnoticed, but he escapes the death penalty by being transported to New South Wales with his pregnant wife Sal and their child. When they arrive, everything divides them'. Indeed, 'William mistrusts the Aborigines and, provided with his patch of land, claims one as his own. His wife makes contact with the Indigenous people more easily' (2009, p. 186). It seems that Grenville has European females better establishing an empathy with Indigenous Australians than do their male counterparts.

European inland exploration and pastoralism: key issues in Australian historical novels

Just imagine you are an outer-space observer of Earth — say, you are on Mars and have a powerful telescope trained on Earth. The Earth year/time is December 1787, and you are fascinated by this large island/continent in the Southern Hemisphere, which seems to be so peaceful in relation to the wars and disruptions occurring in other parts of the world. You have been observing this large island/continent for tens of thousands of years.

Then you notice eleven sailing ships approaching. They are loaded with convicts. You study them as they eventually berth in a beautiful harbour on the east coast of the island/continent. You are intrigued as you study these fair-skinned visitors spread out over the countryside. They begin to strip the land of many of the trees and begin ploughing the ground, and herding the animals they brought with them. You watch with interest as the people originally living here begin to respond to these changes by attacking the newcomers, or by attempting to exist on the fringes of this alien society with its many diseases and the corrupting influence of alcohol.

Soon the rugged range of mountains to the west of the settlement of these white people is crossed by what appear to be three explorers. In increasing numbers, now white-skinned people are using this new path across the mountains as they move their animals across to the lands beyond the mountains. Then the whole process of clearing the land is continued. Then more explorers (or are they scouts for a planned occupation of these lands?) are sent out across the vast interior of the island/continent, preparatory to an ever-increasing settlement of these white-skinned people.

As a Martian who has studied this island/continent for many tens of thousands of years, you are amazed at the changes taking place over such a short period. Despite the many skirmishes on the frontiers of settlement, you wonder at how little interaction there is between the new arrivals and the original inhabitants. These white invaders don't seem at all interested in the fact the dark-skinned original custodians of these lands have been so successful in their care of the land while living off it. What does the future hold for this beautiful country and its original inhabitants as these white people spread out over it, and appropriate its landscape, flora and fauna? How is this history reflected in historical fiction?

Inland European explorers and 'blind' encounters with Indigenous Australian culture

As a student at a New South Wales government school in rural New South Wales during the 1950s, through History lessons, stories in the *School Magazine* and other reading material I was taught the heroic deeds of Australia's European inland explorers, *men* who formed the foundation for pastoral Australia. At university in the 1960s, I read in standard texts, such as Shann's *An Economic History of Australia* (1930/1967) about Major Thomas Mitchell, 'one of [the Duke of] Wellington's Torres Vedras men', who battled 'blacks' and a fierce landscape to 'discover' the New South Wales western rivers: 'he marched back from Glenelg [located in south-west Victoria] in military order, and his cart-tracks, "the Major's line", became the route by which Sydney-side stockmen made their way overland to the Port Phillip district' (Shann, 1930/1967, p. 99). Even at university I was left with no doubt of the debt Australia owed the 'achievements' of these men, whose expeditions were portrayed in military terms.

As Cathcart comments, 'exploration by land was, until the 1970s, one of the preoccupations of Australian popular history' (1994, p. 389). As most school children of the 1950s-1960s can attest, 'history books began with exploration by sea, explaining how the coastline of Australia had been mapped by noble Dutch and British seafarers. This map-making was seen as laying the ground for possession' (p. 389). History lessons were about coloured pencils and blank maps of Australia: 'it was through the act of "filling in the blanks" on the map of the world actually brought the land itself into being, and therefore made it available to its "discoverer". In popular accounts, this process was completed by the land explorers, notably John Oxley … Thomas Mitchell … Ludwig Leichardt' (p. 389). Indeed, 'An account of the principal expeditions undertaken by each of these men was written into the grand narrative of Australian history' (p. 389). The Indigenous Australians were marginalised in this tragic interpretation of the nation's history.

For some Australians, it seems, the careers of these apparently egocentric Europeans inland explorers offer endless fascination. New publications of their histories appear regularly. For example, in November 2011 Evelyn Juers (2011) reviewed John Bailey's *Into the Unknown* (2011) and E.B. Joyce and D.A. McCann's edited collection, *Burke & Wills* (2011). *Into the Unknown* is a rather celebratory, triumphalist, although at times critical, description of the career of Ludwig Leichhardt. Published by the Commonwealth Scientific Industrial Organisation (CSIRO), *Burke & Wills* seeks to establish the scientific achievements of Robert O'Hara Burke and William John Wills in their vainglorious attempt to explore the Australian continent from south to north.

Yet, over fifty years ago, through historical fiction, Australians were given another version of these inland explorers through Patrick White's *Voss* (1957), based on Leichhardt's career as Australian inland explorer. For Huggan, the novel:

> emerges as… as [an] hallucinatory stud[y] in the devasting effects of white (male) monomania: on the family unit, on society at large, and on the fractured individual who, driven by by barely controlled compulsions, allows these to legitimise his twisted impulses to domination and destruction. (Huggan, 2007, p. 86)

Juxtaposed to White's view of Leichardt as depicted in Voss, Huggan offered another, different view. For many historians, the goodness in the land needed to be fought over, against a hostile wilderness. History depicted the conquering of this hostile land of the Australian myth in terms of the sacrifice of many of our pioneering men and women (Tacey, 1995). Yet the European ignorance of the land was due to almost an absence of dialogue with Indigenous Australians. Breslin (1992) argues that the first five decades of contact revealed very little non-Indigenous desire to acquire Indigenous knowledge of the land, and the bounty of food it oftentimes provided Indigenous Australians. To recognise Indigenous people as beneficiaries of an abundant land would have contradicted the myth of the hostility and infertility of the land. Because of the Indigenous Australia's use of fire culture, many historians and anthropologists have come to recognise that the relationship of Indigenous Australians and the land was highly complex.

European inland exploration in historical fiction

By the 1970s and 1980s erudite Australian writers of historical fiction had tuned into this postcolonial understanding of the Australian inland explorers as expressed by Michael Cathcart (1999) — including Peter Carey. As with so many 'blind' European explorers and pastoralists before him who had stumbled into strange Australian lands, Oscar, in Carey's *Oscar and Lucinda* (1988), is unable to comprehend the ancient Indigenous Australian culture. Oscar had,

> drifted up the Bellinger River like a blind man up the central aisle of Notre Dame. He saw nothing. The country was thick with sacred stories more ancient than the ones he carried in his sweat-slippery leather Bible. He did not even imagine their presence. Some of these stories were as small as the transparent anthropods that lived in the puddles beneath the river casuarinas. The stories were like fleas, thrip, so tiny they might inhabit a place (inside the ears of the seeds of grass) he would later walk across without even seeing. In this landscape every rock had a name, and most names had spirits, ghosts, meanings. (Carey, 1988, p. 492, as cited in McCredden, 2005)

This must have been an event that was repeated manifold times during Australia's history of European inland exploration.

Pastoralism and the legend of the 1890s

By the late 1960s, postcolonial historians began to question traditional assessments of pastoralism: its supposedly long-held images of itself, its contribution to national identity, and its connection with the Australian Legend. This was most recognisable in the manner in which Vance Palmer formulated it in the 1950s. According to Palmer, Australian society was based on egalitarianism, white Anglo-Saxon values, mateship, a respect for the practical over the theoretical, frugality, and an individual's right to progress according to *his* (as yet, not *her*) ability.

Palmer described the principal characteristics of the typical Australian male, forming the Australian Legend, this way: 'Tall, yet robust, sardonic in temperament, daring in action, they had the idealistic qualities Lawson was to emphasise in his stories of mateship, just as Masefield was to celebrate their kingly bearing in describing the soldiers of Gallipoli' (Palmer, 1954, p. 15).

For decades, the pioneering legend was more about heroes and 'warriors of the bush', heroes who fought courageous battles against the wilderness. This commenced with the myth that grew around the European explorers. The Australian landscape was constructed in adversarial terms in verse and prose, especially from the 1880s onwards through *The Bulletin*. It proselytised and reinforced the construction of the white Australian male battling the hostile interior. From the 1880s onwards, the description of the land was as a barely fertile, moody and dangerous 'other', with its drought, floods and treacherous 'native blacks', which white men and their loyal women sought to tame (Henningham, 2002). The land and its inhabitants were both threatening and merciless killers, as exemplified in a plethora of verse by such legends as Henry Lawson (see Wilde, Hooton & Andrews, 2000). Generally, Australian histories of the frontier excluded or downplayed the presence and roles of women — notwithstanding that works such as Louis Esson's poem *The Shearer's Wife* portrayed the vagaries confronted by the frontier woman (Henningham, 2002). But postcolonial histories have unearthed a fascinating wealth of women's experiences in the frontier.

The emerging national (male) type was constructed into the heroic pioneer who shaped the hostile country. Handsome in his many graces, tall, fair and strong, it was fitting he would become the hero of Gallipoli, in the guise of the 'warrior bushmen'. The traits and physique of the hero of the Legend were often accepted uncritically by white historians up until the 1950s (R. White, 1981, p. 77). Indeed, this hero-type of the Legend enjoyed broad public appeal, even into the 1980s: witness the film *Crocodile Dundee* (1986) where, despite its setting in northern Australia, Indigenous Australians could only score *supporting* roles.

Sensing they were somehow different from their British ancestors, by the 1880s most Australians — some second and third generation Australians — looked to themselves and were growing tired of being a British colonial antipodean outpost. Self-conscious of their convict heritage, some searched for a heroic past. Ken Inglis has argued that this largely unsuccessful search for a national hero during the years prior to the 1870s, was based on an adulation for the European explorers, as expressed in Henry Kendall's poetry (Inglis, p. 74, as cited in Hirst, 1978, p. 316).

However, this did not always accord with the everyday facts of rural Australia. For while there was an 'active process of building the country up on a democratic base', nevertheless 'a semi-feudal kind of life lingered out on the stations' (Palmer, 1954, p. 15). The Legend owes a debt to A.B. (Banjo) Paterson and other writers such as Henry Lawson, Joseph Furphy, Miles Franklin and Bernard O'Dowd, and the artists from the Heidelberg School, in particular. For Hirst, 'the pioneer legend had had a significant influence on the writing of the formal history. It solved the problem that formal historians could never overcome satisfactorily: the embarrassment of the convict origins of the nation' (1978, p. 331). Indeed, 'the pioneer legend, by proclaiming the settlement of the land as the chief theme in Australia's history, found it easy not to mention convicts at all' (p. 331).

So now Australia's history was shrouded in a myth, in order to disguise what was perceived to be an embarrassing fact. How could European exploration and inland expansion through pastoralism and mining add to, or distract from, this legend of the national type during the decades following? The mad rush during the nineteenth- and twentieth-century into the pastoral industry across Australia's interior was as much driven by an unquestioning acceptance of *terra nullius* (the legal concept that the land was unoccupied) as it was by the quest for fortunes through pastoralism (Tiffen & Lawson, 1994, p. 5). Lamia Tayeb contends that 'colonial processes of appropriation were largely based on myths of human and cultural emptiness. In settler colonies, a pattern of colonisation was developed on the basis or primal beginning and belonging rather than imposed invasion and occupation' (Tayeb, 2006, p. 125). Nevertheless, by postcolonial standards it was 'invasion', inasmuch as it comprised a foreign force occupying lands claimed by a civilisation for millennia. Of course, if the foreign force refused to recognise that a civilisation did indeed exist here, it does nothing to strengthen the argument developed by the invaders.

The Australian rural landscape

The term 'landscape' looms as a troubled term in postcolonial discourse in Australian history and literature. The term, first, is a metaphor. But it is, as Seddon (1998) explains, 'a misleading metaphor: first, because it implies a passive role for the "stage"' and second, because it assumes the landscape was simply "there", waiting'. It was, however, not like that at all: 'The idea of a passive landscape is a biophysical version of the doctrine or *terra nullius*, that the land was not only known: it was available, passively receptive, and, in a sense, already "known" — because, after all, rivers are rivers, plains are plains, forests are forests' (Seddon, 'Landscape', 1998).

The invading Europeans brought their own ways of seeing and naming the landscape. For example, with many of the animals living there, the invaders imposed their existing knowledge: for example, the platypus was first called a 'water mole'. As Seddon observes, 'there has been a long, difficult, and continuing process of mutual readjustment'. An example of this, Seddon states, was the European concept of drought, which is, as R.L. Heathcote observed in *Geographical Review* (1969), 'a problem of perception' (quoted in Seddon, 1998). Seddon suggests that 'To speak of "drought" is to say the rainfall has failed to live up to our expectations; but the failure lies with our expectations, not with the rainfall' (1998).

Just as new arrivals to Australia today must wonder sometimes at old British imperial terms — for example 'the Far East' to describe Asia to our north — which continue to be used in some Australian discourse, much Australian geography and the terminology used to describe it was oriented from Australian eastern seaboard cities. Seddon makes the following observation:

> 'In a country urbanised before landscape was colonised, a "geography" of the land continues to be shaped as much by imagination as by reality ... [The bush] was a cultural reality before the landscape acquired a specific form', remarks the art historian, Ian Burn, in *National Life and Landscapes* (1990). Perhaps its most characteristic form is that of the obsessively ordered, tentacular suburbia of the coastal cities ('sprawling' is inept; to sprawl is to be informal and relaxed). The coast remains central to our consciousness, because that is what 'the outback' and 'the inland', two distinctly Australian terms, are measured from. (Seddon, 1998)

How was this manifest in Australian white settler memory of the past? The historical novel is a great means of understanding this in terms of individual lives.

Deconstructing some the supposed virtues of pastoral Australia

Only challenged with the onset of postcolonial histories, earlier there had been a plethora of published nonfiction histories extolling the virtues of pastoral Australia. Pastoral history until recent decades was the central component of the general history of Australia. Australia was said to ride on the sheep's back, and the history of the nation rode on the back of the pastoral industry. In studying such topics as 'squatters and selectors' and the Robertson Land Acts (officially the *Crown Lands Acts 1861* (NSW)), students of Australian history at universities and secondary colleges during the inter-war years through until the 1960s studied such works as Shann's *An Economic History of Australia*, wherein the squatters appear as exemplars of economic enterprise and the industry itself as 'the principal activity and support of the white man's Australian economy' (Shann, 1930/1967, p. 211).

As Graeme Davison writes, the wanton and careless actions by the pastoralists bore a heavy burden which brought about a dreadful affect on the Australian environment (Davison, 1998a). With the onset of postcolonial literature, Australian historical novelists picked up these new themes. Forever the environmentalist, Nancy Cato alerted readers to the ravages of pastoralist Australia. Witness a paragraph from *Forefathers* (1983):

> When rabbits had crossed the Murrumbidgee, Fergus had completely enclosed his run with wire netting rabbit-proof fencing. By digging out burrows and wholesale poisoning, he soon had his properties free of rabbits. They had been introduced by a squatter near Geelong, Victoria, to provide sport for his guns. Now they were in New South Wales, and the twenty million sheep which had taken over the waterholes and driven the Aborigines from the hunting grounds, were being driven out themselves by fifty million rabbits. The huntin' and shootin' squatters had imported their own destruction. (Cato, 1983, p. 111)

In a work lamenting the decline of the political influence of the pastoralists in Australia, Shann waxed enthusiastic about the early influence of wool on the Australian colonial economy, particularly praising the early work of John Macarthur (Shann, 1930/1967, pp. 84-88). According to Shann, the pastoralists were becoming politically marginalised by the 1930s (pp. 84-88). Certainly, they left their mark on Australian culture and society during the second part of the nineteenth century. And nowhere else is this more evident than in their mansions scattered across the rich Australian pastoral lands. As

Mitchell observes, 'in their heyday the great pastoral families had aspired to status of an Australian aristocracy, a self-image which found expression especially in the building of impressive homesteads' (1998, p. 494). Indeed, by the end of the nineteenth century, portraits of the Australian squattocracy often incorporated illustrated histories of their properties, glorifying the subjugation of the land.

According to Mitchell, after the 'historiographical shifts, and the steady drift of population to the cities, pastoral Australia retains a treasured place in the national imagination' (1998, p. 495). This is perhaps because of the strong presence of the idea of pastoral Australia long after the era of pastoralism has passed. Witness the great range of Australian historical novels from Boldrewood's *Robbery Under Arms* to Bryce Courtenay's *Jessica* (2006).

The romance of pastoral property in Australian historical novels

Robert Dixon writes at length of 'the romance of property' in his *Writing the Colonial Adventure*. He does so through an analysis of Rolf Boldrewood's *The Miner's Right* (Dixon, 1995, Chapter 1). Just as Europeans brought their own meaning to much of the Australian fauna, flora and geography, pioneering Australian literature, too, brought with it its own meanings, bound up in British or European notions of social class and property. Prominent in late nineteenth-century Australian literature, Boldrewood provides a starting point for this discussion.

> According to Pierce:
>
> 'Boldrewood' was not only saluting the literary heritage made available to Australian authors by [Sir Walter] Scott and [Fenemore] Cooper, he was longing for a national future in which the ideals that he presumed their fiction to enshrine would become manifest. In his romances, the confusion of literary and political desires and chronologies which made such a polemic contribution to the writing of Australian literary history, may be sharply discerned. 'Boldrewood's construction of a romantic

> national history was based on the theme of conflict over property and its resolution through the triumph of the pastoralist class (to which he once belonged). (Pierce, 1992, p. 308)

How does the colonial eulogy of pastoralism manifest itself in postcolonial literature? Tayeb's study of David Malouf's *Fly Away Peter* (1981) provides an insight into the manner in which Australian pioneer pastoralists interacted with the natural environment. The novel is set before and during the Great War. The first part of the novel is set on what is now the Gold Coast in Queensland, and the second part on the Western Front.

The central character of the novel is Jim Saddler, a self-contained young man and a devoted ornithologist, particularly of the bird life inhabiting the estuary near his home. Ashley Crowther has recently inherited the farm, which includes the estuary. Ashley and Jim form a close bond when Ashley offers Jim a job as a warden, recording the comings and goings of birds in their 'sanctuary'.

The novel exposes many attitudes associated with pastoralism during the pre-war period. First, there is a desire to *subdue* nature rather than *inhabit* it. In the novel, 'Jim Saddler moves between the polarities of imperial relations — New and Old Worlds, Southern and Northern hemispheres, peace and war — in order to recognise the need for an overarching communion between man and his physical world' (Tayeb, 2006, p. 176). Jim has not entirely freed himself of 'imperial, or Old World cartographic and historical holds' (p. 176). To name something, in a sense places some form of ownership over it:

> Jim too had rights here ... Such claims were ancient and deep. They lay in Jim's knowledge of every blade of grass and drop of water in the swamp, of every bird's foot that was set down there; in his having a vision of the place and the power to give that vision breath; in his having, most of all, the names for things and in that way of possessing them. (Malouf, 1981, p. 141, as cited in Tayeb, 2006, p. 176)

As Tayeb states, 'the terms of imperial exploration are explicitly evoked in this passage through the correlation of naming and possession' (p. 176).

'Language and inscription' underpin the claims and empowerment of imperial knowledge. In the colonial drive to appropriate the 'unmade' landscape, epistemic knowledge is paramount:

> In Jim's and Ashley's exploratory dream of Queensland, there is a curbing tendency to fill in a colonial void by bringing that void into linguistic and epistemic plenitude. This is ultimately similar to the violent transposition of Europe on Australia characterizing pioneer forms of settlement. An ironical narrative vision seems to play down Jim's and Ashley's project of the sanctuary, since their appropriative claims are unsettled by a spatial self-sufficiency, which tends to free the landscape from the temporal and epistemic fetters of the project to create a natural sanctuary in the Queensland bush. (Tayeb, 2006, p. 177)

For the landscape to be truly 'ours' and not belong to the 'other', the flora and fauna must bear English names: koalas are commonly called 'native bears', wombats are called 'badgers'. But this is not simply about giving familiar names to the unfamiliar. It is also about appropriating the landscape.

Social stratification in colonial pastoralist Australia

There have been a vast number of Australian nonfiction social histories describing the social stratification of late nineteenth-century pastoral Australia (for example, Serle, 1963; Serle 1971). Of course, this notion of Australian nineteenth-century and early twentieth-century society has appeared in an even more extensive range of Australian historical fiction. For example, commenting on Malouf's *Fly Away Peter*, Tayeb writes, 'Queensland society is profoundly marked by European notions of social hierarchy: the whole pre-war community of Queensland settlers is 'bound to conventions of class'. This transposing of ideas of British social hierarchy to the nineteenth-century pastoral Australian is really about 'the construction of home in the white settler collective consciousness [and] is subject to the psychic contingencies of "habitation" in both the physical and epistemic sense of the word' (Tayeb, 2006, p. 177).

With the onset of postcolonialism and postmodernism, our understanding of the history of Australian inland European explorers has undergone massive changes. One significant development has come with the voices of Indigenous Australians offering versions of this history previously ignored or hidden. Just as the treatment of this history has been transformed, so, too, has the manner in which historical novelists treat this subject matter. With the passing of the Australian historical saga with its accompanying eulogy of the Australian Legend, has come historical novels which now look to the anxiety of a nation reflecting on what this 'exploration' meant to the original inhabitants of the land.

Australia's pastoral industry quickly followed in the footsteps of the European 'explorers'. Prevailing interpretation of the history of this epoch in Australian history also has undergone changes. It is now widely recognised there were some serious losers in this history, none more so than the Indigenous Australians. Just as historical novelists have changed their focus with the treatment of European explorers as a subject matter for novels, so, too, have historical novelists looked to better include Indigenous Australians in the pastoral epoch. As an accompaniment to these changes, gone are any fanciful ideas about the Australian Legend being a product of pastoral Australia.

Indigenous Australians write their own historical fiction

How does one Indigenous Australian use the historical novel genre to portray the frontier? In *The Guardian* in December 2012, Carol Birch highly praised Kim Scott's 2010 novel *That Deadman Dance*:

> *That Deadman Dance*, winner of a raft of awards in Australia, including the country's prestigious Miles Franklin prize, is an exercise in lush impressionism, evoking a time when the aboriginal Noongar people of western Australia first encountered the 'horizon people': British colonists, European adventurers, and whalers from America, ghost-like white people intent upon establishing a settlement in a land both forbidding and primevally beautiful. (Birch, 2012)

While according to Birch, Scott's novel is not without its flaws, 'where it truly succeeds is in its glorious descriptions of landscape and wildlife, and the evocation of an ancient and mysterious place that seems to exist outside of time' (2012).

Scott's is a novel about first contact between Indigenous Australians and Europeans, viewed from the Indigenous Australian side of the frontier. For me, the novel is particularly enlightening because of the way in which it shows how at the frontier it was not the Europeans who did all the appropriating, but the Indigenous Australians did their fair share of the same, to meet their own social and economic needs. Morag Fraser put it this way:

> And because he [Scott] embodies understanding across culture, and not just a desire for it, because he doesn't subscribe to reductive binaries, black-white, superior-inferior etc, his work has about it the shimmer of possibility even as it traces tragedy. No matter how deep the rift, this has been, and can be again. (Fraser, 2011)

That Deadman Dance is a welcome addition to Australian literature, and should find a ready readership amongst students in Australian schools and colleges undertaking History.

Changing European attitudes to Indigenous Australians in Australian historical fiction

While not strictly historical fiction (according to the definition from the Historical Novel Society noted in Chapter 4 of this book) and perhaps at the time partly autobiographical, Mary Durack's *Keep Him My Country* deserves some space in this book, if only as an example to explain changing attitudes to European/Indigenous Australian relations. The novel, first published in 1955, was set in Western Australian's Kimberley in the early 1950s. There are aspects of the novel, especially some treatment of Indigenous Australians, that surely raise questions fifty years following its publication — but which would not have caused concern at the time of publication. Thus, when Davies contends that 'when completed, a literary work has a life independent of that of the author/s' and that 'the meaning of the work is fixed and can no more be changed by interpretations offered by its authors than by its critics', he raises some serious issues (Davies, 1996, p. 23). The statement is problematic, I suggest, A historical novelist writes according to the values, attitudes, understandings and interpretations of the time, the society in which he or she is a part of. In an important way, any historical novel encapsulates the social milieu of the time in which it is written. Discussions offered by critics are not about changing the novel's meanings, but rather about the way in which the historical generalisations offered by the historical novelist are interpreted. Witness Durack's and Scott's novels, both with powerful Indigenous Australian themes, written less than sixty years apart.

Much of *Keep Him My Country* is about the relationship between Rolt, the White owner of the isolated Kimberley cattle station, and his Indigenous partner, Dalgerie. While Durack never gives Dalgerie a voice in the novel, importantly, it is Dalgerie who brings Rolt to an understanding of the land, so hostile at times to whites but yet home to Dalgerie's people for millennia.

Durack wrote the novel virtually at the end of a literary era: eugenic views concerning Indigenous Australians and their relationships with white society would undergo massive changes during the late 1960s and 1970s, as the original inhabitants of the land were recognised, not least by novelists, as possessing complex cultures (Maddison, 2011).

Anderson has researched the influence of the Australian eugenicist/educators on the Australian 'racial type', and the government-sponsored drive towards a virile, white race (Anderson, 2002). With a single-minded and zealous striving, the goal of racial betterment could be achieved by what those who were considered to be at the time progressive reformers. Published at the time and in the same city as depicted in *Follow the Rabbit Proof Fence* (1996) and the accompanying horrors facing the Stolen Generations, the following appeared in the Perth *Sunday Times* in 1927: 'Australia's half-caste problem must be tackled boldly and immediately. The greatest danger, experts agree, is that three races will develop in Australia — white, black and the pathetic third race which is neither' (*Sunday Times*, 1927). The plight of a 'pathetic third race' in Australia had been a part of white public discourse for decades, and was represented in *The Chant of Jimmy Blacksmith* (1972).

In writing about Patrick White's *Voss* (1957) and *Fringe of Leaves* (1976), Collins claims that 'it is here, in the necessarily lacunary relation of the subject of history and memory, that the fragmented, incomplete, dialectical structure of allegory becomes relevant for understanding historical fiction as a *potential* antidote to, rather than the instance of, myth-making' (2008, p. 57, emphasis in original). Indeed, 'it is no coincidence that the dispute between historical truth and postmodernist relativism in Australia returns obsessively to the "traumatic scene", or "holocaustal event" of frontier violence between indigenous and settler Australians' (p. 57).

Although the frontier had long past in the New South Wales central west, this statement equally could well apply to Thomas Keneally's *The Chant of Jimmie Blacksmith*. Based on the exploits of Jimmy Governor, the infamous Wiradjuri outlaw on whom the character of Jimmie Blacksmith is based, Keneally's novel is intertwined powerfully with myth and tradition, but it is Indigenous Australian myth and tradition as interpreted by a white Australian novelist:

> In June of 1900 Jimmie Blacksmith's maternal uncle Tabidgi — Jackie Smolders in the white world — was disturbed to get the news that Jimmie had married a white girl in the Methodist Church at Wallah.
>
> Therefore, he set out with Jimmie's initiation tooth to walk the hundred miles to Wallah. The tooth would be a remonstration and lay a tribal claim on Jimmie. For Tabidgi, Jackie Smolders was full-blooded and of the Tallum section of the Mungindi tribe. To his mind, people should continue to wed according to the tribal pattern. (Keneally, 1972/78, p. 1)

I have already alluded to the massive changes in Australian society during the 1960s. By the time he wrote *The Chant of Jimmie Blacksmith*, Keneally had become a part of these massive changes, a generational re-evaluation and re-examination of society. Indigenous/non-Indigenous relationships were a part of these changes. As one commentator put it, 'race relations in Australia's past, and by implication, present, are the accepted theme' of the novel (Tiffin, 1978, p. 121). However, 'Keneally himself [had] gone further, calling the novel a "parable"; implying, thereby, that these historical events have contemporary meaning and relevance' (Molloy, 1984, p. 25).

With *The Chant of Jimmie Blacksmith* opening with an Indigenous Australian perspective, albeit one imaged by a non-Indigenous novelist, there is a strong and decisive break with traditional white perspectives of Indigenous Australian culture. Moreover, the mixed-blooded Jimmie, himself, is established as being Indigenous Australian, and indeed Jimmy Governor was identified as Indigenous in the massive coverage of his exploits in the Australian colonial press (Ramsland, 1996, pp. 75-81). Keneally wrote the novel soon after the massive surge of postcolonial thought into Australian literature, both fiction and nonfiction, beginning sometime during the 1960s.

In practical terms, the 1967 referendum recognised the rights of Indigenous people as Australian citizens who, inter alia, would be counted in a part of the Australian population. From here flowed such momentous events as the Freedom Rides of the early mid-1960s, advocating Indigenous Australian access to public utilities in New South Wales. It would be an over-simplification to suggest these events *in themselves* influenced Keneally's writing of the novel. However, given the rapid decline of the blatant paternalism and racism marking white/Indigenous Australian relations in Australia, thoughtful Australians such as Keneally were likely motivated to reflect on these old and tragic values and attitudes. What better medium than a historical novel associated with the 'notorious' Jimmy Governor, the memory of whom was still in the minds of many living Australians?

For decades a renowned postcolonial author of many nonfiction works depicting Indigenous Australian/European conflict on Australia's 'pioneering' frontier, Henry Reynolds is responsible for generating considerable public awareness and debate. His works include *Frontier: Aborigines, settlers and land* (1987), *Dispossession: Black Australia and White invaders* (1989), *Why Weren't We Told?* (2000) and *The Law of the Land* (2003). Commenting on Keneally's *The Chant of Jimmie Blacksmith*, Reynolds observes the novel was 'written, published, read and reviewed in that period between 1969 and 1972 when white liberal opinion rediscovered the Aborigine — in the past and the present, in history and in politics' (1987, p. 14). Reynolds goes on to state that 'the book reflected many of the preoccupations of the period with its emphasis on white racism and black resistance, guilt and violence' (p. 14). Moreover, 'at best it captured an important aspect of the national mood at the time. At worst it shared faults with some contemporary Government policies which, though superficially well meaning, were paternalistic in execution and burdened an unconscious legacy of ancestral racism' (p. 14). He is referring to segregation policies in place in many country towns at the time.

Many of the myths Keneally attempts to dismiss in *The Chant of Jimmie Blacksmith* are associated with the Australian Legend. First, there is the 'heroic white settler' view of Australian colonisation. Jimmie is a man cheated at every turn because he is seen as 'half black', potentially treacherous and, above all, powerless. In the popular mind, the 'half-caste' is perceived as inheriting the worst of what was considered to be Indigenous Australian nature — lazy, deceitful, thieving, treacherous — as well as the worst of white working-class nature.

But first, some attention needs to be paid to the original 'Jimmie Blacksmith', in particular his motives for his notorious exploits. *The Chant of Jimmie Blacksmith* was based on the story of Jimmy Governor. Governor, together with his brother Joe and another Wiradjuri man, Jacky Underwood, had been involved in the so-called Breelong Outrage — the murder by tomahawk of several members of the Mawbey family at Breelong Station, near Gilgandra, on the evening of 30 July 1900. Underwood was captured separately soon afterward. Jimmy, with his brother Joe, had been on the run ever since the Mawbey killings, raiding and robbing homesteads and creating terror in a large number of small, isolated communities, over a large tract of country in north-central New South Wales. Jimmy was finally captured by civilian settlers at Bopin, near Wingham on the Manning River, in the early hours of 27 October 1900; Joe had died soon after near Singleton, by a shot from another settler's gun.

The colonial police had mounted a massive manhunt, the biggest in the colony's history, ranging over fourteen weeks, with little success. It was later estimated the outlaws had travelled about 2000 miles in different directions in that time to elude the police. They displayed sophisticated bush lore and physical endurance by moving rapidly backwards and forwards across the rugged and inaccessible Liverpool Ranges, raiding huts and small homesteads in both coastal and inland areas. They shifted camp as frequently as possible, doubled back on their tracks from time to time, rode fast and hard on stolen horses, walked along the tops of station fences for miles and frequently wrapped rabbit skins around their shoeless feet to leave no tracks for the black trackers hired by the police. The outlaws' methods of deception had been brilliant and the huge force of pursuing police soon faced a barrage of biting criticism from all sections of the colonial press. In his trial, Governor confessed to wanting to be another Ned Kelly, gaining national notoriety (Ramsland, 1996, pp. 75-81).

West (2009) provides a study of Australian nationalism, and analysis of what was often banditry shaped by social protest and a struggle between Australians and the largely British staffed colonial government. This book fills in the historical details of the struggle between the state and the outsiders defined by John Hillcoat and Nick Caves's 2005 film, *The Proposition*, and also provides an explanation of why Governor would harbour ambitions of becoming another Ned Kelly. Jimmy Governor (Blacksmith), an outsider, was pushed by European society to performing the atrocities, to gain notoriety as a Wiradjuri Ned Kelly.

Jimmie Blacksmith was conceived under problematic circumstances: 'the man who impregnated the giddy Dulcie Blacksmith must have been of a pensive nature; a man who perhaps hated the vice of sleeping with black women, yet could not master it' (Keneally, 1972/1978, p. 3). Thus, in tune with popular thought and eugenic thinking, whites and Indigenous Australian having a sexual relationship was seen as a 'vice'. And conceived in this 'vice', Jimmie is born into the no-man's land of the 'half-caste', a character trapped between two cultures and societies, shunned by both. However, 'Jimmie was destroyed precisely because he had learned the ways of white Australia so well. For him, typically Australian possession was a sacred state, and in effect the women he kills are sacrifices offered up to his shrine' (Brady, 1979, p. 76).

Another myth *The Chant of Jimmy Blacksmith* seeks to address also concerns the Australian Legend, the taming of the land by the white pioneers. For Mitchell (1998), the novel shows very strongly the contribution made by Indigenous Australians who had 'come in' and who had played such a vital role in the development of the Australian pastoral and mining industry. Indeed, in *The Australian Legend* (1958), Mitchell argues, 'Russell Ward argued that "a specifically Australian outlook grew up first and most clearly among the bush workers of the pastoral industry", a view which, in spite of Ward's academic critics, remains a fruitful source of popular myths" (Mitchell, 1998). The conviction the Indigenous Australians were a 'fossil race' inexorably bound for extinction did little to advance any argument for their role in supposed nation building through the pastoral industry.

Also concerning the Australian Legend, *The Chant of Jimmie Blacksmith* challenges the myth of Australian mateship and equality. In the history of Indigenous/non-Indigenous relations up until the time of the writing of the novel, this myth only applied to non-Indigenous society. To be black was likely to mean state-condoned repression, violence, economic exploitation and degradation, all of which Jimmie Blacksmith faced in the novel. This terrible treatment is also connected to the view of the Indigenous Australians as a 'doomed race', accelerated with the onset of Social Darwinism. As Richard White explains: 'previously Europeans had been convinced of the inferiority of the Aborigines, but that did not justify their extinction. Social Darwinism did. Racial conflict was reduced to a question of the Struggle for Life and the Survival of the fittest' (1981, p. 69). Although Darwin himself was not a proponent of Social Darwinism, White notes that 'Darwin himself, visiting Australia in 1836 while groping towards his theory of evolution, had seen the havoc inflicted on Aborigines by white technology, white customs and white disease' (1981, pp. 69-70). White goes on to state that 'before Darwin had published *The Origin of Species*, the extinction of Aborigines was explained away as "the design of Providence". Darwin's theories gave such sentiments an aura of scientific legitimacy' (1981, p. 70).

Another myth Keneally seeks to explode in *The Chant of Jimmie Blacksmith* concerns the assimilation policies in Australia, which only at the time of the writing of the novel were being challenged in public discourse. Andrew Markus has outlined the various strategies and lifestyles Indigenous Australians adopted to ensure the survival and cultural identity, which included survival in pastoral properties and fringe camps (Markus, 1998).

Those very same influences — postcolonialism and postmodernism — asserted such powerful influences over the way in which historians now interpret European exploration and pastoralism in Australian history, were bound to assert the same influence over the history of European attitudes to Indigenous Australians. In turn, these developments are reflected in Australian historical fiction with themes associated with Indigenous/non-Indigenous Australian relations. Consequently, a novel such as Durack's *Keep Him My Country*, written nearly sixty years ago, stands in stark contrast with Keneally's *Chant of Jimmie Blacksmith*. The former was written in a society deeply imbedded in colonialist literary values while the latter was responding to postcolonialist values.

Her Majesty's loyal Australian colonies: patriotism, nationalism and empire in historical novels

Many Australians have felt a familiar surge of patriotism during national days such as Australia Day and Anzac Day, or at times when the national focus has been on our performance in sporting events such as the Olympic Games. But let us travel back in time 120 years or so, when there were no such national days or national sporting events. What was the nature of Australia's patriotism and sense of nationalism in, say, 1885?

During that time, Australian colonials thought of themselves first as being British — Australian colonial British. Mainstream patriotism was framed in that context — Australian British colonials. I have discussed in various places in the book how Australians by the 1870s, 1880s and 1890s were developing a sense of nationhood, and what it was that fashioned this. Pastoral Australia was central to this developing sense of identity, and was revealed in such novels as Boldrewood's *Robbery Under Arms* (1888) and Praed's *Outlaw and Lawmaker* (1893). What were some other aspects to this developing sense of nationhood and patriotism during the second half of the nineteenth century?

Whose patriotism? 'The last refuge of a scoundrel'?

Many Australian historical novels draw on themes associated with patriotism, including Patrick White's *A Fringe of Leaves* (1976). Here White rejects notions of official patriotism — see, for example, Ungari (2010). But White's is a very different notion of patriotism, than, for example, that expressed by John Howard when he was Prime Minister (McKenna, 2008). Because of its place in Australian historical fiction, the notion of patriotism warrants some study.

Soutphommasane (2009) has sought to research a fresh insight into our understanding of Australian patriotism and nationalism. In reviewing Soutphommasane's book, Burchell writes: 'the paradox of patriotism is that it enlists the best and worst of human impulses, frequently at the same time'. He goes on to state: 'everybody loves to recite Samuel Johnson's old tavern-tankard witticism about patriotism being the last refuge of a scoundrel. Often, though, we have an uneasy sense that what Johnson meant was not exactly what we want to think he meant' (Burchell, 2009, p. 24). Indeed, for Burchell, 'even James Boswell, Johnson's devoted friend, wasn't sure he'd grasped Johnson's meaning, though he did loyally insist that Johnson was not impugning a real and generous love of country but only pretended patriotism that served as a cloak for self-interest' (p. 24).

There is a cynical aspect to the notion of patriotism; it can be many things to many people. Witness appeals to patriotism by a whole spectrum of politicians in Australian during the last twenty years alone. Patriotism can be a game for all players, so long as everybody observes the ground rules of expressed love of nation. Burchell explains again: 'patriots usually appeal to our nation's grand past, often warning of an endangered future; it is often claimed patriots of true and simple hearts will always see through corrupt politicians and other public figures, while others (usually much more numerous) will be fooled by fine phrases and empty sentiments' (2009, p. 24). He goes on to say: 'couched in these terms, patriotic oppositionalism has had — and will long continue to have — a profitable career as a tool of populists and malcontents of all persuasions' (2009, p. 24).

Nevertheless, patriotism in the fledgling Australian colonies was very real to many Australians during the latter part of the nineteenth century. This was especially the case with second- and third-generation Australians already speculating on a unified Australian nation. In attempting to distinguish patriotism from nationalism, Soutphommasane writes that nationalists, whatever creed they may be, are convinced in the superiority of their nation, often with racist, political and ideological undertones, whereas patriots advance ideas about the cultural unity of their country: 'expressions of nationalism are inevitably political or ideological: political actors frequently appeal to ideas about a national destiny or cultural integrity to justify their decisions or mobilise public support. Patriotism, meanwhile, is an attitude that almost inevitably draws on a sense of cultural affinity' (2009, p. 40). However, as Soutphommasane recognises, 'the dividing line between political and the cultural is a blurry one at best' (2009, p. 40).

It is important to first remember the dominant socio-political ideology of the time was utilitarianism. As Richard White notes, in this age national culture had a definite purpose:

> It existed, not for its own sake, but for the sake of morality. The prophet of this new 'moral aesthetic' was John Ruskin, whose ideas on cultural matters were to dominate Britain for half a century from the 1840s. He had found moral purpose in art: the greatest art was that which conveyed 'the greatest number of the greatest ideas'. (R. White 1981, p. 61)

Richard White also observes: 'the moral purpose of culture was also widely accepted in the Australian colonies, and it was with that justification that they vied with each other to erect cultural monuments. The first wave of universities, the major art galleries, the museums, the large public libraries and government education systems all appeared between the 1840s and the end of the century' (p. 61). Indeed, 'all were intended, as W.C. Wentworth said of the University of Sydney, opened in 1852, "to enlighten the mind, to refine the understanding, to elevate the soul of our fellow men"' (White, 1981, p. 61).

While the first of the universities in the Australian colonies were 'established to defeat materialism, these cultural symbols themselves embodied the view culture was measured in material terms'. One drive for this was 'national greatness' and this was 'commonly measured by the extent to which a nation had erected the machinery for the moral improvement of its population' (R. White, 1981, p. 61).

Furthering Roe's (1965) writings on culture and its links with patriotism in Australian society, White argues, 'such visible symbols of "Culture" encouraged the immense pride of the colonial bourgeoisie in their own progress. It bolstered their position: they were the leaders of a cultured, not debased, community, and they saw themselves as responsible for its moral improvement' (R. White, 1981, p. 61). Of course, by the 1880s and the development of 'Marvellous Melbourne' this manifestation of patriotism had reached its high-water mark.

The Australian Legend defines patriotism, nationalism and the Australian 'warrior' from the bush

With an ancestry in pioneer and pastoral Australia, the 'warrior' bushmen of the Legend stood as if a colossus in our national thinking. As Richard White has commented: 'Russell Ward has pointed out that the "noble frontiersman" provided Western culture with an escape from urban, industrial civilisation, a romancing of imperial expansion, and a focus for patriotic nationalist sentiment, especially in "new" societies' (1982, p. 103). Indeed, for White, 'Ward himself was concerned with the third element, and argued that the national image of the Australian bushman had a distinctively Australian inheritance of the nomadic bush-workers of the outback. However, all three elements are so closely interwoven that the isolation of any one is distorting' (1982, p. 103). Moreover, White (1982) suggests that 'it must also be remembered that the bush-worker was an integral part of empire and, when he was ennobled as "the Bushmen"' (p. 103), reinforcing the place of the bushmen in the Australian Legend.

The new imperialists pinned their hopes on this 'Coming Man'. It was to such men, 'the men who could shoot and ride' as Kipling put it, the empire looked for 'its superior cannon fodder'. So Australians, just as the New South Wales Parliament had done in 1885 in sending the NSW Contingent to the Sudan, chose to send off contingents of 'Bushmen' to the Boer War, and was 'thrilled when Chamberlain was impressed enough to ask for more' (White, 1982, p. 103). Of course, the same thing had occurred with the dispatch of the NSW Contingent to the Sudan.

'The idealisation of the bush-worker', asserts White, 'by Tom Roberts, A.B. Paterson and others was a reaffirmation the wool industry was the "real" basis of the Australian economy and of Australian prosperity' (White, 1982, p. 103). Moreover, the stereotype of the bush warrior was that of the bush-worker, not the agricultural worker, or the urban office- or factory-worker.

Patriotism and the anti-Mahdi fervour in Australia following the murder of General Gordon

In Khartoum in early 1885, the Muslim leader, labelled the Mahdi, had the British General Gordon put to death. This sent shockwaves throughout the British Empire, and today is most popularly remembered through films such as The Four Feathers.

There has been a suggestion there were parallels with the anti-Mahdi fervour in Australia following the murder of General Gordon and that in modern-day Australia in regard to Islam/Christian relations (Kuhn, 2007). While there is no doubting the strength of the anti-Mahdi fervour, and the associated moral outrage, there is no real trace of Islamophobia in the Australian colonies during 1885. Why should there have been? There were few Muslims in Australia — a small number of Afghan camel drivers, maybe a few remaining Macassan trepangers, and few Malay pearlers — and these were in isolated areas situated away from population centres (Saeed, 1998). But there was certainly ample jingoism and moral outrage at the Mahdi's role in the death of General Gordon, as Inglis describes in Chapter 5 of his *The Rehearsal* (1985).

Huggan argues that Australian literature, generally, has had an ambivalent role in Australia's racial and religious relations: 'Australian literature has been constitutive, rather than merely reflective, of the history of social relations in Australia, and ... this constitutive role ... is perhaps most visible in the discourse it has produced, and continues to produce, about race, both within the national context and beyond' (2007, p. vi). For Huggan, 'this argument is hardly new; indeed, it is the consensus among many contemporary Australian literary critics (p. vi).

Huggan (2007) looked to Dixon (1995), Sheridan (1995) and Whitlock (1999) to develop his argument. He concluded: 'Australian literature, so the argument runs, is both producer and product of continuing racial tensions and anxieties, born in part out of a legacy of settler colonialism, but also attributable to the changing place of a nominally postcolonial nation in an increasingly globalized world' (Huggan, 2007, p. vi).

Patriotism is tested with the death of General Gordon and the developing Sudan campaign

With regard to their relationship with the British Empire, the Australian colonies were considerably different in the mid-1880s than they were forty or so years previously. Robert Dixon comments: 'studies of British imperialism normally cover the period from the 1870s to World War 1. During the early Victorian years, from the 1830s down to 1870, "the colonies" and the colonial interests' of the British Empire were certainly familiar terms, but the word "imperialism" was not applied to British, as distinct from French, contexts until the 1870s' (1995, p. 2). Indeed, for Dixon, 'The "imperialism" of the later period differed from the early and mid-Victorian decades in so far as it expressed both a greater assertiveness and a greater anxiety about the Empire. Before 1870 British attitudes to the colonies were confident and expansionist' (1995, p. 2).

Thus, the moral outrage surrounding the death of General Gordon came at a time when the relationship between the Australian colonies with Britain was undergoing some change. The 1870s was 'a watershed, marking qualitative change away from the confidence of the early Victorian period to a time of doubt about the civilising mission of British commerce, worries about national efficiency, and fears of racial decline and cultural decadence' (Dixon, 1995, p. 2). It was a period 'of mounting complexity and contradiction, an era in which the empire was subject to both centripetal and centrifugal forces'. Apart from the growing rivalry from Germany, Belgium and the United States 'more than any other events before the Boer War, the invasion of Egypt in 1882 and the death of Gordon at Khartoum in 1885 fuelled British anxieties' (p. 2).

Ken Inglis is by far the most recognised authority on the history of the 1885 NSW Contingent to the Sudan. As Inglis (1985) records, '"Chinese" Gordon, the most famous soldier in Victorian England, had been installed as governor-general of the Sudan in Khartoum on 18 February 1884. He had held that office once before, adding to his legend of putting down the slave trade' (1985, p. 3). Through the marvels of the electric telegraph, on 6 February 1885 people in Australia learned the Arab insurgent known as the Mahdi had captured Khartoum, and Gordon probably had been taken prisoner. By 12 February 1885 the *Sydney Morning Herald* reported in fact Gordon had been killed. Inglis adds: 'The death of Gordon provoked shock and outrage. ... Gordon was mourned more intensely than any other. He had seemed invincible. What must be done to avenge him? The question was asked as vehemently in Sydney as in London' (1985, p. 11).

As Inglis (1985) explains: 'Gordon's death was the gravest single item of news carried to Australia by the cable in its twelve years of operation. Colonial adults and children learned of his legendary triumphs in China and his works of philanthropy among poor boys' (1985, p. 12). Gordon was the very essence of the values associated with *Victorian Boys' Own*. For Inglis, 'The feats of Gordon Pasha, servant of the Khedive of Egypt and liberator of African slaves, had been recorded in newspapers and illustrated papers and retailed in schools. Australian boys and girls had been told, truly, that he was a devout reader of the Bible and cared nothing for money or comfort' (p. 12). It was all about Empire. Inglis continues: 'stories of his deeds had dwelt on the spiritual power of a lone Englishman standing up for right: Chinese Gordon leading his men into battle against the Taipings armed only with a cane; Gordon Pasha riding a camel into the camp of Suleiman the slave dealer and putting the man to shame' (p. 12). Here in Khartoum in 1885 was a wonderful lesson for boys of the Empire: 'Gordon ... fitted the image perfectly after his only two English companions left the town in September. As mediated to Australians young and old, Gordon embodied the virtues of the three great imperial types: the warrior, the philanthropist and the missionary' (p. 12). Indeed, for Inglis, 'now he was a martyr. Editors enlarged their papers to mourn him. Clergymen preached sermons on his life and death. Poets grieved' (12). It was not simply a case of one man's demise. For Inglis (1985), 'in the colonies, as at home, the vigorous public mourners were people who disliked Gladstone's government already and who saw the tragedy of Khartoum as caused by its vacillation in London' (p. 12). Inglis shows how in private even devout liberals decried Gladstone's failure to act decisively and in a timely manner in rescuing Gordon.

The 1885 formation of the NSW Sudan Contingent highlighted mixed expressions of patriotism as expressed in New South Wales. In respect to mixed expressions of patriotism, Inglis (1985) describes the central role of Major-General Sir Edward Strickland, retired imperial soldier and prominent Catholic, in the idea of the NSW Contingent by having published in the *Sydney Morning Herald* a letter flagging the idea of a contingent to the Sudan. Dr Andrew Garran, Editor of the *Sydney Morning Herald*, published the letter in order to gauge public opinion for such an adventure. William Bede Dalley, acting premier of New South Wales, also played a central role in having Whitehall approve the sending of the NSW Contingent to the Sudan. Along with analysing the motives of the Contingent's supporters, Inglis then examines the motives of the people in New South Wales who opposed the sending of the Contingent — the pro-Gladstone liberals and the many Catholic Irish in London (1985, p. 14). Even in 1885 patriotism found complex expressions in New South Wales.

Militarism and war in Australian historical fiction

An impartial outside observer could argue that conquest and war have dominated Australian history. Conquest came first in 1788, with the 'assault' on Botany Bay by the British, led by Captain Arthur Phillip with his First Fleet. Then came a series of bloody encounters over the remainder of the Australian continent during the next 100 years or so. Then there was an attempted invasion of far-off Turkey by Anzac troops, under the command of the British. Then followed the other horrific battles of the Great War in Europe, all of which were followed by the battles of the Second World War, and the other wars that followed. Australia's history is, in part, a series of forgotten battles on its own soil and in foreign lands.

Many Australians enjoy reading about their wars, celebrating and remembering them. Successive governments have contributed to our National War Memorial, and scattered throughout Australia in town squares, mechanic institutes, churches, halls, schools, gateways to public ovals, and other places are the thousands of other memorials. But there are few memorials to those who suffered in the wars with Indigenous Australians.

Pride in our past, or militarising our history?

There is a plethora of published works on Australia's involvement in various wars. On the eve of Remembrance Day 2009, Paul Ham wrote in *The Weekend Australian*: 'I'm searching for a collective noun to describe the writers about war. It would help because 15 books have just landed on my desk demanding to be reviewed ahead of Remembrance Day' (2009, p. 18). Indeed, for Ham 'some of these books create legends; others exploit legends. Some are brutally honest and beautifully written; others, formulaic and pedestrian; some wring tears of sorrow from the reader; others leave you cold' (p. 18).

Himself an author of considerable Australian war nonfiction (e.g., Ham, 2007), Ham goes on to declare, 'a "glut" of war writers is no good; it suggests an oversupply, which is misplaced given the public's passing fascination with our martial past' (2009, p. 18). While many Australians may question Ham's use of the word 'passing' there is no doubt about Australians' current fascination for our martial past. To reinforce his message concerning the apparently ever-increasing popularity of war histories in the Australian book industry, Ham's review of five war publications released to coincide with Anzac Day 2010 was headed 'war history is a contested zone' (Ham, 2010, p. 18). A glut there surely is.

In the lead up to Anzac Day, there is usually a book or film, and often both, released to in a carefully programmed market strategy. For example, in mid-April 2010, Jeremy Sim's film *Beneath Hill 60* was released in Australian theatres. It was the story of the exploits of the 1st Australian Tunnellers in tunnelling under Hill 60 on the Western Front in Belgium. In reviewing the film, Evan Williams reminded readers that 'our history is rich in military engagements, crucial battles, charismatic leaders and legendary wartime characters' (Williams, 2010, p. 17). During the first week of the month leading up to Anzac Day 2012, Ashley Ekins's (with Ian McNeill) *Fighting to the Finish: the Australian Army and the Vietnam War (1968-75)* (2012) appeared beside Kevin Blackburn's *The Sportsmen of Changi* (2012).

Every year on 25 April, many Australians pause to remember. At cenotaphs and shrines across cities, at memorials in country towns, and, indeed, on the sandy ridges of Gallipoli, the sweating jungle of Kokoda, and the misty old battlefields of Belgium, some Australians greet the dawn with solemn patriotism. Anzac Day is for many Australians our true and authentic national day (see, for example, *The Australian*, 2010 and J. Green, 2012). But for some, it is a day that evokes ambivalence, rather than pride. Why, some people ask, should we lend such importance to a day glorifying death, savagery and war? What is there to be inspired by when the original landing at Gallipoli was nothing short of a failed attempt to invade Turkey, and a manifest product of British imperial folly?

Two highly respected Australian historians — Henry Reynolds and Marilyn Lake — challenged what they argue is the Anzac myth with their 2010 book, *What's Wrong With Anzac?* For them, the commemoration of Anzac Day involves the militarisation of Australian history. Australia's national self-understanding would be better, they contend, with an acceptance of the Anzac legend as an aberration of Edwardian militarism, and not as a cathartic moment in Australian nationhood.

But while enjoying some support from academic historians, Reynolds and Lake's message is, I argue, drowned out by the march of tens of thousands of feet at dawn services around Australia, and weeping tears of tens of thousands of Australians attending dawn services around the world. It is not surprising, then, that militarism and war feature so forcibly in Australian historical fiction.

The bush warriors as soldiers of the Queen

In accounting for this 'glut' of published works on war, it is useful to return to an examination of the bush warriors as soldiers of the Queen. Richard White makes clear what the 1885 Sudan campaign meant to the Australian colonies: 'At a time when military superiority was accepted as the ultimate measure of national fitness, by far the greatest, most glorious test was war' (1981, p. 72). Indeed, for White, 'the greatest heroes in the colonies, as in Britain, were soldiers of the Empire. When General Gordon was killed in the Sudan in 1885, the colonies went into mourning, Melbourne school-children wrote essays on "General Gordon as Hero" and statues were erected to commemorate his sacrifice to Empire' (1981, p. 72). There were even ramifications: 'James Service, Premier of Victoria, put aside inter-colonial rivalry and said that the Sudan had "precipitated Australia, in one short week, from a geographical expression to a nation"' (Serle, *The Rush to be Rich*, 1971, as cited in R. White, 1981, p. 72).

Rightly, Inglis (1985) titled his study of the dispatch of the NSW Sudan Contingent in 1885 as 'The Rehearsal', for, in retrospect, it was a rehearsal for the Boer War and the Great War that would soon follow. And in this respect Pierce reminds us: 'the "coming race" which he [speaking of Rolf Boldrewood] envisaged would be fit, most of all, for services as "Soldiers of the Queen" in the climactic war which he accurately anticipated. Thus imperial history would subsume Australian history' (1992, p. 308). The new racial type evolving in the Australian colonies had an imperial destiny. Indeed, for Pierce, 'a further dispossession would occur, our literary history — whatever its authentic local subjects — would be unfolded within one stream of the literary history of Britain' (p. 308).

The NSW Sudan Contingent was first and foremost about a drive by New South Wales politicians to link arms with Britain to avenge the death of General Gordon, and curry to the dominant moral outrage then occurring. But it exemplified much more. There would be other wars, and there would be tragic loss of human life on a gigantic scale, but there would also be individual loss, and the loss of individual and national innocence. How is this represented in Australian historical fiction?

War and the loss of innocence in historical fiction

Lamia Tayeb writes of Malouf's *Fly Away Peter*. Jim, a central character in the novel, is a changed man on returning from the trenches of Flanders. As Tayeb puts it:

> Jim's metamorphosis stems from loss … [His] loss is aligned with Australia's lost innocence following involvement in the [Great War], and, is, therefore, associated with the 'childhood' of nature. Through his experiences of exile in the world of the trenches, which is evocative of the hellish image of the Old World, Jim comes to discover the cruel and, by image extension, adult side of his nature … Jim undergoes a painful process of self-discovery; what he experiences, during the war, is not so much the difference of place as it is a more disturbing difference within himself: the world he 'found himself in was unlike anything he had ever known or imagined. It was as if he had taken a wrong turning in his sleep, arrived at the dark side of his head, and got stuck there'. (Tayeb, 2006, p. 179, including quote from *Fly Away Peter*, p. 58)

Like so many novels based on experiences in the Great War, *Fly Away Peter* is about homecoming, and how the individual copes with the experience. In *Fly Away Peter*, Malouf,

> exposes the colonial pre-given conception of landscape and subjectivity, and negotiates a deeper correspondence between them that is based on communion and integration. … [I]t charts a 'homecoming project' that is rather induced by exposure to the centre and a maturing journey from the childhood of the nation to the adulthood of Europe and European history. Reconciliation is again based on the transcendence of present divisions through a direct intercourse (almost an interfusion) with the womb of nature. (Tayeb, 2006, p. 179)

For other novels, the war experience and the homecoming are treated as a form of liberation. In reviewing David Brooks's *The Umbrella Club* (2009), Jose Borghino writes '*The Umbrella Club* is not a World War I novel. Brooks doesn't downplay the horrors of war, but he doesn't dwell on them either. Edward [the principal character] and Axel [Edward's companion] survive the trenches, weary and, yes traumatised, but in some ways the experience opens their eyes' (2009, pp. 14-15). They discover ballooning, and eventually go off to New Albion, an island to the north of Australia on a ballooning adventure.

Xavier Herbert's *Poor Fellow My Country* (1975) won the Miles Franklin Literary Award. It is the story of Jeremy Delacy and his illegitimate grandson, Prindy. It is set during the years leading up to World War Two, and includes some memorable scenes depicting the homefront during the war. It covers matter on Aboriginal affairs, particularly with respect to dispossession, Australian patriotism and nationalism, subjects also dealt with in Herbert's 1938 novel *Capricornia*.

Australian historical novels with war as a backdrop and addressed to a younger audience, increasingly are being used as a medium to give voice to social issues other than war. In respect to feminist history, in *A Rose for the Anzac Boys* (2008), Jackie French demonstrates this through the use of speech and letters throughout the entire novel. A general societal attitude towards women in the early twentieth century is evident in French's novel when Midge is thinking about what her life will be like after the war and is dreaming of the fields of Glen Donal (French, 2008, p. 32). In the passage Midge is aware that it is not socially acceptable for her to be dreaming of running Glen Donal by acknowledging she should be thinking about marriage and children, not running a sheep property in country New Zealand.

'Wars' with the Indigenous Australians

Of the 'glut' of nonfiction dealing with memories of Australian wars, very few dealt with wars between Indigenous/non-Indigenous Australians on Australian soil. First, it is worth noting of traditional methods of warfare in Indigenous Australian society. Dennis et al. write that 'although there were regional variations, the tactics used were generally quite similar across Australia. Aboriginal tactics were almost entirely based on their pre-existing hunting and fighting practices' (1995, p. 4). Consequently, 'this raises the question of why Aboriginal people, unlike indigenous people in New Zealand and North America, did not radically adapt their fighting techniques to changed circumstances' (p. 5):

> it is not enough to point to the absence in Aboriginal society of the concept of war as understood by Europeans: in the nineteenth century the Zulus of South Africa were able to achieve a military revolution which took them in a short time to from small-scale fighting like that of Australian Aborigines to mass warfare involving conquest ... nor is it sufficient to identify Aboriginal 'conservatism' as the reason why they did not adapt their military tactics. Aboriginal culture had changed before and would change again in many ways after the invasion. (Dennis et al, 1995, p. 6)

For Indigenous Australians, fighting was a highly ritualised, rule-governed activity. It had to be in order to preserve their population. Moreover, their military resources came from the land, and were not produced in factories. They simply did not have an economic base for sustained warfare in the Western sense.

But occasionally, Indigenous Australians did attack whites in relatively open country, and something like a conventional battle ensued. Here, the Indigenous Australians tried to take advantage of their superior numbers, advancing in crescent formation, perhaps with the aim of outflanking and surrounding the invading Europeans. Once they learnt not to break ranks in the face of gunfire, attacking *en masse* they could sometimes be quite effective, particularly before the improvements in firearms technology that occurred following the Crimean War (1853-56). At times disciplined groups of fighters could wait for the first volley of shots then hurl their spears while the invading force was reloading. Yet, 'open battle was usually more costly to Blacks than to Whites, and as their numerical advantage disappeared Aborigines generally abandoned it' (Dennis et al., 1995, p. 6). For Dennis et al., 'perhaps the most famous battle was that at Battle Mountain near Cloncurry, Queensland in 1884, which resulted in an overwhelming defeat of the ... [Kalkadoon] people and put an end to their six-year war against the invader' (p. 6).

Indigenous Australian/Europeans battles/massacres and skirmishes in historical fiction

Very early Australian historical novelists used the frontier violence between European settlers and the Indigenous Australian custodians of the land as critical and defining events in their novels. For example, Nettlebeck writes:

> When violence erupted in April 1841 between overlanders bringing stock from NSW and the Maraura people of the upper Murray districts between Lake Bonney, Lake Victoria and the Rufus River near the two colonies' border, public attention was readily captured. The previous year, settler anxiety about the potential for Aboriginal 'aggression' had been sparked by a case — the Maria massacre, in which twenty six Europeans from the shipwrecked brig Maria were killed by the

Milmenrura people along the Coorong's coastline — which would later become mythologised as exemplary of the sufferings and risks of pioneer life…

As well as being retold, in numerous versions, in settler memoirs and stories, this event became immortalised in Simpson Newland's popular historical fiction *Paving the Way: A Romance of the Australian Bush* (1893) (Nettlebeck, 1999)

Of course, postcolonial history and historical fiction have exposed these myths, and often describe the colonial frontier as a brutal place where raids and reprisals were common place as colonists fought to establish pastoral or mining industries.

The Battle for Battle Mountain and the events leading to it, along with the Kalkadoon society and culture are described in Grassby and Hill's *Six Australian Battlefields* (1988) and David Lowe's *Forgotten Rebels: Black Australians who fought back* (1994). This work seeks to explode the myths associated with Australia's supposed 'peaceful' settlement.

* * *

Spurred on by Australia Day celebrations, and reflected in the number of publications, there is a rising demand for nonfiction convict histories. Moreover, it is a history subject to almost constant revision. There is also a demand for the publishing of historical novels with convicts as subject matter. Like their nonfiction cousins, historical novels portraying convict history have undergone changes during the century and half of their writing: from Clarke's *His Natural Life* through to Grenville's *Sarah Thornhill*. This is a genre reflecting national aspirations, moods and anxieties. Here was a continuing link with Australia's convict heritage, and this has been reflected in many Australian historical novels.

The term 'landscape' — colonial landscape — loomed as a troubled term in postcolonial discourse in Australian history and literature. It was a landscape appropriated by Europeans. This chapter has provided an opportunity to examine the metaphorical use of the word 'landscape'. Of course, this was the means by which Europeans appropriated the land they were settling — land cared for by Indigenous Australians for tens of thousands of years. These, postcolonial and postmodernists ideas also are reflected in historical novels as they have been in nonfictional interpretations of Australian history.

During the early history of the Australian historical novel, and only challenged with the onset of postcolonial histories, there had been a plethora of published histories extolling the virtues of pastoral Australia. The strong social stratification of pastoral society was rarely examined by historians and historical novelists. Typically, these were the historical sagas. But over recent decades, much has changed. Histories dealing with capitalising 'their' land — the construction of home in the white settler memory of the past — provide a powerful means in historical novels to re-examine the process and purpose of pastoralism, as seen in the way in which homesteads feature in Australian historical novels. This is all a part of unwrapping the myths of pastoral Australia and romancing property and society in pastoral Australia.

Patriotism is a troubled term, and the meaning of which has undergone many changes as Australian society and culture evolves. With the rising tide of nationalism in Australia during the decades leading up to the Great War, patriotism was nurtured in the fledgling universities of the colonies. An excellent example of this is W.C. Wentworth and his role in the University of Sydney.

To a large extent, the Australian Legend defined patriotism and nationalism, as the Australian 'warrior' from the bush developed and was to eventually take his place in the world's terrible twentieth-century conflagrations. As a prelude to all of this, patriotism was nurtured in the Australian colony of New South Wales in the anti-Mahdi fervour following the murder of General Gordon in far off Khartoum.

From evidence advanced by Ham (2009), I have attempted to illustrate how Australians love their military histories, perhaps in fictional form more than in its more traditional form. In the recent research by Reynolds and Lake — published as *What's Wrong With Anzac?* — the two prominent historians identify what they contend to be the problematic virtues of Anzac myth in contemporary Australia.

The bush warriors, as soldiers of the Queen, first tasted the excitement of being armed and trained, departing for foreign shores for a military campaign in the inglorious 1885 Sudan Campaign. But as this was occurring, other terrible battles were being fought on Australian soil, for example in outback Queensland — a war without monuments, despite the fact that this battle involved the only recorded cavalry charge in Australian history. Perhaps one day tourists will wander through our National War Memorial to observe the Kalkadoons of Western Queensland, an example of fierce Indigenous Australians and their battle for their Battle Mountain.

Conclusion

Taken as a part or as a whole, once teachers have used historical novels and their sub-genres as a teaching/learning strategy in their History lessons, they come to appreciate the huge contribution they can make to their students' appreciation of history. Many students immediately engage with their historical novels, and this is, I suggest, not surprising.

Historical novels currently enjoy huge popularity amongst the readership of the Australian public, as does children's historical fiction through the writings of such fine authors as Jackie French. While some commentators may lament this rising tide of popularity for historical fiction, with the onset of the National History Curriculum, History teachers in Australian schools are poised to make full use of the genre in their pedagogy. Certainly, this is the message given at recent HTAA conferences. The use of historical novels in the classroom is more than a device simply to pique the interest of History students, who may otherwise be losing their interest in the topic being taught. Historical novels are able to provide deep understanding of historical events and personages, as well as assisting in the development of historical literacy.

The field of historical novels and its sub-genres is ever increasing, and at the same time greatly enriching the historical understanding of readers. This provides a marvellous opportunity for the teachers of History from the beginning of schooling through to the senior years.

While long gaining the attention of historians and historical novelists, the apparently vexed relationship between history and historical novels is being re-evaluated by teachers of History, as they grow in confidence in responding to the imperatives of the ACARA History, and as they recognise the need to develop engaging teaching/learning experiences for their students. Witness the contribution historical novelists make to history conferences around the world. Here are very serious historiographical questions, often concerned with the historians' use of facts, and the general question of 'what is history?' Enthusiasts of the use of historical fiction as a pedagogical strategy in the History curriculum will confirm its special role in generating imagination in our students, and most History teachers will relate how this an important objective or ideal in the teaching of History. Indeed, some History teachers will go as far to say imagination and a sense of wonder are the principal aims in the teaching of History.

Engaging in a narrative is a unique and personal experience for the reader — as well as the author. Indeed, this matchless and precious relationship between the author and the reader of historical fiction forms the basis of a powerful pedagogy — students are able to engage with contentious issues, points of view in a historical context. Since the 1980s, generally, massive changes have come over Australian classrooms in the form of 'the new pedagogies' / constructivist pedagogy and essential learnings. By the second decade of the twenty-first century, many Australian teachers have a new confidence in progressive methods in the classroom. Consequently, many teachers across all grades as they work towards the new national History curriculum are looking to the teaching historical literacy through historical novels.

Teachers of History are now realising historical novels can be used in the classroom in ways textbooks have been long found to be wanting. This is no more so than in developing an understanding of historical agency, something which ought to be a major objective in the teaching of History. Typically, textbooks obscure issues of agency, as they often do with masking the voice of minority social and cultural groups. Textbooks do so by presenting the past as the result of abstract and impersonal forces appearing beyond human control. Teachers are now being encouraged to interrogate a historical novel for historical agency, using interrogation criteria long found to be successful in History lessons.

In the same manner, teachers embrace historical novels because of the way in which they link the past to the present and the future. Researchers have found historical novels assist in understanding history as the 'extended present', rather than as a chronological series of events — the past, present and future — thus enhancing their understanding of the historical process. Because of the personal nature of the narrative — the author sharing something unique with the reader — historical novels often provide a narrative allowing for intersecting and often conflicting narratives. For example, how can we best deal with contentious topics such as asylum seekers, the so-called 'boat people'? I argue that historical novels are an ideal way to present manifold voices on such a topic. This ideal is all about using historical novels to connect and engage with students. Engaging students with quality historical novels enhances their historical understanding — as well as their understanding of present issues from various points of view — through a number of metacognition reading strategies

Historical novels, as with memory, assist in ameliorating social and cultural groups who have tragic collective memories. This helps to explain the rise in popularity of the historical novel, as well as pointing to one reason for its usefulness as a pedagogical device in the teaching of history. Historical novels provide access to the inner workings of the human psyche, furnishing their universal appeal.

Teachers of History are now realising that adult historical fiction, along with historical fiction written for younger readers, now encompasses an open honesty, pulling few punches, and avoiding sugarcoating treatment of difficult topics. Authors now openly deal with gender issues, race issues, and a host of other difficult issues, discussing them openly and transparently.

Particularly in the senior grades, teachers of History are realising the value of the use of counterfactual history, particularly in respect to deepening students' understanding of historiography. Through asking deliberate 'what if …?' questions, teachers can probe the historiography of a particular topic or issue in history. Thus, students are led to think of history as being a chance affair. As odd as it might sound, when students understand this, they have developed considerable capacities of historical literacy.

References

Adams, H. (2001) 'Bringing History into the Classroom', *Classroom*, 21, 7, pp. 10-14.

Adams, H. (2004) 'Using Historical Fiction in the Classroom', *Classroom*, 24, 6 pp. 8-10, http://search.informit.com.au.ezproxy.cdu.edu.au/fullText;dn=138755;res=AEIPT (retrieved 14 September 2010).

Alternate History Discussion Board (n.d.) http://www.alternatehistory.com/discussion/showthread.php?t=99061 (retrieved 16 July 2011).

Alternatives: AH Directory (n.d.) 'The Australian War of Independence (David Atwell) An independence crisis emerges in Australia in 1975', http://www.alternatehistory.com/ahdirectory.html (retrieved 12 July 2011).

Althistory Wiki (n.d.) 'Commonwealth of Australia and New Zealand (1983-Doomsday)' http://althistory.wikia.com/wiki/Commonwealth_of_Australia_and_New_Zealand_(1983:_Doomsday) (retrieved 14 July 2011).

Anderson, D. (2008) 'Dark Heart of Desire', *The Australian*, 8 November, http://www.theaustralian.com.au/news/richard-flanagan-wanting/story-e6frg8no-1111117941468 (retrieved 20 November 2009).

Anderson, W. (2002) *The Cultivation of Whiteness: science, health, and racial destiny in Australia*, Melbourne, MUP.

Apol, L.S., S. Aki, T.M. Reynolds, & S.K. Rop (2003) '"When Can We Make Paper Cranes?": examining preservice teachers' resistance to critical readings of historical fiction', *Journal of Literacy Research*, 31, no. 4, pp. 429-464.

Armstrong, J. (1999) 'Truth in Storytelling', *Riverbank Review* (Summer), pp. 14-16.

Atwood, Margaret (1998) 'In Search of *Alias Grace*: On Writing Canadian Historical Fiction', *The American Historical Review (AHR Forum: Histories and Historical Fictions)*, 103, no. 5 (December), pp. 1503-1516.

Australian Historical Association (AHA) (n.d.) http://www.theaha.org.au/conferences/aha_conferences.htm (retrieved 15 July 2011).

Banivanua, T. & J. Evans (eds), *Writing Colonial Histories: comparative perspectives*, University of Melbourne, Department of History, 2002, http://search.informit.com.au/documentSummary;dn=743609709909884;res=IELHSS (retrieved 6 November 2009).

Bantick, C. (2012) 'Schools Become the Dustbin of History', *The Age* (Melbourne), 5 March.

Bateman, D. & C. Harris (2008) 'Time Perspectives: examining the past, present and futures', in C. Marsh (ed.), *Studies of Society and Environment: Exploring the Teaching Possibilities* (5th edn) Sydney, Pearson Education.

Battle of Vinegar Hill Memorial (n.d.) http://www.blacktown.nsw.gov.au/our-city/history/the-region/vinegar-hill_home.cfm (retrieved 24 April 2010).

Beston, J. (2007) 'Mythmaking in Patrick White's Novels', *AUMLA*, vol. 107.

Beston, J.B. (1973) 'An Interview with Thomas Keneally', *World Literature Written in English*, 12, p. 55.

Birch, C. (2012) 'Review, That Deadman's Dance', *The Guardian*, 7

December, http://www.guardian.co.uk/books/2012/dec/07/that-deadman-dance-kim-scott-review (retrieved 17 March 2013).

Bird, C. (2009) 'Past Master', *The Australian Literary Review*, 3 June, p. 20.

Birns, N. (2005) 'Receptacle or Reversal? Globalization Down Under in Marcus Clarke's *His Natural Life*', *College Literature*, 32, No. 2, Spring, pp. 127-145.

Birns, N. & R. McNeer (2007) *A Companion to Australian Literature since 1900*, Rochester, N.Y., Camden House.

Blainey, G. (2011) 'Australian Stories', *Weekend Australian Review*, 5-6 November, pp. 21-22.

Boldrewood, R. (2005) *Robbery Under Arms*, Scoresby, Vic., The Five Mile Press.

Borghino, J. (2009) 'Poetic Vehicle Carries Heavy Moral Freight', *Weekend Australian Review*, 3-4 October, pp. 12-13.

Bracey, P., A. Gove-Humphries & D. Jackson (2006) 'Refugees and evacuees: enhancing historical understanding through Irish historical fiction with Key Stage 2 and early Key Stage 3 pupils', *Education 3-13*, 34, no. 2, pp. 103-112.

Bradley, J. (2009) 'Once Upon a Time in America', *Weekend Australian Review*, 31 October-1 November, pp. 19-20.

Bradley, J. (2011a) 'Remembering What History Forgets', *Weekend Australian Review*, August 20, pp. 20-21.

Bradley, J. (2011b) 'Caught in Time's Cruel Machinery', *Weekend Australian Review*, 26-27 November, p. 22-23.

Brady, V. (1979) 'The Most Frightening Rebellion: the recent novels of Thomas Keneally', *Meanjin*, 38, pp. 74-86.

Brantlinger, P. (1998) *Rule of Darkness: British literature and imperialism, 1830-1914*, Ithaca, Cornell University Press.

Breslin, B. (1992) *Extermination with Pride: Aboriginal-European relations in the Townsville-Bowen Region to 1869*, Dept of History and Politics, James Cook University.

Brewer, M. (2007) 'Using Novel Studies in the Classroom', *Teacher Timesavers*, http://teachertimesavers.com/Novels%20in%20Classroom.pdf (retrieved 24 April 2010).

Bristow, J. (1991) *Empire Boys: Adventures in a Man's World*, London, Harper Collins.

Britt J. (n.d.), Historical fiction in the next generation's method of how we learn about history, *Ezine @rticles*, http://ezinearticles.com/?Historical-Fiction-Is-the-Next-Generations-Method-of-How-We-Learn-About-History&id=4691875 (retrieved 24 April 2010).

Brodie, J. (1996) *Going for the Gold*, Environmental Education and Volunteer Programs, http://www.blm.gov/education/going_4_the_gold/classroom.html (retrieved 24 April 2010).

Bulhof, J. (1999) 'What If? modality and history, *History and Theory*, 38, pp. 145-168.

Bunzl, M. (2004) 'Counterfactual History: a user's guide', *American Historical Review*, 109, no. 3, pp. 845-858.

Burchell, D. (2009) 'Fresh Refuge for Patriots', *Weekend Australian Review*, 17-18 October, p. 24.

Byrnes, P. (2009) 'Review Van Diemen's Land', *Sydney Morning Herald*, 28 September, http://www.smh.com.au/news/entertainment/film/film-reviews/van-diemens-land/2009/09/28/1253989859814.html (retrieved 13 March 2013).

Caddie, 1976 (n.d.) Australian Screen, http://aso.gov.au/titles/features/caddie/ (retrieved 2 November 2011).

Campbell, F. (2008) 'History as Fiction', *The Australian*, 1 March, http://www.theaustralian.com.au/news/history-as-fiction/story-e6frg8kf-1111115651259 (retrieved 25 February 2010).

Carey, P. (1998) *Oscar and Lucinda*, St Lucia, UQP.

Carr, E.H. (1987) *What is History?* (2nd edn) Penguin, London.

Carroll, K. (2009) 'Picture Books, Perspectives & Pedagogy: using historical fiction in stages 4 and 5 History', paper presented at the NSWHTA State Conference, 2 May 2009, http://www.kaycarroll.org/uploads/3/0/4/6/3046475/picture_pedagogyfinish.pdf (retrieved 14 June 2011).

Cathcart, M. (1999) 'Exploration by land' in G. Davison, J. Hirst, S. MacIntyre (eds) *The Oxford Companion to Australian History*, Melbourne, OUP.

Cato, N. (1983) *Forefathers*, London, New English Library.

Chamberlain, G. (1986) 'Afterword: allohistory in science fiction', in C.G. Waugh & M.H. Greenberg (eds) *Alternative Histories: Eleven Stories of the World as It Might Have Been*, New York, Garland, pp. 281-300.

Chandler, A. Bertram (1983) *Kelly Country*, New York, Daw Books.

Clark, A. (2008) *History's Children: history wars in the classroom*, Sydney, UNSW Press.

Clarke, R. (2006) 'Truth, History, and Fiction: History and Historical Fiction in the Contemporary Australian Public Sphere', UNAUSTRALIA, Proceedings, Annual Conferences Cultural Studies Association of Australia, Canberra, http://www.unaustralia.com/electronicpdf/Uncraik.pdf (retrieved 2 December 2009).

Clarke, S. (2008) 'Still Not Settled', *The Australian*, 1 October, http://www.theaustralian.com.au/news/arts/still-not-settled/story-e6frg8px-1111117565650 (retrieved 20 November 2009).

Clarke, S. (2011) 'Kate Grenville creates a personal history in a colonial setting', *Weekend Australian Review*, 27-28 August, pp. 18-19.

Clendinnen, I. (1996) 'Fellow Sufferers: history and imagination', *Australian Humanities Review*, http://www.australianhumanitiesreview.org/archive/Issue-Sept-1996/clendinnen.html (retrieved 2 December 2009).

Clendinnen, I. (2003) *Dancing with Strangers*, Melbourne, Text Publishing.

Clendinnen, I. (2006) 'The History Question: who owns the past', *Quarterly Essay*, 23.

Clendinnen, I. (2007) 'The History Question: response to correspondence', *Quarterly Essay*, 23.

Clendinnen, I. (2008) 'Blurb', in Anna Clark (2008) *History's Children: history wars in the classroom*, Sydney, UNSW Press.

Clendinnen, I. (2011) 'Stirring Stories in the White Pages', *Weekend Australian Review*, February 19-20, pp. 28-29.

Clode, D. (2002) *Killers in Eden*, Sydney, Allen & Unwin.

Club Troppo (n.d.) Australian Alternate History Week, http://clubtroppo.com.au/2010/09/01/australian-alternate-history-week/ (retrieved 12 July 2011).

Cohen, S. & L.M. Shires (1998) *Telling Stories: a theoretical analysis of narrative fiction*, London, Routledge.

Collins, F. (2008) 'Historical Fiction and the Allegorical Truth of Colonial Violence in *The Proposition*', *Cultural Studies Review*, March 1, pp. 55-71.

Collins, W.J. (1990) 'Paths Not Taken: the development, structure, and aesthetics of alternative history', PhD dissertation, University of California.

Cooper, H. (2002) *History in the Early Years* (2nd edn), Routledge, London.

Cosic, M. (2011) 'A History in Fiction', *Weekend Australian Magazine*, 25-26 August, pp. 5-6.

Coulthard-Clark, C. (1998) *The Encyclopaedia of Australia's Battles*, Sydney, Allen & Unwin.

Courtney, B. (1999) *Solomon's Song*, Melbourne, Viking.

Crawford, P. & V. Zygouris-Coe (2008) 'Those Were the Days: Learning About History Through Literature', *Childhood Education*, 84, no. 4, p. 197.

Critical Dialogue (1997) Stuart Macintyre, 'The genie in the bottle: putting history back into the school curriculum', Alan Barcan, 'History in a pluralist culture: responses to Stuart Macintyre', Stuart Macintyre, 'Rejoinder to Alan Barcan', *Australian Journal of Education*, 41, no. 2, pp. 189-215.

Croome, A. (2011) 'Cloak and Dagger with a Conscience', 9-10 July, pp. 28-29.

Curthoys, A. (2006) 'Is History Fiction?', *Q History*, 44, 2, pp. 10-17.

Curthoys, A. & J. Docker (2010) *Is History Fiction?* (2nd ed.), Sydney, UNSW Press.

Dalton, H. Scott (2006) 'What is Historical Fiction?' Vision: a resource for writers, http://fmwriters.com/Visionback/Issue34/historicalfic.htm (retrieved 21 May 2011).

Damico, J., M. Baildon & D. Greenstone (2010) 'Examining How Historical Agency Works in Children's Literature', *Social Studies Research and Practice*, 5, no. 1, pp. 1-12.

Darian-Smith, K. (2003) *Australia*, London, Belinda Press.

Davies, S. (1996) 'Interpreting Contextualities', *Philosophy and Literature*, 20, pp. 20-38.

Davis, K.S. (1998) 'Postmodern Blackness', *Twentieth Century Literature*, 4, no. 2, p. 245.

Davison, G. (1983) 'The City Bred Child and Urban Reform in Melbourne, 1900-1940', in P. Williams (ed.) *Social Process and the City*, Sydney, Allen & Unwin.

Davison, G. (1998a) 'Environment' in G. Davison, J. Hirst, S. MacIntyre (eds) *The Oxford Companion to Australian History*, Melbourne, OUP.

Davison, G. (1998b) 'Kindergarten', in G. Davison, J. Hirst & S. MacIntyre (eds) *The Oxford Companion to Australian History*, Melbourne, OUP.

Demos, J. (1998) 'In Search of Reasons for Historians to Read Novels…' *The American Historical Review, (AHR Forum: Histories and Historical Fictions)*, 103, no. 5 (December): pp. 1526-1529.

Dennis, P., J. Grey, E. Morris, R. Prior & J. Connor (1995) *The Oxford Companion to Australian Military History*, Melbourne, OUP.

Dirlik, A. (2002a) 'Revolution in History and Memory: the politics of cultural revolution in historical perspective', in D. Jurago and M. K. Booker, *Rereading Global Socialist Culture After the Cold War: the Reassessment of Tradition*, New York, Praeger Publishing.

Dirlik, A. (2002b) 'Whither History? Encounters with Historicism: postmodernism and postcolonialism', *Futures*, 34, no. 1, February, pp. 75-90.

Dixon, R. (1986) 'Rolf Boldrewood's *War to the Knife*: Narrative Form and Ideology in the Historical Novel', *Australian Literary Studies*, 12, no. 3, May, pp. 324-334.

Dixon, R. (1995) *Writing the Colonial Adventure: race, gender and nation in Anglo-Australian popular fiction, 1875-1914*, Melbourne, CUP.

Donelson, K.L. & A.P. Nilsen (1997) *Literature in Today's Young Adults* (5th edn), New York, Addison Wesley/Longman.

Drane, R. (2008) *Fighters by Trade: a highlights of Australian boxing*, Sydney, Harper Collins.

Dutton, G. (1985) *The Australian Collection: Australia's greatest books*, North Ryde, NSW, A&R.

Dwyer, J. & J. Caughey (2007) *Let's Read History*, Melbourne, Wizard Ideas.

Easton, M., S. Shapman, D. Young, M. Saldais and P. van Noorden (2004) *SOSE Alive 2*, Milton, Qld, John Wiley & Sons.

Edmonds, C. (1977) *Caddie, A Sydney Barmaid* (D. Cusack introduction), Melbourne, Sun Books.

Eggert, P. & E. Webby (n.d.) '*Robbery Under Arms*: Rolf Boldrewood', http://hass.unsw.adfa.edu.au/ASEC/completed_projects/academy_editions_aus_lit/titles/RUA_Blurb.html (retrieved 27 August 2009).

Elks, S. & B. Packham (2012), 'States Rewrite History Lessons', *The Weekend Australian*, 29-30 September.

Erlandson, B. & J. Bainsbridge (2001) 'Living History Through Canadian Time-Slip Fantasy', vol. 3, 2, pp. 1-11, https://ejournals.library.ualberta.ca/index.php/langandlit/article/view/17654/14011 (retrieved 27 November 2011).

Falconer, D. (2006) 'Historical Novels', *Eureka Street*, July, http://www.eurekastreet.com.au/article.aspx?aeid=1298 (retrieved 3 October 2009).

'Fatal Shore Author Robert Hughes Dies at 74', (2012) *Sydney Morning Herald*, 7 August, http://www.smh.com.au/entertainment/art-and-design/fatal-shore-author-robert-hughes-dies-at-74-20120807-23r0l.html (retrieved 13 March 2013).

Fentress, J. & C. Wickham (1992) *Social Memory: new perspectives on the past*, Oxford, UK/Cambridge, US, Blackwell.

Ferguson, N. (1997a) 'Introduction: Virtual History: Towards a 'chaotic' theory of the past', in Niall Ferguson (ed.) *Virtual History: alternatives and counterfactuals*, London, Picador.

Ferguson, N. (1997b) 'Afterword: A Virtual History, 1646-1996', in Niall Ferguson (ed.) *Virtual History: alternatives and counterfactuals*, London, Picador.

Ferguson, N. (ed.) (1997) *Virtual History: alternatives and counterfactuals*, London, Picador.

Ferguson, N. (2011) 'History has never been so unpopular', *The Guardian*, 29 March, http://www.guardian.co.uk/education/2011/mar/29/history-school-crisis-disconnected-events (retrieved 28 October 2011).

Ferrari, J. (2010) 'Letters, Sounds at Core of New Curriculum, *The Australian*, 25 February.

Fitzgerald, R. (2011) 'Revisionist Look at a Fleeting History', *Weekend Australian Review*, February 19-20, p. 29.

Fogel, R.W. (1964) *Railroads and American Economic Growth*, Baltimore, MD, Johns Hopkins University Press.

Follett, K. (2010) *The Fall of Giants*, London, Pan Books.

Follett, K. (1989) *The Pillars of the Earth*, London, Macmillan.

Frank, Anne, *The Diary of a Young Girl: The Definitive Edition*, O.H. Frank and M. Pressler (eds) (1947/91), Susan Massotty (Translator), New York, Doubleday.

Fraser, M. (2011) 'Review, That Deadman's Dance', *Sydney Morning Herald*, 13 January, http://www.smh.com.au/entertainment/books/that-deadman-dance-20110113-19p63.html (retrieved 17 March 2013).

Frederic, J. (1977) 'Ideology, Narrative Analysis and Popular Culture', *Theory and Society*, 4, pp. 543-559.

Freeman, E. (1988) 'Recreating the Past: historical fiction in social studies curriculum', *The Elementary School Journal*, 88, no. 4, pp. 23-33.

French, J. (1994) *Somewhere Around the Corner*, Sydney, Harper Collins.

French, J. (2007) 'History is the Best Adventure: now, where can we put the mummies?' *Teacher: the national education magazine*, 181, pp. 59-63.

French, J. (2008) *A Rose for the Anzac Boys*, Sydney, Harper Collins.

French, J. (2010) 'Turning History into Stories and Stories into History — Subtitle: What We can learn from Queen Victoria's Underpants', History Teachers' Association of Australia Conference, Sydney, http://www.historyteacher.org.au/htdocs/conferences/2010/programdetails.htm#dennett (retrieved 14 June 2011).

Funnell, L. (2012) 'Robert Drewe, *Our Sunshine*, Review', *The Newtown Review of Books*, http://newtownreviewofbooks.com/2012/02/11/robert-drewe-our-sunshine/ (retrieved 29 May 2013).

Gaddis, J.L. (2002) *The Landscape of History: how historians map the past*, New York, OUP.

Gaile, A. (2005) *Fabulating Beauty: perspectives on the fiction of Peter Carey*, Amsterdam, Rodopi.

Galda, L. & B.E. Cullinan (2002) *Literature and the Child* (5th edn), Belmont, Wadsworth.

Gillin, T. (2012) 'Ned's last stand not a solo affair', *Weekend Australian Review*, 24-25 March, pp. 22-23.

Gore, J. (2001) 'Pedagogy Rediscovered', *Curriculum Support*, vol. 6, no. 1, \\uofa\users$\users1\a1603421\Desktop\Pedagogy rediscovered.mht (retrieved 13 April 2011).

Graham, J. (2005) 'Essential Learnings', AEU — Victoria, http://www.aeuvic.asn.au/professional/papers/Essential_Learnings/ (retrieved 12 February 2008).

Grassby, A. & M. Hill (1988) *Six Australian Battlefields*, Angus & Robertson, Sydney.

Green, E. (2008) *Adam's Empire*, Heatherton, Vic., Hinkler Books.

Green, J. (2012) 'Anzac Day is about their deaths, not our lives', *The Drum*, ABC Online, http://www.abc.net.au/news/2012-04-25/green-anzac-day-lest-we-forget/3971574 (retrieved 17 March 2013).

Greene, M. (1995) *Releasing the Imagination: essays on Education and the Arts, and social change*, San Francisco, Jossey-Bass Publishers.

Grenville K. (2005), interview with Ramona Koval, *Books and Writing*, ABC Radio National, 17 July.

Griffiths, T. (1989) '"Cultural History of Melbourne": the culture of Nature writing in Victoria, 1880-1945', *Historical Studies*, 23, no. 93, pp. 339-65.

Groce, E. & R. Groce (2005) 'Authenticating Historical Fiction: rationale and process', *Education Research and Perspectives*, 32, no. 1 p.p. 99-119; June 2005, http://search.informit.com.au.ezproxy.cdu.edu.au/fullText;dn=145850;res=AEIPT (retrieved 14 September 2010).

Grossman, L. (2010) 'In Favour of Ripping Yarns', *The Weekend Australian Review*, 16-17 January, pp. 16-17.

Ham, P. (2007) *Vietnam: the Australian war*, Sydney, Harper Collins.

Ham, P. (2009) 'Beyond Myth: heroism and self-sacrifice are perennial themes of Remembrance Day', *Weekend Australian Review*, 7-8 November, pp. 18-19.

Ham, P. (2010) 'The First Casualty: war history is a contested zone', *Weekend Australian Review*, 7-8 November, p. 18.

Hamilton, K.G. (ed.) (1978) *Studies in the Recent Australian Novel*, St Lucia, UQP.

Hamilton, P. (2003) 'Imaginary Histories', seminar (with Kate Grenville, Andy Kissane and Diana Simmonds), University of Technology, Sydney, 15 August.

Hancock, M.R. (2004) *A Celebration of Literature and Responses: children, books, and teachers in k-8 classrooms* (2nd edn), Upper Saddle River, NJ, Merrill/Prentice Hall.

Harris-Hart, C. (2008) 'History or SOSE: Where to Know?' *Curriculum Perspectives*, 28, no. 1, pp. 75-82.

Harrison, D. (2010) 'History curriculum "could fail"', *The Age* (Melbourne), http://www.theage.com.au/national/education/history-curriculum-could-fail-20100228-pb7q.html (retrieved 24 April 2010).

Harrison, J. (1992) *Timothy's Teddy*, Harper Collins, London.

Hasluck, N. (2011) *Dismissal*, Sydney, Fourth Estate.

Healy, T. & P. Cropper (1994) *Out of the Shadows: mystery animals of Australia*, Sydney, Ironbark.

Hedeen, J. (2010) 'Teaching with Historical Fiction: Why teach with Historical Fiction?', http://www.indianahistory.org/teachers-students/teachers/teacher-resources/lesson-ideas/WHYTEA.PDF (retrieved 13 September 2010).

Hellekson, K. (2001) *The Alternate History: refiguring historical time*, Kent, Ohio, Kent State University Press.

Henningham, N. (2002) 'A Mother of Heroes For Our New Home: representations of white women as victims of frontier violence in Colonial North Queensland', in T. Banivanua and J. Evans (eds) *Writing Colonial Histories: comparative perspectives*, University of Melbourne, Department of History http://search.informit.com.au/documentSummary;dn=743609709909884;res=IELHSS (retrieved 6 November 2009).

Hergenhan, L.T. (1983/1993) *Unnatural Lives: studies in Australian fiction about convicts*, St Lucia, UQP.

Herz, S. (2010) 'Using Historical Fiction in the History Classroom', Yale-

New Haven Teachers Institute, http://www.yale.edu/ynhti/curriculum/units/1981/cthistory/81.ch.10.x.html (retrieved 14 May 2010).

Heseltine, H.P. (1964) 'Australian Fiction Since 1920', in G. Dutton (ed.) *The Literature of Australia*, Ringwood, Vic., Penguin.

Hickman, J. (2001) 'Truth as Patchwork: developing female characters in historical fiction', in S. Lehr (ed.) *Beauty, Brains and Brawn: the construction of gender in children's literature*, Portsmouth, Heinemann.

Hicks, A. & D. Martin (1997) 'Teaching English and History Through Historical Fiction', *Children's Literature in Education*, 28, 2, pp. 49-59.

Hill, E. (1948) *My Love Must Wait*, Angus & Robertson, Sydney.

Hirst, J. (2005) *Sense and Nonsense in Australian History*, Melbourne, Black Inc.

Hirst, J.B. (1978) 'The Pioneer Legend', *Journal of Historical Studies*, 18, pp. 316-337.

Historical Novel Society (n.d.) http://www.historicalnovelsociety.org/definition.htm (retrieved 15 July 2011).

HistoricalNovelsinfo, http://www.historicalnovels.info/Australasia.html (retrieved 3 March 2011).

Hodge, B. & V. Misha (1991) *Dark Side of the Dream: Australian literature and the postcolonial mind*, North Sydney, Allen & Unwin.

Hoge, J. (1988) *Teaching history in the elementary classroom*, ERIC Clearinghouse for Social Studies/Social Science Education, http://www.ericdigests.org/pre-928/history.htm (retrieved December 12 2009).

Holderhead, S. (2012) 'Humanities takes a hit: students decide maths adds up', *The Advertiser* (Adelaide), 27 March.

Hopkins, G. (2009) *Timeline of Historical Fiction*, Education World: The educators best friend, http://www.educationworld.com/a_lesson/03/

lp301-03.shtml (retrieved 10 March 2011).

Howard, J. (2006) 'Australia Day Address to the National Press Club, Parliament House, Canberra', Australianpolitics.com, http://australianpolitics.com/news/2006/01/06-01-25_howard.shtml (retrieved 24 April 2008).

HTAA (2010) February Newsletter.

HTAA (2010) March Newsletter.

HTAA National History Conference, 2010, conference program details, http://www.historyteacher.org.au/htdocs/conferences/2010/programdetails.htm#dennett (retrieved 14 May 2011).

Huggan, G. (2007) *Australian Literature: postcolonialism, racism, transnationalism*, Melbourne, OUP.

Hunt, L. (1998) '"No Longer an Evenly Flowing River": Time, History, and the Novel', *The American Historical Review (AHR Forum: Histories and Historical Fictions)*, 103, no. 5 (December): pp. 1517-1521.

Hutchinson, G. (2006) 'The Great War', *Sydney Morning Herald*, 13 November http://www.smh.com.au/news/book-reviews/the-great-war/2006/11/13/1163266443502.html (retrieved 14 May 2011).

Independent Australia (n.d.) 'Anti-government bias', http://www.independentaustralia.net/tag/murdoch-media-bias/ (retrieved 16 July 2011).

Inglis, K.S. (1970) *C.E.W. Bean: Australian historian*, St Lucia, UQP.

Inglis, K.S. (1985) *The Rehearsal*, Adelaide, Rigby.

Jenkins, K. (1991) *Re-Thinking History*, London, Routledge.

Johnson, S. (2002) 'What Are the Rules for Historical Fiction?' http://www.historicalnovelsociety.org/historyic.htm (retrieved 4 September 2009).

Juers, E. (2011) 'Ambitious Expeditions to the Interior', *Weekend Australian Review*, 19-20 November, p. 22.

Keneally, T. (1972/1978) *The Chant of Jimmie Blacksmith*, Sydney, Fontana.

Keneally, T. (1975) 'Doing Research for Historical Novels, *Australian Author*, 7, 1, p. 27.

Kersey Group (2010) Interview (29 July), (pseudonym) a group of three practicing principals, Inveresk.

King, S. (2011) *11.22.63*, London, Hodder & Stoughton.

Kossew, S. (2007) 'Voicing the "Great Australian Silence": Kate Grenville's Narrative of the Settlement of the Secret River', *The Journal of Commonwealth Literature*, 42, 7, pp. 7-18.

Kuhn, R. (2007) 'The Rise of Anti-Muslim Racism in Australia: who benefits', paper presented to the Humanities Research Centre Work in Progress Seminar, Australian National University, 20 February.

Lake, M. & H. Reynolds (2008) *Drawing the Global Colour Line: white men's countries and the question of racial equality*, Melbourne, MUP.

Lasky, K. (1990) 'The Fiction of History: or, what did Miss Kitty really do?', *The New Advocate*, 3, no. 3, pp. 157-166.

Le Goff, J. (1992) *History and Memory*, trans. by S Rendall & E. Clamantr from the French, New York, Columbia University Press.

Leadbetter, B. (2006) 'Telling Tales Inside School', HTAA Conference, Fremantle, http://www.historyteacher.org.au/files/leadbetter_tellingtales.pdf (retrieved 12 March 2010).

Lebow, R.N. (2007) 'Counterfactual Thought Experiments: a necessary teaching tool', *The History Teacher*, 40, no. 2, pp. 153-76.

Lee, P. & R. Ashby (2000) 'Progression in Historical Understanding Ages 7-14', in P.N. Stearns, P. Seixas & S. Wineburg (eds) *Knowing, Teaching, and Learning History*, New York, New University Press.

Lee, R. (2000) 'History is but a fable agreed upon: the problem of truth in history and fiction', Historical Novel Society, http://www.

historicalnovelsociety.org/historyis.htm (retrieved 2 October 2009).

Levstik, L.S. & K.C. Barton (2011) *Doing History: investigating with children in elementary and middle schools* (4th edn) New York, Routledge.

Lewis, C., P. Enciso & E. Moje (eds) (2007) *Reframing Sociocultural Research on Literacy: identity, agency and power*, Mahwah, N.J., Lawrence Erlbaum.

Lindquist, T. (2002) 'Why and How I Teach with Historical Fiction', *The Reading Teacher*, http://teacher.scholastic.com/lessonrepro/lessonplans/instructor/social1.htm (retrieved 4 March 2010).

Loosley, S. (2011) 'Portrait of a Catastrophe', *Weekend Australian Review*, 5-6 November, p. 23.

Lowe, D. (1994) *Forgotten Rebels: Black Australians who fought back*, Melbourne, Permanent Press.

Lukacs, G. (1937/1963) *The Historical Novel*, Boston, Beacon Press.

Lusted, D. (1986) 'Why Pedagogy?', *Screen*, 27, no. 5, pp. pp. 2-14.

Lynch, G. (2007) 'New Preface: Historical Fiction Writers Explicate Their Practice', proceedings of the 12th Conference of Australian Association of Writing Programs, Canberra http://www.aawp.org.au/files/u280/lynch.pdf (retrieved 12 November 2009).

Macdonald, J. (2008) 'Building the Knowledge Around Historical Fiction: some strategies for grade 3 students', *Literacy Learning: the middle years*, February, http://findarticles.com/p/articles/mi_6949/is_1_16/ai_n31417998/ (retrieved 14 May 2010).

Macintyre, S. (2006) 'What if Australia's baptism of fire had occurred at the Cocos Islands?' in Stuart Macintyre & Sean Scalmer (eds) *What if?* Melbourne, MUP.

Macintyre, S. & S. Scalmer (eds) (2006) *What if?* Melbourne, MUP.

MacMillan, M. (2009) *The Use and Abuse of History*, London, Profile Books.

Maddison, S. (2011) *Beyond White Guilt*, Sydney, Allen & Unwin.

Malouf, D. (1990) *The Great World*, London, Chatto & Windus.

Marcus, A.S. (ed.) (2003) *Celluloid Blackboard: Teaching History With Film*, Stanford, Stanford Uni. Press.

Markus, A. (1998) 'Aboriginal Resistance', in G. Davison, J. Hirst, S. MacIntyre (eds) *The Oxford Companion to Australian History*, Melbourne, OUP.

Marsh, C. (2008) *Studies of Society and Environment: exploring the teaching possibilities* (5th edn), Frenchs Forest, Pearson Education Australia.

McCredden, L. (2005) 'Sacred Exchange', in Andreas Gaile (ed.) *Fabulating Beauty: perspectives on the fiction of Peter Carey*, Amsterdam/New York, Pub Rodopi.

McKenna, M. (2002) *Looking for Blackfella's Point*, Sydney, UNSW Press.

McKenna, M. (2008) 'Values and Patriotism in John Howard's Australia', in Gare, D. & D. Ritter, *Making Australian History: Perspectives on the Past Since 1788*, South Melbourne, Thompson, pp. 592-600.

McKnight Jr, E.V. (1994) 'Alternative History: the development of a literary genre', PhD dissertation, University of North Carolina, Chapel Hill.

McLaren, G. (1999) *Life's Been Good: the children of the Great Depression*, Fremantle, Fremantle Arts Centre Press.

McManus, J.M. (2008) 'A Novel Idea: historical fiction and social studies', *Social Education*, 72, no. 4,http://go.galegroup.com/ps/i.do?id=GALE%7CA179615556&v=2.1&u=adelaide&it=r&p=AONE&sw=w (retrieved 29 October 2011).

McWilliams, E. (1994) *In Broken Images: feminist tales for a different teacher education*, New York, Teachers College, Columbia University.

Miller, E.M. (1940) *Australian Literature 1795-1938* (facsimile edn) Sydney University Press, first published by Melbourne University Press, 1940.

Miller, P.B. (2004) 'Counterfactual History: "not if?" but "why not"', *The Chronicle of Higher Education*, 50, no. 23 (Feb. 13), pp. B10-B11.

Mitchell, B. (1998) 'Pastoral History', in G. Davison, J. Hirst, S. MacIntyre (eds) *The Oxford Companion to Australian History*, Melbourne, MUP.

Mitchell, K. (2010) 'Australia's "Other" History Wars: Trauma and the Work of Cultural Memory in Kate Grenville's *The Secret River*', in Marie-Louise Kohlke and Christian Gutleben (eds), *Neo-Victorian Tropes of Trauma: The Politics of Bearing After-Witness to Nineteenth Century Suffering*, Amsterdam and New York, Rodopi Press.

Molloy, F.C. (1984) '*The Chant of Jimmie Blacksmith*: cultural conflict and the individual', *The Teaching of English*, 46, pp. 21-27.

Moorehead, A. (1996) *The Fatal Impact: an account of the invasion of the South Pacific, 1797-1840*, Middlesex, Penguin.

Moran, M. (2005) 'Why Historical Fiction Belongs in Your Classroom', *Random House, For High School Teachers*, http://www.randomhouse.com/highschool/RHI_magazine/active_citizens/moran.html (retrieved 24 April 2010).

Mordhorst, M. (2008) 'From Counterfactual History to Counternarrative History', *Management and Organizational History*, 3, no. 1, pp. 5-26.

Morris-Suzuki, T. (1994) 'Collective Memory, Collective Forgetting: Indigenous People and the Nation-state in Japan and Australia', *Meanjin*, 53, no. 4, Summer 1994, pp. 597-612, http://search.informit.com.au/documentSummary;dn=885656110402132;res=IELLCC (retrieved 1 March 2013).

Morrison, T. (1987) *Beloved*, London, Chatto & Windus.

National Centre for History Education (n.d.) http://www.hyperhistory.org/ (retrieved 12 August 2011).

National Curriculum Board (2009) *Shape of the Australian Curriculum: History*.

Nawrot, K. (1996) 'Making Connections with Historical Fiction, *The Clearing House*, vol. 69, 6, July/August, pp. 343-345.

Nelson, C. (2007) 'Faking it: History and Creative Writing', *TEXT*, 11 no. 2, October, http://www.textjournal.com.au/oct07/nelson.htm (retrieved 2 December 2009).

Nettlebeck, A. (1999) 'Mythologising Frontier: Narrative Versions of the Rufus River Conflict, 1841-1899', in R. Nile (ed.) *Imaginary Homelands: Journal of Australian Studies no 61*, St Lucia, UQP.

New South Wales Board of Studies (n.d.) 'HSC History Extension', http://www.boardofstudies.nsw.edu.au/syllabus_hsc/history_extension_faq.html (retrieved 14 May 2011).

Nile, R. (2008) 'The Conceits of Silence', *The Australian*, 16 April.

Norton, D. (1999) *Through The Eyes of a Child: an introduction to children's literature* (5th edn) New Jersey, Prentice-Hall.

Olick, J.K. (2007) *The Politics of Regret: on collective memory and historical responsibility*, New York/London, Routledge.

Palmer, V. (1954) *The Legend of the Nineties*, Melbourne, Currey O'Neil.

Papert, S. (1993) *The Children's Machine: Rethinking School in the Age of the Computer*, New York, Basic Books.

Parkes, R. (2009) 'Teaching History as Historiography: engaging narrative diversity in the curriculum', *International Journal of Historical Learning Teaching and Research*, 8, no. 2. pp. 118-132.

Parkes, R.J. (2011) *Interrupting History: rethinking history curriculum after 'the end of History'*, New York, Peter Lang.

Paton Walsh, J. (1977) 'History is Fiction', in Paul Heins (ed.), *Crosscurrents of Criticism*, The Horn Book, Boston.

Sunday Times (1927) 'Our Nation's Future: the Half-Caste Problem', Perth, 23 August.

Pierce, P. (1992) 'Preying on the Past: Contexts of Some recent Neo-Historical Fiction', *Australian Literary Studies*, 15, no. 4, pp. 304-312.

Pierce, P. (2007) '*Robbery Under Arms* (review)', *Textual Cultures: Texts, Contexts, Interpretation*, vol. 2, 1, pp. 157-159, http://muse.jhu.edu/login?auth=0&type=summary&url=/journals/textual_cultures/v002/2.1.pierce.pdf (retrieved 13 March 2013).

Porter, B. (1984) *The Lion's Share: a short history of British Imperialism, 1850-1983*, London, Longman.

Potts, D. (2006) *The Myth of the Great Depression*, Melbourne, Scribe.

'Pride in the past isn't Necessarily a Lost Cause' (2010) *The Australian*, 24 April, http://www.theaustralian.com.au/opinion/pride-in-the-past-isnt-necessarily-a-lost-cause/story-e6frg6zo-1225857323308 (retrieved 17 March 2013).

Pybus, C. (2009a) 'A Novelist's Eye', *The Weekend Australian Review*, 29 August, pp. 10-11.

Pybus, C. (2009b) 'Within Reasonable Doubt', *The Weekend Australian Review*, 14-15 November, pp. 16-17.

Quartly, M. (1998) 'Convict History', in G. Davison, J. Hirst, S. MacIntyre (eds) *The Oxford Companion to Australian History*, Melbourne, OUP.

Ragland, R.G. (2007) 'Changing Secondary Teachers' Views of Teaching American History', *The History Teacher*, 40, no. 2, pp. 219-247.

Ramsland, J. (1996) *With Just But Relentless Discipline: a social history of corrective services in New South Wales*, Sydney, Kangaroo Press.

Raye, K., 'E-how: Historical Fiction to Teach History?' (n.d.) http://www.ehow.com/list_6828703_benefits-historical-fiction-teach-history_.html#ixzz1B9lhoyOI (retrieved 8 March 2011).

Read, D. (ed.) (1982) *Edwardian England*, London, Croom Helm.

Reed, A. (1994) *Reaching Adolescents: the young adult book and the school*. New York, Macmillan.

Review, *Sydney Daily Telegraph*, (n.d.) inside front page, Mary Durack, *Keep Him My Country*, 1955, Corgi edn, 1983.

Reynolds, H. (1979) 'Jimmie Governor and Jimmie Blacksmith', *Australian Literary Studies*, 9, no. 1, pp. 14-25.

Reynolds, H. & Lake, M. (2010) *What's Wrong With Anzac?* Sydney, UNSW Press.

Reynolds, R. (2006) 'The Values of Historical Fiction: avenues to global citizenship. *Social Educator*, 24, no. 3, pp. 28-33.

Reynolds, R. (2008) 'The Use of Historical Fiction to Promote Critical Citizenry', *Curriculum Perspectives*, 28, no. 1, pp. 1-10.

Richie, J. (1996) 'Edmonds, Catherine Beatrice (Caddie) (1900-1960)' *Australian Dictionary of Biography*, http://adb.anu.edu.au/biography/edmonds-catherine-beatrice-caddie-10098 (retrieved 2 November 2011).

Ricoeur, P. (2004) *Memory, History, Forgetting*, trans. by K. Blamey & D. Pellauer, Chicago Uni. Press, Chicago/London.

Roberts, G. (1997) 'On "What is History?": From Carr and Elton to Rorty and White', *History and Theory*, 36, no. 2, pp. 249-260.

Roberts, S.L. (2011) 'Using Counterfactual History to Enhance Students' Historical Understanding', *The Social Studies*, 102, no. 3, pp. 117-123.

Robin, L. (1998) 'Natural History', G. Davison, J. Hirst & S. MacIntyre (eds) *The Oxford Companion to Australian History*, Melbourne, OUP.

Rodwell, G. (2008) '"Death by a thousand cuts": a History of the Tasmanian Essential Learnings Curriculum: 2000-06', PhD thesis, University of Tasmania.

Rodwell, G. (2010) 'Historical Novels: engaging student teachers in K-10 history pre-service units', *Australian Journal of Teacher Education*, 35, no. 7, pp. 15-29.

Rosenfeld, G. (2002) 'Why Do We Ask "What If?" Reflections on the Function of Alternate History', *History and Theory*, Theme Issue 41, December, pp. 90-103.

Rosenfeld, G.D. (2005) *The World Hitler Never Made: alternative history and the memory of Nazism*, New York, Cambridge University Press.

Rossi, John (2002) 'Churchill and the revisionist historians', *Contemporary Review*, 280, 1634, , http://findarticles.com/p/articles/mi_m2242/is_1634_280/ai_8537054 (retrieved 12 May 2011).

Routman, R. (2003) *Reading Essentials*, New York, Heinemann.

Ryan, A. (1998) 'Developing a Strategy to Save History', *AHA Bulletin*, 87, pp. 39-50.

Rycik, M. & B. Rosler (2009) 'The Return of Historical Fiction: teaching tips', *The Reading Teacher*, 63 no. 2, pp. 163-167.

SACE Board of South Australia (2010) *History 2011 Subject Outline Stage 1 and Stage 2*, http://www.sace.sa.edu.au/subjects/stage-2-in-2010/society-and-environment/modern-history (retrieved 14 May 2011).

SACE Board of South Australia (2012) 'Data Information Release', http://www.sace.sa.edu.au/about/key-information/data-reports (retrieved 14 April 2012).

Sackville-O'Donnell, J. (2002) *The First Fagin: The True Story of Ikey Solomon*, Ackland Press, Melbourne.

Saeed, A. (1998) 'Islam', in G. Davison, J. Hirst & S. MacIntyre, *The Oxford Companion to Australian History*, Melbourne, OUP.

Sansom, C. (1987) 'Concepts, skills and content: A developmental approach to the history curriculum', in C. Portal (ed.) *The History Curriculum for Teachers*, London, The Falmer Press.

Sarandis, C. (n.d.) 'Teacher Guide: Roses for Anzac Boys', http://www.harpercollins.com/harperimages/ommoverride/teacher_guides_rose_for_anzac_boys.pdf (retrieved 29 March 2010).

Saylor Bibliography (n.d.) http://www.stevensaylor.com/bio.html (retrieved 1 March 2013).

Saylor, S. (2004) *The Judgement of Caesar*, St Martins, Minotaur.

Scalmer, S. (2006) 'Introduction', in Stuart Macintyre & Sean Scalmer (eds) *What if?*, Melbourne, MUP.

Schultz, J. (2007) 'The Future of SOSE? Integrative Inquiry is the Answer', *Social Educator*, 25, no. 3, pp. 11-16.

Schumnk, R.B. (2010) 'Uchronia: the alternative history list', *Uchronia*, http://www.uchronia.net/ (retrieved 26 October 2011).

Schwartz, L. (2004) 'Ikey Stirs up Storm 200 years on' *The Age* (Melbourne), http://www.theage.com.au/articles/2004/07/13/1089694358255.html (retrieved 12 October 2009).

Scott, K. (2010) *That Deadman Dance*, Melbourne, Picador.

Seddon, G. (1998) 'Landscape', in G. Davidson, J. Hirst & S. MacIntyre (eds) *The Oxford Companion to Australian History*, Melbourne, OUP.

Seixas, P. (1999) 'Beyond "Content" and "Pedagogy": in search of a way to talk about history education', *Journal of Curriculum Studies*, 31, no 3, pp. 317-337.

Seixas, P. (2001) 'Review of Research in Social Studies', in V. Richardson (ed.) *Handbook of Research on Teaching* (4th edn), Washington DC, American Educational Research Association.

Seixas, P., D. Fomowitz & P. Hill (2005) 'History, Memory and Learning to Teach', in R. Ashby, P. Gordon & P. Lee, *Understanding History: recent research in history education*, vol. 4, London and New York, Routledge Falmer.

Shann, E. (1967) *An Economic History of Australia* (students' edn) Georgian House, Melbourne, 1967 (first published CUP, 1930).

Sheridan, S. (1995) *Along the Fault Lines: sex, race and nation in Australian women's writing, 1880s-1930s*, St Leonards, NSW, Allen & Unwin.

Sim, C. (2001) 'Transforming the Subject: a case study of subject matter preparation in teacher education', *Queensland Journal of Educational Research*, 17 no. 1, pp. 29-47.

Sipe, L.R. (1997) 'Enhancing history; within historical fiction', *Slide Share Historical Fiction Revision*, http://www.slideshare.net/skrobert/historical-fiction-revision (retrieved 8 March 2011).

Sipe, L.R. (1997) 'In their own words: author's views on issues in historical fiction', *The New Advocate*, 10, no. 3, pp. 243-255.

Smith, B. (1990) *Minnie and Ginger*, Clarkson N. Potter, New York.

Smith, B. (2010) 'How our convict colonists put us in a class of our own', *The Weekend Australian*, 23-24 January, Enquirer, p. 4.

Sobchack V. (ed.) (1996) *The Persistence of History: cinema, television and the modern event*, New York/London, Routledge.

Soutphommasane, T. (2009) *Reclaiming Patriotism: nation-building for Australian progressives*, Melbourne, CUP.

Sparrow, J. (2006) 'The Myth of the Great Depression', *The Age* (Melbourne) http://www.theage.com.au/news/book-reviews/the-myth-of-the-great-depression/2006/07/28/1153816369701.html (retrieved 29 October 2011).

Spence, J. (1998) 'Margaret Atwood and the Edges of History', *The American Historical Review (AHR Forum: Histories and Historical Fictions)*, 103, no. 5 (December): pp. 1522-1526.

State Library of NSW: Discover Collections: Samuel Marsden (n.d.) http://www.sl.nsw.gov.au/discover_collections/history_nation/religion/

foundations/marsden.html (retrieved 24 April 2010).

Stearns, P.N., P. Seixas & S. Wineburg (eds) (2000) *Knowing, Teaching and Learning History*, New York, New University Press.

Steele K. (n.d.) 'Historical Fiction', *Kims Korner for Teacher Talk*, http://www.kimskorner4teachertalk.com (retrieved 24 April 2010).

Stephens, J. (1992) *Language and Ideology in Children's Fiction*, London, Longmans.

Sutherland, E. & T. Gibbons (2009) 'Historical fiction and History: members of the same family', *Text*, 13, 2, http://www.textjournal.com.au/oct09/sutherland_gibbons.htm (retrieved 29 October 2011).

Swain, S. (1998) 'Philanthropy', in G. Davison, J. Hirst & S. MacIntyre, *The Oxford Companion to Australian History*, Melbourne, OUP.

Tacey, D. (1995) *The Edge of the Sacred: transformation in Australia*, Blackburn North, Vic., Harper & Collins.

Tambyah, M. (n.d) 'What do SOSE Teachers Know? The significance of subject content knowledge among middle school teachers and teachers', professional identity, School of Cultural and Language Studies in Education, Faculty of Education, Queensland University of Technology, www.aare.edu.au/06pap/tam06849.pdf (retrieved 9 March 2011).

Taraporewalla, R. (2011) 'The Value and Utility of History and the Challenge of the New Curriculum', *Australian Policy and History*, February, http://www.aph.org.au/files/articles/theValue.htm (retrieved 24 October 2011).

Tayeb, L. (2006) *The Transformation of Political Identity From Commonwealth Through Postcolonial Literature: the cases of Nadine Gordimer, David Malouf and Michael Ondaatje*, Lewiston, The Edwin Mellen Press.

Taylor, A. (1987) *Reading Australian Poetry*, St Lucia, QUP.

Taylor, L. (2009) 'Keneally's Novel Trade Solution', *The Weekend Australian Review*, 29-30 August, pp. 13-14.

Taylor, T. (2000) *The Future of the Past. Executive summary of the report of the National Inquiry Into School History*, Canberra, Department of Education, Science and Training.

Taylor, T. (2006) *An overview of the Teaching and Learning of Australian History in Schools*, Prepared for the Australian History Summit, Canberra, 17 August 2006, http://www.htansw.asn.au/home/nationalcurriculum/HistorySummit_Tony%20Taylor.pdf (retrieved 10 March 2010).

Taylor, T. (n.d.) 'Teaching historical literacy: the National History Project', *Civics and Citizenship Education*, maintained by Education Services Australia, sponsored by Australian Government Department of Education, Employment and Workplace Relations, http://www.curriculum.edu.au/cce/default.asp?id=9323 (retrieved 3 March 2010).

Taylor, T. & C. Young (2003) *Making History: a guide for the teaching and learning of history in Australian schools*, Commonwealth Department of Science, Education and Training, http://hyperhistory.org/images/assets/pdf/complete.pdf (retrieved 18 December 2009).

Tetlock, P. & A. Belkin (1996) 'Counterfactual Thought Experiments in World Politics: logical, methodological, and psychological perspective,' in P. Telock & A. Belkin, *Counterfactual Thought Experiments*, Princeton, Princeton University Press.

Tharoor, S. (2010) 'Review of Madhustree Mukerjee *Churchill's Secret War*', *Time*, 29 November 2010, p. 43.

The Australian (2011) 'H.V. Evatt and New Allegations of Espionage', 15 April, http://search.news.com.au/related/id%3Astory_1226039594251/0/Evatt-espionage-charge-denied/?us=ndmtheaustralian&sid=910&as=TAUS&ac=search&r=related (retrieved 20 July 2011).

The Australian Women's Register, 'Nancy Cato', http://www.womenaustralia.info/biogs/AWE0104b.htm (retrieved 9 September 2009).

The Australian Women's Register, 'Mary Durack', http://www.womenaustralia.info/biogs/IMP0027b.htm (retrieved 18 September 2009).

The Essay: What is History, Today? (2011) BBC Radio 3, 14 Nov., http://www.bbc.co.uk/programmes/b017575t (retrieved 14 December 2011).

The Rocks — Heritage & History (n.d.) http://www.therocks.com/sydney-Education_and_Tours-Heritage_and_History.htm (retrieved 13 March 2013).

The University of Melbourne (n.d.) Prof. Stuart Macintyre, http://history.unimelb.edu.au/about/staff/macintyre.html (retrieved 15 May 2011).

The Weekend Australian (2012) Editorial: 'A Balanced View of History', 29-30 September.

Tiffin, C. (1978) 'Victims Black and White: Thomas Keneally's *The Chant of Jimmie Blacksmith*', in K.G. Hamilton (Ed.) *Studies in the Recent Australian Novel*, St Lucia, UQP.

Tiffin, C. & A. Lawson (eds) (1994) *De-Scribing Empire: postcolonialism and textuality*, London, Routledge.

Tolstoy, L. (1869) *War and Peace*, trans. by A. Mandelker (2010), London, Oxford World Classics.

Tomlinson, C.M., M.O. Tunnell & D.J. Richgels (1993) 'The Content and Writing of History in Textbooks and Trade books', in M.O. Tunnell, & R. Ammon (eds) *The Story of Ourselves: teaching history through children's literature*, Portsmouth, Heinemann.

Tourism Tasmania (n.d.) 'History and Heritage', http://travelmedia.tourismtasmania.com.au/about/history/convict.html (accessed 25 March 2010).

Tripp, V. (2011) 'The Vitamins in the Chocolate Cake: Why Use Historical

Fiction in the Classroom', *Teaching History.org*, September, http://teachinghistory.org/nhec-blog/24679 (retrieved 24 October 2011).

Troughton, E. (1941/1954) *Furred Animals of Australia*, Sydney, A&R.

Trounson A. (2012) 'Why history's losing its lustre', *The Australian*, 7 March.

Trove, Boat People (n.d.) http://trove.nla.gov.au/result?q=%22%20Boat%20people%20Australia%22 (retrieved 16 July 2011).

Tumarkin, M. (2012) 'I, Witness: the Holocaust memoir remains our best weapon against historical revisionism', *Weekend Australian Review*, 23-24 June, pp. 18-19.

Turner, F.J. (1906/1965) *Rise of the New West: 1819-1829*, New York, Collier Books.

Uchronia (n.d.) http://www.uchronia.net/ (retrieved 15 July 2011).

Unexplained-Mysteries.com. http://www.unexplained-mysteries.com/forum/index.php?showtopic=142322 (retrieved 12 April 2010).

Ungari, E. (2010) 'Patrick White's Sense of History in A Fringe of Leaves', *Australian Studies*, 2.

Vamplew, W. & D. Adair (1998) 'Sport and Leisure', G. Davison, J. Hirst & S. MacIntyre, *The Oxford Companion to Australian History*, Melbourne, OUP.

Van Sledright, B. (2004) 'What Does It Mean to Think Historically ... and How Do You Teach It? *Social Education*, 68, no. 3, pp. 230-233.

Vernay, J.F. (2010) *The Great Australian Novel: a panorama*, trans. by Marie Melbourne, Ramsland, Brolga Publishing.

Villano, T. (2005) 'Should Social Studies Textbooks Become History? A look at alternative methods to activate schema in the intermediate classroom', *International Reading Association*, 59, no. 2, pp.122-130.

Wakeling, L. K. (1998) 'Theorising Creative Processes in the Writing of Neo-

Historical Fiction Watermark', PhD thesis, University of New South Wales.

Walsh, J. P. (1972) 'History is Fiction', *The Horn Book*, 48, February, pp. 17-18.

Wesseling, E. (1991) *Writing History as a Prophet: Postmodernist Innovations of the Historical Novel*, Amsterdam and Philadelphia, J. Benjamin.

'What Are the Benefits of Using Historical Fiction to Teach History?', *eHow.com*, http://www.ehow.com/list_6828703_benefits-historical-fiction-teach-history_.html#ixzz0zYK2GCd8 (retrieved 24 April 2010).

White, H. (1982) 'The Politics of Historical Interpretation: discipline and de-sublimation, *Critical Enquiry*, 9, Sept., pp. 113-137.

White, H. (1996) 'The Modernist Event'. in V. Sobchack (ed.) *The Persistence of History: cinema, television and the modern event*, New York, Routledge.

White, R. (1981) *Inventing Australia: images and identity, 1788-1980*, Sydney, Allen & Unwin.

Whitlock, G. (1999) 'Australian Literature: points for departure', *Australian Literary Studies*, 19, no. 2. pp. 95-102.

Wilde, W. H., J. Hooton & B. Andrews (1994) *The Oxford Companion to Australian Literature* (2nd edn), Melbourne, OUP.

Willbanks, R. (1992) *Speaking Volumes*, Ringwood, Vic, Penguin.

Williams, E. (2010) 'Deep and Meaningful', *The Weekend Australian Review*, 17-18 April, pp. 17.

Williams, P. (ed.) (1983) *Social Process and the City*, Sydney, Allen & Unwin.

Williamson, G. (2012) 'Keneally's Triumph', *The Weekend Australian Review*, 5-6 May, pp. 18-19.

Windschuttle, K. (2002) *The Fabrication of Aboriginal History, Vol. One, Van Diemen's Land, 1803-1847*, Sydney, Macleay Press.

Wineburg, S. (1991) 'Reading Historical Texts: notes on the breach between school and academy', *American Educational Research Journal*, 28, pp. 495-519.

Winthrop-Young, G. (2009) 'Fallacies and Thresholds: Notes on the Early Evolution of Alternate History', *Historical Social Research*, 34, no. 2, pp. 99-117.

Wright, E. (2012) 'New Australian Fiction', *Weekend Australian Review*, 7-8 April, p. 21.

'Wyatt Shares Stolen Generation Stories' (2010) *The Epoch Times* (Eng edn), 20 September, http://www.theepochtimes.com/n2/australia/koori-minister-tells-stolen-generation-memories-43406.html (retrieved 1 March 2013).

Wyndham, D. (2003) *Eugenics in Australia: Striving for National Fitness*, London, Galton Institute.

Yeager, E.A. (2000) 'Thoughts on Wise Practice in the Teaching of Social Studies', *Social Education*, 64, no. 6, pp. 352-353.

Ying, Z. (2006) *Fiction and the Incompleteness of History, Toni Morrison, V.S. Naipaul and Ben Okri*, Bern, Peter Lang.

Yu, O. (1995) 'Australian Invention of Chinese Invasion: a century of paranoia, 1888-1988', *Australian Literary Studies*, 17, no. 1, pp. 74-84.

Zinn, C. (2000) 'Nancy Cato: novelist and poet capturing the spirit of the Australian outback', *The Guardian*, 12 July, http://www.guardian.co.uk/news/2000/jul/12/guardianobituaries.books (retrieved 8 September 2009).

This book is available as a free fully-searchable PDF from
www.adelaide.edu.au/press

www.ingramcontent.com/pod-product-compliance
Lightning Source LLC
Chambersburg PA
CBHW080023110526
44587CB00021BA/3833